European Union Sanctions and Foreign Policy

Sanctions are an important tool within the foreign policy of the European Union, which have until now remained obscure to both scholars and the general public. This book examines sanctions as a political tool of influence and evaluates the efficacy of sanctions imposed by the EU against third countries and their ability to bring about the desired outcome.

While the principal sanctions activity of the EU takes place under the Common Foreign and Security Policy, the author also considers the suspension of development aid under the ACP-EU Partnership Agreement, the withdrawal of trade privileges under the Generalized System of Preferences and other sanctions outside these frameworks. Reviewing the sanctions practice of the EU in its virtual entirety, Portela assesses the relevance of classical sanctions theory by testing a series of hypotheses with empirical case-studies attempting to identify the determinants of success of EU sanctions.

Enhancing our understanding of the EU's international role, this book will be of interest to students and scholars of international politics, security studies, EU studies, human rights and democracy, conflict management, IPE and development studies.

Clara Portela is currently an Assistant Professor of Political Science at Singapore Management University.

Routledge Advances in European Politics

1 **Russian Messianism**
Third Rome, revolution, Communism and after
Peter J.S. Duncan

2 **European Integration and the Postmodern Condition**
Governance, democracy, identity
Peter van Ham

3 **Nationalism in Italian Politics**
The stories of the Northern League, 1980–2000
Damian Tambini

4 **International Intervention in the Balkans since 1995**
Edited by Peter Siani-Davies

5 **Widening the European Union**
The politics of institutional change and reform
Edited by Bernard Steunenberg

6 **Institutional Challenges in the European Union**
Edited by Madeleine Hosli, Adrian van Deemen and Mika Widgrén

7 **Europe Unbound**
Enlarging and reshaping the boundaries of the european union
Edited by Jan Zielonka

8 **Ethnic Cleansing in the Balkans**
Nationalism and the destruction of tradition
Cathie Carmichael

9 **Democracy and Enlargement in Post-Communist Europe**
The democratisation of the general public in fifteen Central and Eastern European countries, 1991–98
Christian W. Haerpfer

10 **Private Sector Involvement in the Euro**
The power of ideas
Stefan Collignon and Daniela Schwarzer

11 **Europe**
A Nietzschean perspective
Stefan Elbe

12 **European Union and E-Voting**
Addressing the European Parliament's internet voting challenge
Edited by Alexander H. Trechsel and Fernando Mendez

13 **European Union Council Presidencies**
A comparative perspective
Edited by Ole Elgström

14 **European Governance and Supranational Institutions**
Making states comply
Jonas Tallberg

15 **European Union, NATO and Russia**
Martin Smith and Graham Timmins

16 **Business, the State and Economic Policy**
The case of Italy
G. Grant Amyot

17 **Europeanization and Transnational States**
Comparing Nordic central governments
Bengt Jacobsson, Per Lægreid and Ove K. Pedersen

18 **European Union Enlargement**
A comparative history
Edited by Wolfram Kaiser and Jürgen Elvert

19 **Gibraltar**
British or Spanish?
Peter Gold

20 **Gendering Spanish Democracy**
Monica Threlfall, Christine Cousins and Celia Valiente

21 **European Union Negotiations**
Processes, networks and negotiations
Edited by Ole Elgström and Christer Jönsson

22 **Evaluating Euro-Mediterranean Relations**
Stephen C. Calleya

23 **The Changing Face of European Identity**
A seven-nation study of (supra)national attachments
Edited by Richard Robyn

24 **Governing Europe**
Discourse, governmentality and European integration
William Walters and Jens Henrik Haahr

25 **Territory and Terror**
Conflicting nationalisms in the Basque country
Jan Mansvelt Beck

26 **Multilateralism, German Foreign Policy and Central Europe**
Claus Hofhansel

27 **Popular Protest in East Germany**
Gareth Dale

28 **Germany's Foreign Policy towards Poland and the Czech Republic**
Ostpolitik revisited
Karl Cordell and Stefan Wolff

29 **Kosovo**
The politics of identity and space
Denisa Kostovicova

30 **The Politics of European Union Enlargement**
Theoretical approaches
Edited by Frank Schimmelfennig and Ulrich Sedelmeier

31 **Europeanizing Social Democracy?**
The rise of the party of European socialists
Simon Lightfoot

32 **Conflict and Change in EU Budgetary Politics**
Johannes Lindner

33 **Gibraltar, Identity and Empire**
E.G. Archer

34 **Governance Stories**
Mark Bevir and R.A.W. Rhodes

35 **Britain and the Balkans**
1991 until the present
Carole Hodge

36 **The Eastern Enlargement of the European Union**
John O'Brennan

37 **Values and Principles in European Union Foreign Policy**
Edited by Sonia Lucarelli and Ian Manners

38 **European Union and the Making of a Wider Northern Europe**
Pami Aalto

39 **Democracy in the European Union**
Towards the emergence of a public sphere
Edited by Liana Giorgi, Ingmar Von Homeyer and Wayne Parsons

40 **European Union Peacebuilding and Policing**
Michael Merlingen with Rasa Ostrauskaite

41 **The Conservative Party and European Integration since 1945**
At the heart of Europe?
N.J. Crowson

42 **E-Government in Europe**
Re-booting the state
Edited by Paul G. Nixon and Vassiliki N. Koutrakou

43 **EU Foreign and Interior Policies**
Cross-pillar politics and the social construction of sovereignty
Stephan Stetter

44 **Policy Transfer in European Union Governance**
Regulating the utilities
Simon Bulmer, David Dolowitz, Peter Humphreys and Stephen Padgett

45 **The Europeanization of National Political Parties**
Power and organizational adaptation
Edited by Thomas Poguntke, Nicholas Aylott, Elisabeth Carter, Robert Ladrech and Kurt Richard Luther

46 **Citizenship in Nordic Welfare States**
Dynamics of choice, duties and participation in a changing Europe
Edited by Bjørn Hvinden and Håkan Johansson

47 **National Parliaments within the Enlarged European Union**
From victims of integration to competitive actors?
Edited by John O'Brennan and Tapio Raunio

48 **Britain, Ireland and Northern Ireland since 1980**
The totality of relationships
Eamonn O'Kane

49 The EU and the European Security Strategy
Forging a global Europe
Edited by Sven Biscop and Jan Joel Andersson

50 European Security and Defence Policy
An implementation perspective
Edited by Michael Merlingen and Rasa Ostrauskaitė

51 Women and British Party Politics
Descriptive, substantive and symbolic representation
Sarah Childs

52 The Selection of Ministers in Europe
Hiring and firing
Edited by Keith Dowding and Patrick Dumont

53 Energy Security
Europe's new foreign policy challenge
Richard Youngs

54 Institutional Challenges in Post-Constitutional Europe
Governing change
Edited by Catherine Moury and Luís de Sousa

55 The Struggle for the European Constitution
A past and future history
Michael O'Neill

56 Transnational Labour Solidarity
Mechanisms of commitment to cooperation within the European Trade Union movement
Katarzyna Gajewska

57 The Illusion of Accountability in the European Union
Edited by Sverker Gustavsson, Christer Karlsson, and Thomas Persson

58 The European Union and Global Social Change
A critical geopolitical-economic analysis
József Böröcz

59 Citizenship and Collective Identity in Europe
Ireneusz Pawel Karolewski

60 EU Enlargement and Socialization
Turkey and Cyprus
Stefan Engert

61 The Politics of EU Accession
Turkish challenges and Central European experiences
Edited by Lucie Tunkrová and Pavel Šaradín

62 The Political History of European Integration
The hypocrisy of democracy-through-market
Hagen Schulz-Forberg and Bo Stråth

63 The Spatialities of Europeanization
Power, governance and territory in Europe
Alun Jones and Julian Clark

64 European Union Sanctions and Foreign Policy
When and why do they work?
Clara Portela

European Union Sanctions and Foreign Policy

When and why do they work?

Clara Portela

Routledge
Taylor & Francis Group
LONDON AND NEW YORK

First published 2010
by Routledge
2 Park Square Milton Park Abingdon Oxon OX14 4RN

Simultaneously published in the USA and Canada
by Routledge

711 Third Avenue, New York, NY 10017, USA
Routledge is an imprint of the Taylor & Francis Group, an informa business.

Typeset in Times New Roman by
Taylor & Francis Books

British Library Cataloguing in Publication Data
A catalogue record for this book is available from the British Library

Library of Congress Cataloging in Publication Data
A catalog record for this book has been requested

ISBN 978-0-415-55216-5 (hbk)
ISBN 978-0-203-84751-0 (ebk)

Contents

Tables

Acknowledgements

My gratitude goes primarily to Prof. P. Vennesson and Prof. M. Cremona for their guidance in completing this work. I would also like to thank Prof. T. Biersteker, Prof. K. Smith, Prof. M. Brzoska and Prof. D. Cortright, as well as three anonymous reviewers for their valuable comments.

Special thanks to Dr H. Hazelzet, and to all EU officials who kindly agreed to an interview, in particular Mr A. De Vries and Mr A. Straver, Mr J. Fernández and Ms M. Pérez-García. I would also like to thank Prof. T. de Wilde d'Estmael, Dr H. Kramer, and Dr C. Wagemann for supporting my work and for providing me with inspiration, and Routledge's editorial team, Mrs H. Bagtazo, H. Frammingham and L. Dunne for their help.

My thanks go also to my family for their support and to the Ministries of Foreign Affairs and Education of Spain for generously funding my research at the European University Institute in Florence.

Abbreviations

ACP	African, Caribbean and Pacific group
CCP	Common Commercial Policy
CFSP	Common Foreign and Security Policy
CPA	Comprehensive Peace Agreement
EC	European Community
ECHO	European Community Humanitarian Aid Office
EDF	European Development Fund
EU	European Union
EP	European Parliament
EPC	European Political Co-operation
EUBAM	European Union Border Assistance Mission
FRY	Federal Republic of Yugoslavia
GNP	gross national product
GSP	Generalized System of Preferences
ICTY	International Criminal Tribunal for the Former Yugoslavia
ILO	International Labour Organisation
IMF	International Monetary Fund
LDC	Least Developed Country
MFN	Most-Favoured Nation
NPT	Non-Proliferation Treaty
OSCE	Organisation for Security and Co-operation in Europe
PCA	Partnership and Co-operation Agreement
QCA	Qualitative Comparative Analysis
SAA	Stabilisation and Association Agreement
SADC	Southern African Development Community
SPLM	Sudan People's Liberation Movement
TACIS	Technical Assistance for the Commonwealth of Independent States
TEU	Treaty on European Union
UNSC	United Nations Security Council
WTO	World Trade Organisation

Introduction

Why investigate the efficacy of EU sanctions and how to go about it

Member states of the European Community (EC), later the European Union (EU), have been wielding sanctions against third countries in the absence of United Nations Security Council mandates since the early 1980s. This practice has evolved substantially over the past decade, with sanctions regimes being imposed with increasing frequency. The scarce attention devoted to this EU foreign policy practice contrasts with intense scholarly interest in the EU as an international actor. The very few works that have taken into account the existence of EU sanctions have focused on exploring the factors leading to the decision to use sanctions (Hazelzet 2001) or their imposition through the EU rather than other frameworks (Jones 2007); or they limit their work to description (Anthony 2002, Kreutz 2006, Eriksson 2005). The present study has the objective of ascertaining the determinants of success and failure of EU sanctions. Do EU sanctions work, and if so, under what conditions?

Why explore the *efficacy* of EU sanctions? Firstly, about forty years of research into the determinants of sanctions' success has not yet produced any satisfactory, comprehensive explanation of when and how sanctions work. The determinants of success of sanctions still need to be ascertained. Secondly, this state of affairs is compounded by the fact that while researchers were busy searching for the determinants of success, sanctions themselves have undergone a profound transformation. While classical sanctions were economic in nature, a new type of sanction came to the fore during the 1990s: the so-called *targeted* or *smart* sanction. These kinds of sanctions seek to focus harm on the individuals responsible for the objectionable behaviour, rather than on society as a whole, and include measures as diverse as visa bans, financial sanctions, arms embargoes and flight bans. The past decade has also witnessed an increased use of sanctions for crisis management; that is, sanctions applied in situations of violent conflict. All of this opens up new questions about the usefulness of this instrument in new contexts. Given these transformations, a reassessment of their efficacy is in order.

The present investigation is located within the broader framework of the study of EU foreign policy, examining a theme as yet absent from mainstream debate. The current debate on European foreign policy does not feature investigations which systematically explore the impact and efficacy of EU actions.

The question of efficacy has major consequences for the debate on the nature of the EU as an international actor. What can the efficacy of EU sanctions teach us about its role in the international system? What does it reveal about the EU's *power* in international relations? Due to their traditional position as the ultimate coercive foreign policy tool before military force, sanctions can be indicative of the EU's capacity to compel policy changes in third countries without having recourse to, or even threatening, military force. In other words, if the EU is able to coerce third countries into changing their behaviour, if its sanctions *work*, then we can draw conclusions about the EU as a civilian power that go beyond the traditional characteristics of this concept. Therefore, an analysis of these actions can be especially useful in ascertaining the potential and limits of EU influence.

The present study endeavours to ascertain the *conditions* under which sanctions imposed by the EU bring about desired changes in the behaviour of the target. It also aims to explain *why* these particular conditions, or combination(s) of factors, are conducive to success. The aim is to determine the *independent* effect of EU sanctions, to the extent that it is possible to discern the influence of EU sanctions among the wider spectrum of international actions applied in any particular situation. A set of criteria delimits the sanctions universe in this study. The first defining characteristic is the unilateral nature of the measures. Sanctions applied by the EU in implementation of UN Security Council Resolutions are omitted from the investigation. Only autonomous EU sanctions, accompanied or not by measures from other international actors of a non-universal vocation, are considered. The second criterion is the non-commercial character of the aims pursued by sanctions. The rationale for this choice is the existence of an international organisation, the World Trade Organisation (WTO), which foresees the imposition of sanctions in cases of the infringement of rules among its members, thereby reducing the leeway for determining the nature and duration of the sanctions otherwise enjoyed by the senders. The present study includes sanctions of different types levied by the EU since the signature of the Treaty on European Union (TEU) in 1991. It encompasses measures adopted within the Common Foreign and Security Policy (CFSP), aid sanctions imposed within the Community framework and decisions on the withdrawal of trade privileges under the Generalized System of Preferences. These types of measures are complemented by a fourth group, namely sanctions adopted 'informally' outside any of these legal frameworks. Thus, the present exploration of EU coercive measures that fit into the academic definition of sanctions brings together a range of instruments that are normally examined separately, due to their diverse legal nature.

The standard of success by which efficacy is measured is the ability to contribute to change in the political behaviour of the target. The methodology of this study is inspired by the landmark study on sanctions efficacy, the work authored by economists Hufbauer, Schott and Elliot, *Economic Sanctions Reconsidered*, the first edition of which appeared in 1985. However, the present investigation attempts to correct some of the deficiencies that mar their evaluation. In addition to its goal of assessing the efficacy of EU sanctions, the present study also seeks to improve the general methodology on sanctions evaluation.

The investigation proceeds as follows. Firstly, a number of hypotheses on the efficacy of EU sanctions are formulated on the basis of theoretical works in the field of sanctions research, occasionally complemented by other theoretical sources. After that, a dataset comprising EU sanctions episodes since the signing of the Treaty on European Union (which created the CFSP), up to the present day is presented. The hypotheses are then tested against the empirical cases, in an attempt to ascertain the variables that account for efficacy and inefficacy. Once this combination of factors has been determined, the success and failure of sanctions are explained with the help of existing theories.

One of the main challenges in this enterprise consists in dissociating the effects of EU sanctions from those brought about by concurrent factors. This difficulty, typical in sanctions research, is resolved by ascertaining the 'sanctions contribution' rather than the 'policy result'. In the present study, only sanctions' contributions are ascertained. On the basis of the determinants identified by the vast literature on the efficacy of sanctions, the present investigation explores those variables likely to affect the outcome, with the objective of discovering the factors under which EU sanctions contributed to the desired results, i.e. to induce a change in the behaviour of the target. Whenever possible, the independent effect of EU sanctions should be determined.

In methodological terms, the study consists of a qualitative investigation. It is preceded by a QCA (Qualitative Comparative Analysis). This method, often employed for hypothesis generation, is particularly appropriate for the purpose of ascertaining particular combinations of factors accounting for a specific outcome, due to its ability to identify *necessary* and *sufficient* conditions. Once the relevance of the variables has been identified by means of this method, a 'reality check' is conducted in the form of case studies. The objective of the case studies is to test the results of the analysis. Exploring a small number of cases in detail serves the purpose of confirming or disconfirming the hypothesis that the factors identified by QCA really account for the success of sanctions in the specific example at hand. The insights arising from the case studies are decisive for validating or falsifying the QCA results. Having identified the determinants of success of EU sanctions, the investigation returns to the broader theoretical framework accounting for the effects of sanctions, in order to test their explanatory power. Conclusions are drawn regarding the applicability of general sanctions theory to EU sanctions, and the contribution that insights gained from the study of EU sanctions practice can make to the discipline.

The present investigation has a triple objective. First, it aims to refine the methodology for the evaluation of sanctions' success. Second, it attempts to ascertain the mode of operation of sanctions, and particularly of targeted sanctions. Third, it also hopes to throw some light on the nature of the EU's influence in international relations.

The findings of the study confirm the continued validity of some factors stemming from classical sanctions theory, but also illuminate new aspects. Although EU sanctions are more likely to be effective where they can inflict economic damage on the target, the investigation also shows that sanctions can be efficacious by stigmatising leaders. Some factors hardly noticed in the current body of scholarship, such as the sound management of the sanctions strategy, or the activism of the sender in lifting sanctions, emerge as potential determinants for the efficacy of the attempt to influence. Finally, the investigation uncovers the relationship between the choice of institutional framework within which the EU decides to wield sanctions and the prospects of success of the measures.

The investigation concludes that EU sanctions work either when aid to ACP countries is suspended, or when CFSP sanctions are employed against third states strategically exposed – or unprotected by a major power – interested in reaping the economic benefits of cooperation with the EU and in augmenting their international prestige. Thus, albeit manifestly targeted and mostly non-economic in nature, EU sanctions work by withholding the prospect of increased prosperity and the prestige and international recognition associated with dealing with the EU. Finally, the study reveals the EU as an accommodating and responsive sender of sanctions.

1 Sanctions and their efficacy

Notwithstanding the fact that the debate on the efficacy of sanctions has been in existence for four decades, the investigation of their efficacy has not yet yielded satisfactory results. The determinants for the success and failure of sanctions have not yet been ascertained. The inherent difficulty of the task has been further compounded by a transformation of the instrument itself. Classical comprehensive trade embargoes have given way to more sophisticated measures, so-called 'targeted' sanctions. After addressing some essential definitional questions, this chapter outlines the progress made in International Relations (IR) scholarship in identifying the determinants of the success and failure of sanctions. It then proceeds to describe the emergence of the new concept of targeted sanctions, and to discuss its implications for the sanctions debate, paying special attention to the case of sanctions imposed by the EU.[1] The final section of the chapter discusses a number of methodological issues related to the analysis and measurement of success, and identifies flaws, with a view to obviating them in the design of the present study. What are targeted sanctions? How do they differ from classical embargoes? How have they affected IR scholarship on sanctions evaluation, and how well has the methodology of evaluation been adapted to study their impact?

International sanctions as an object of study

The methodological debate on sanctions held in the late 1990s between Hufbauer et al.–Pape–Baldwin generated a fruitful discussion on the definition of the object of study. Although the debate was confined to economic sanctions, it offers useful insights for a definition of sanctions as tools of influence. In the classical definition, sanctions entail 'the deliberate government-inspired withdrawal of … trade or financial relations [to obtain] foreign policy goals' (Hufbauer et al. 1985:2). According to this formulation, two central definitional elements can be discerned in the concept of economic sanctions: the coercive measure needs to be *economic* in nature and its aim needs to be *political*. This effectively excludes measures to attain economic policy goals. In his critique of *Economic Sanctions Reconsidered*, Pape specified this distinction in order to illustrate the difference between *economic sanctions* and *trade wars*. According to this author, *economic sanctions* 'seek to lower the economic welfare of a target state by reducing international trade in order to coerce the target government to change its political behaviour' (Pape 1997:93–94). By contrast, a *trade war* takes place 'when a state threatens to inflict economic harm … in order to persuade the target state to agree to terms of trade more favourable to the coercing state' (1997:94). In Pape's view, trade wars and economic sanctions should be studied separately, primarily because the *basis of decision making* by the target is different:

> States involved in trade disputes decide whether to make concessions depending on which choice they expect would maximise their wealth. Targets of economic sanctions, on the other hand, understand that they would be better off economically if they conceded to the coercer's demands, and make their decisions based on whether they consider their political objectives to be worth the economic costs.
>
> (Pape 1997:96)

With this observation, Pape exposes the core difference between the target state's compliance and non-compliance in both situations: decisions follow economics-based, as opposed to purely political, calculations. Therefore, 'there is good reason to believe that the variables that dominate target states' decision making in response to different types of demands are often different' (Baldwin and Pape 1998). In view of this fundamental difference, Pape's claim that theories of the determinants of success in trade disputes are of limited applicability to decision making on compliance with economic sanctions seems to be warranted. Indeed, consensus has emerged among researchers that economic sanctions and trade disputes are analytically distinct and that their study should not be conflated.

However, an additional, often overlooked reason underlies the differences in the bases of decision making between trade and non-commercial disputes. International trade disputes are subject to international legal regulation, mostly through the legal system put in place by the World Trade Organisation (WTO). The WTO has its own system of sanctions applicable as countermeasures in response to breaches (Charnovitz 2005). Thus, there is a higher degree of predictability for decisions on sanctions imposed as a result of breaches of WTO rules. The same applies for EU measures of commercial defence, such as anti-dumping measures or remedies: EC legislation specifies the sorts of infractions which might trigger the adoption of countermeasures. In contrast, in foreign policies falling outside the narrowly defined trade realm, the EU has greater discretion in deciding on sanctions against third countries. While some international norms such as human rights have achieved a high degree of codification under international law, countermeasures in response to the violations of these norms are not foreseen in the relevant treaties. The UN Security Council is endowed with the capacity to impose mandatory multilateral sanctions once it has determined a 'threat to international peace and security'.[2] No enforceable norm stipulates that the outbreak of violent conflict, nuclear proliferation or the imprisonment of political opponents should trigger sanctions by third countries, especially when the UN Security Council refrains from taking action. EU measures featured in this book are thus agreed on a purely voluntary basis by the Council of Ministers. In view of this fundamental difference, the study of sanctions in commercial and non-commercial disputes should be kept separate in order to accurately ascertain their coercive power in each realm.

Theory on the operation of sanctions

In order to analyse the success and failure of sanctions, the following section outlines the theory according to which sanctions are expected to attain their objectives.

The point of departure: the 'naïve' theory and its critics

The classical formulation of how sanctions are expected to operate stems not from any official statement by the leadership of a state which has levied sanctions – a 'sender' state in sanctions terminology – but from a critical academic. Galtung formulated a general theory on the operation of sanctions, which he coined the 'naïve' theory of sanctions. It postulates that the economic disruption caused by sanctions is expected to translate into political pressure that will eventually compel the leadership in the target country to change its policies, or will lead to its overthrow (Galtung 1967). According to Galtung's classical formulation of the 'naïve' theory of sanctions, these tools operate in a similar way to military warfare. Both share the same end, the 'political disintegration of the enemy so that he gives up the pursuit of his goals. The method used is value-deprivation' (Galtung 1967:386). The theory foresees a roughly proportionate relation between both phenomena; the more intense the value-deprivation, the more widespread the political disintegration:

> The idea is that there is a limit to how much value deprivation the system can stand, and that once this limit is reached (resulting in a split in leadership or between leadership and people), then political disintegration will proceed very rapidly and will lead to surrender or willingness to negotiate.
> (Galtung 1967:388)

A clear parallel thus exists with the use of force. In his essay *Arms and Influence* (Schelling 1966), Schelling inquires about the causes of success or failure of this tool. According to Schelling, the purpose of inflicting suffering is to influence somebody's behaviour: it is the threat of damage that can make somebody yield. One of the points of confluence between the logic underlying the use of force and sanctions concerns the conditions that Schelling lists for the efficacy of the use of force as a political instrument: to be coercive, violence has to be anticipated, and be avoidable by accommodation, for it is not the threat alone that is effective, but the corresponding assurance that the target can avoid pain. Both force and sanctions operate by inflicting pain and by imposing the prospect of continued suffering unless the target complies.

Under Galtung's description of the expected functioning of sanctions, two different modes of operation can be discerned which are meant to produce different outcomes through different mechanisms. One follows the objective of overthrowing the existing leadership by popular upheaval. It presupposes that a 'societal transmission belt' exists that will produce political pressure that will eventually lead to the overthrow of the leaders, allowing the opposition to take power. The overthrow of the Trujillo's regime in the Dominican Republic as a result of US economic sanctions can serve as an example of this form of operation.

The second mode of operation consists in inducing the leadership of the target country to modify its policies according to the preferences of the sender. This shift comes about because 'decision-makers change their calculation of costs and benefits' (Cortright and Lopez 2000:22). For this to happen, the existence of the 'societal transmission belt' that transforms economic damage into political pressure is not a necessary precondition. The change of heart in the leadership concerned can be prompted by societal or opposition pressure, but may also respond to other considerations, such as personal damage, or loss of international prestige. Thus, this mode of operation can accommodate targeted sanctions, since they are expected to operate without damaging the economy as a whole.

While the desired policy change can be effected either through the overthrow of the targeted leaders or through their coercion, some authors tend to conflate the two modes of operation without making explicit this duality. Since EU sanctions do not contemplate the goal of destabilising the target government, but aim only at changing the target leader's policies, the former remains excluded from the present study.

Explaining inefficacy

If, according to the naïve theory, the economic pain inflicted by sanctions is expected to motivate the target to comply with the sender's demand, why does this not always occur in practice? Scholarship has long established that there is no automatic link between the effectiveness of economic sanctions in inflicting economic pain and in compelling policy changes in the target (Cortright and Lopez 2000:3, van Bergeijk 1999:98). Sanctions regimes with a remarkable economic impact have failed to induce changes in the conduct of target governments. Conversely, the mere threat of sanctions has sometimes succeeded in bringing about the desired policy change (van Bergeijk 1994:23, Buchet de Neuilly 2003:102, Barber 1979:389). Nevertheless, it remains that economic and political effectiveness are not totally unrelated; the quest for accurate determinants for successful sanctions has thus persisted over the decades.

Early explanations of the inefficacy of sanctions contested the assumptions regarding the operation of the 'societal transmission belt'. Galtung notes that the naïve theory disregards the target society's capacity to adapt to new circumstances, from both the psychological and the economic point of view: 'one gets used to life under hardship' (Galtung 1967). As for political impact, he observes that value-deprivation may lead to political integration rather than disintegration, producing what he terms the 'rally around the flag' effect (Galtung 1967:388–89; 391). Both aspects have been widely documented in subsequent scholarship: an economy under siege can find ways of successfully adapting to shortages, as do external providers. For their part, leaders can capitalise on externally imposed sanctions to secure their grip on power (Kirshner 1997).

Intent on identifying the determinants of success of sanctions, authors have presented increasingly sophisticated approaches since the mid-1990s (Kirshner 1997, Morgan and Schwebach 1997, Drezner 1999, Blanchard and Ripsman 2002). A number of authors follow the naïve theory while expanding the number of determinants for success (Kaempfer and Lowenberg 1999, Cortright and Lopez 2000). Indeed, improvements to the theory have been virtually limited to the consecutive addition of new variables. Scholars have also attempted to sharpen the naïve theory by taking a closer look at the internal make-up of the target society. This subfield sets out to explain why economic sanctions do not manage to harm the societal fabric of the target society in a way that leads to the unseating of the leadership, as posited by the naïve theory. These authors seek to unravel what happens inside the society of the targeted state under the pressure of sanctions. They put forward various accounts of why the societal conveyor belt does not work – either because of the economic dynamics unleashed by the disruption produced by sanctions (Kirshner 1997), or because of the adverse ways in which opposition groups are affected in authoritarian states (Kaempfer and Lowenberg 1999). Their central innovation consists in the introduction of a variable endogenous to the target, namely whether it is a democratic or an autocratic political system (Grünfeld 1999, van Bergeijk 1999). Kaempfer and Lowenberg draw attention to the importance of a 'reasonably well organized opposition group whose political effectiveness potentially could be enhanced as a consequence of sanctions' (Kaempfer and Lowenberg 1999:52). Cortright and Lopez conclude that assessing the efficacy of sanctions requires an examination of 'how sanctions affect the ability of opposition groups to challenge the policies of the targeted state' (Cortright and Lopez 2000:23). Although none of these authors elaborates on how to operationalise this factor, they point to one of the central questions of sanctions theory, namely, how, exactly, economic distress galvanises political change in the target country. The idea that the internal composition of the target country is a central determinant of efficacy is still somewhat underdeveloped and has not yet been operationalised in sanctions evaluation. In any case, these attempts reflect the widely held belief that the naïve theory can be transformed into a workable model capable of explaining the success and failure of sanctions by incorporating some variables – so far neglected – that might hold the key.

A second subfield seeks to explain the failure of sanctions on the basis of rational-choice approaches. These authors elaborate more sophisticated explanations for the relatively low success rate of sanctions. Their approaches depart from the 're-shuffling of variables' witnessed in the mainstream literature, as they point to structural problems with the operation of sanctions. The explanations by Drezner and Tsebelis are representative of the increasing application of models borrowed from the field of economic theory to explain the effectiveness of sanctions (Tsebelis 1990, van Bergeijk 1994, Morgan and Schwebach 1997, Drezner 1999). Drezner formulates what he calls the 'sanctions paradox' on the basis of a conflict-expectation model. Departing from the premise that conceding in the face of economic coercion implies a redistribution of political assets between target and sender, Drezner finds that the expectation of future conflict will render the sender more willing to impose sanctions and the target less willing to concede. Hence, sanctions between allies will be less likely but more effective, while sanctions between adversaries will be more likely but less effective (Drezner 1999:5). Other authors question the belief that sanctions fail because they do not obtain compliance, positing that sanctions work primarily at the threat stage (Hovi et al. 2005):

> Sanctions are … imposed only if the target refuses to comply. [I]f a credible threat of sanctions fails, it is usually a sign that the target does not intend to comply even if sanctions are imposed. [W]hen sanctions are imposed, there are often good reasons to expect them to fail.
>
> (Hovi et al. 2005:482)

In conclusion, over forty years after Galtung criticised the naïve theory of sanctions, it still constitutes the basis for the evaluation of sanctions efficacy. The permanence of the naïve theory as the foundation on which evaluations are premised, notwithstanding the fact that its fallacy has been widely demonstrated, is probably due to the fact that no better explanatory model for the success of sanctions has yet been developed.

Sanctions that 'create conditions'

Sanctions that have failed to coerce a target into acquiescing to the sender's demands are, nonetheless, frequently credited with having created the 'necessary conditions' for a policy change. This assumption equates to the identification of a third mode of operation, in which the leadership is eventually unseated, although not with the immediacy originally expected. Examples abound. Cortright and Lopez argue that while sanctions against South Africa were not originally judged successful, they 'set the stage for other internal events that led to the dismantling of apartheid', making 'a major contribution to fundamental political change' (Cortright and Lopez 1996:8). Commenting on the Rhodesian case, Elliot contends that the 'impact of sanctions over time increased the pressure on the white regime and ultimately contributed in a modest way to the desired outcome' (Elliot 1998:56). According to Hufbauer and his collaborators, Indian sanctions against Nepal in 1989/90 triggered a democratisation crisis that ultimately led to the desired reorientation of Nepalese security policy (quoted in Pape 1997:105).

The way in which sanctions accomplished their objectives in these cases differs from the definition of success formulated above: sanctions failed to bring about a change in the conduct of the target government. Still, they are held to have been successful in *setting the stage* for internal change. These authors thus suggest that there exists an indirect path for sanctions to reach their objectives. The problem here is that these claims are difficult to demonstrate. Pape has expressed some methodological uneasiness with the linking of economic sanctions to internal political change in the abovementioned case of the Indian sanctions against Nepal. He contends that although the Indian sanctions did cause some dissatisfaction with the regime in 1989, 'we do not know what role they played in the opposition leader's decision in February 1990 to call the general strikes that led to the regime's collapse' (Pape 1997:105). This point highlights the pertinence of Kaempfer and Lowenberg's claim that the capacity of sanctions to enhance opposition groups' potential to challenge leadership or its policies is central to success. This particular question may hold the key to explaining different outcomes, illuminating the mechanisms that empower opposition groups in some cases, or that allow leaderships to weaken opposition groups in others.

Targeted sanctions entering the sanctions debate

The emergence of targeted or 'smart' sanctions in the mid-1990s profoundly transformed the landscape. This concept is of major importance to the EU. Vocal advocates of smart sanctions, EU member states have levied only targeted measures since the early 1990s. Because they differ from classical sanctions in their nature and expected mode of operation, their emergence has significant theoretical implications in the study of their efficacy. Under the term 'economic sanctions', classical scholarship understands three kinds of coercive economic measures:

- a *boycott* restricts the demand for certain products from the target country
- an *embargo* restricts the exports of certain products to the target economy
- *financial sanctions* include two main types of measures: restriction or suspension of lending to and investment in the target economy, and the freezing of foreign assets (van Bergeijk 1994:20).

The notion of targeted sanctions resulted from a serious crisis in the application of comprehensive trade sanctions at a time when UN sanctions on Iraq came under strong criticism. Their severe humanitarian impact on the Iraqi population caused an outcry in European public opinion which made the continued use of this tool politically unsustainable. The notion of targeted sanctions was developed as a reaction to that situation. Targeted sanctions 'are meant to focus their impact on leaders, political elites and segments of society believed responsible for objectionable behaviour, while reducing collateral damage to the general population and third countries' (Hufbauer and Oegg 2000:3). The concept encompasses various types of limited sanctions likely to inflict direct damage on those individuals responsible for the objectionable policy, while sparing the general population. Two categories of targeted measures with different modes of operation can be distinguished:

1. *Personal* measures, which cause personal discomfort to decision makers and their immediate associates. This group includes the freezing of personal financial assets, travel and visa bans.
2. *Selective* measures, which reduce the availability of means to implement the contested policies. This group includes arms embargoes, sanctions on particular commodities, such as oil, diamonds or timber, the freezing of state assets and flight bans.

This dual classification of what can be called *personal sanctions* and *selective sanctions* illustrates that, as with comprehensive trade sanctions, two modes of operation are foreseen, and the types of measures involved are heterogeneous. Moreover, the second group does not totally depart from the logic of comprehensive sanctions. It consists of trade measures and can be situated as an intermediate type between personal sanctions, which exclusively affect individuals, and general trade embargoes (Brzoska 2003:522).

Targeted sanctions appear to be expected to operate in a similar fashion to that posited by the naïve theory of sanctions, and simply transpose the naïve theory to the individual or group level. It is still unclear whether targeted sanctions are expected to work on the basis of the disutility they cause their targets in terms of the disruption of their day-to-day habits, inability to travel and to conduct business and/or lack of access to financial resources, or by virtue of the stigma they inflict. The uncertainty over the specific mode of operation of targeted sanctions emanates not only from lack of precision in the formulation of the theory, but also from the unavailability of empirical evidence which would allow to ascertain the relative importance of psychological as opposed to material aspects in bringing about target compliance. Sanctions scholars unconvinced by the notion of targeted measures base their scepticism on the absence of economic harm inflicted on the target (Hufbauer et al. 2007). In this point of view, the present investigation provides some initial insights into the ability of blacklist-based sanctions to challenge the logic of measures affecting the economy.

The employment of targeted sanctions instantly provoked scholarly interest in the topic (Cortright and Lopez 2002, Tostensen and Bull 2002). This attention also spread to the level of states interested in replacing traditional economic sanctions with this tool. A series of conferences on UN targeted sanctions, known as the sanctions reform process, were organised by three European countries: Switzerland, Germany and Sweden. The conference reports from the Interlaken process, the Bonn–Berlin process and the Stockholm process produced useful guides aimed at improving the design and technical implementation of these sanctions (Biersteker 2001, Brzoska 2001, Wallensteen et al. 2003).

Three major caveats have been expressed with regard to the feasibility of targeted sanctions. First, their alleged lack of humanitarian consequences has been questioned (Tostensen and Bull 2002). An often-cited example is the aviation ban that the UN Security Council planned to levy on Sudan. Following the assessment by the expert panel that it would bear grave humanitarian consequences for the delivery of supplies for the population, the Security Council refrained from imposing it. A second caveat is of a more technical nature. As targeted sanctions are far more sophisticated measures than general trade bans, their implementation requires administrative and technical capacities that many states lack. This is particularly the case since targets are often located in the developing world; thus, neighbouring states are often underdeveloped countries with weak capacities to implement sanctions. Capacity-building activities currently under way in the framework of the UN's Counter-Terrorism Committee are helpful in attenuating this problem, as they simultaneously support the infrastructure required for the enforcement of targeted sanctions (Ward 2005).

The final caveat concerns efficacy. The concern that targeted sanctions might not be more effective than comprehensive embargoes responds to the uncertainty about 'whether the move towards targeted sanctions is due to a view that they work as or more effectively than general economic sanctions or simply a response to the humanitarian impact of sanctions when there is no certainty that they work at all' (Chesterman and Pouligny 2003:506). Whatever the case, there is general agreement among experts that only targeted sanctions are politically feasible – classical trade embargoes are unlikely to garner enough support from the international community to ensure that they are properly implemented and enforced (Cosgrove 2002). Some authors have expressed scepticism as to whether targeted sanctions are capable of hitting leaders to such a degree that they will change their behaviour: 'the danger with smart sanctions is that the naïve theory of "political gain through economic pain" is substituted by a similar naïve theory of "political gain through nauseating the powerful"' (Brzoska 2003). Due to the novelty of the concept, we still rely on a relatively limited amount of empirical experience as to whether targeted sanctions episodes achieve their expected results. The interim assessments expressed so far are rather negative – the overall percentage of success of targeted sanctions is lower than the average, which does not augur well, especially given that such assessments stem from proponents of sanctions (Cortright and Lopez 2000, Hufbauer and Oegg 2000).

What is wrong with how scholarship has evaluated sanctions so far?

The evolution of success evaluation: from sanctions 'never *work' to* 'sometimes *work'*

Early sanctions literature presented an unequivocally negative assessment of their efficacy, thus expressing pessimistic prospects for their future use (Galtung 1967, Wallensteen 1968, Doxey 1972). The overall judgement on the efficacy of sanctions was that they *never* worked, judging by their disappointing record. Scholars reached this assessment primarily on the basis of case studies, such as that of the UN's sanctions against Southern Rhodesia. Consequently, scholarship at that time set out to explain the lack of success of sanctions. The failure of sanctions was ascribed to the fallacy of the underlying theory, the naïve theory. They did not work because their expected mode of operation was premised on erroneous assumptions. The societal transmission belt failed to transform economic pressure into political disintegration. Beyond determining that the naïve theory was wrong, some authors even identified some counterproductive effects in the operation of sanctions (Galtung 1967).

A breakthrough occurred with the publication of the work *Economic Sanctions Reconsidered* by a team of economists in 1985, followed by a second edition in 1990, whose aim was to ascertain the determinants under which sanctions are most likely to be efficacious (Hufbauer et al. 1990:13). They analysed a dataset composed of over 100 sanctions episodes of the twentieth century, and found that sanctions had been at least partially successful in 34 per cent of cases. This finding instilled a new optimism into sanctions research. However, its scientific soundness does not remain without caveats. The study was criticised on the basis of both methodological (Pape 1997 and 1998) and statistical considerations (Bonetti 1991, Cooper Drury 1998), while some of the authors of the 1960s and 1970s continued to defend their pessimistic line. One of the features characterising today's sanctions research landscape is the fact that much of the academic literature is authored by either proponents (de Jonge Oudraat 2000, Rogers 1996, Hufbauer et al. 1990, Cortright and Lopez 2000) or detractors of this instrument (Lektzian 2003, Rosas 2003).

From 'one goal can be evaluated' to 'more goals can be evaluated'

It is commonplace to judge success on the basis of whether sanctions 'appeared to contribute to the achievement of stated policy goals' (Elliot 1995:52). While this criterion might seem straightforward at first sight, it appears much less so if we take into account that sanctions fulfil *several* functions and that the accomplishment of stated goals is only one of these. Some scholars acknowledge that sanctions do not exclusively pursue the goal of achieving the target's compliance with the sender's goals, but that they are also intended to achieve other effects (Barber 1979, Lindsay 1986, Elliot 1995). The multiplicity of functions fulfilled by sanctions was recognised at a relatively early stage in sanctions scholarship. Barber identified a variety of possible roles for sanctions beyond their coercive purpose (Barber 1979). He distinguishes between primary, secondary and tertiary objectives of sanctions. Primary objectives are concerned with the actions and behaviour of the target state or regime. Secondary objectives relate to the status, reputation and position of the sender government(s) and are directed at both domestic and international audiences. 'Positively, they are intended to demonstrate the effectiveness of the imposing government … the purpose of sanctions here is to demonstrate a willingness and capacity to act. Negatively, the purpose may simply be to anticipate or deflect criticism' (Barber 1979:380). Tertiary objectives are concerned with broader international considerations. They may include efforts by the senders to ensure 'a certain pattern of behaviour in international affairs', or 'support for a particular international structure, such as the League of Nations' (Barber 1979:382).

The categorisation by Barber constitutes a useful analytical point of departure. The imposition of sanctions with the *objective* of bringing about change in another state can simultaneously perform other *functions*: that of satisfying public opinion, on the one hand, and supporting norms and multilateral structures, on the other. Galtung puts forward a further element when he defines sanctions as 'actions ... with either or both of two purposes: to punish the receivers by depriving them of some value and/or to make the receivers comply with certain norms' (Galtung 1967:409). Barber also provides some insights into the relationship between objectives. The relative weight of the different categories of objectives may shift when sanctions are applied over a lengthy period (Barber 1979:372). This draws attention to the fact that the different functions of sanctions have, by definition, long-term effects whose importance may go well beyond the realisation of the stated objectives. Following up on the identification of a multiplicity of goals, Lindsay posits that states pursue five aims when they impose sanctions, adding 'subversion' and 'deterrence' to the categories put forward by Barber (Lindsay 1986). There is some disagreement as to whether the punitive effect of sanctions qualifies as a goal. While punishment is sometimes regarded as one of the objectives of sanctions (Galtung 1967), Lindsay argues that punishment is more adequately characterised as a means for the operation of sanctions (Lindsay 1986:156).

As these scholars recognised the multiplicity of goals of sanctions, they also acknowledge that different goals should be measured separately. Still, they disagree as far as the feasibility of the assessment is concerned. While Barber dismisses the assessment of the secondary and tertiary functions of sanctions as virtually unfeasible, Lindsay attempts to evaluate the effectiveness of all five of the goals he identifies. Yet, the study by Hufbauer, Schott and Elliot published the same year sets out to assess the efficacy of sanctions exclusively in terms of achieving compliance. The acknowledgement that sanctions have goals other than 'compliance' helps to assuage the concerns of a strand of scholarship puzzled or dismayed at the continued use of sanctions despite their alleged ineffectiveness. Barber and Lindsay not only concede that compliance is far from being the only goal of sanctions, and that the importance allocated by senders to the different objectives pursued through sanctions might vary over time (Barber 1979); they also suggest that compliance might not be the most important goal, or that it may not even be among the objectives of a sanctions regime (Lindsay 1986). In fact, in order to make an accurate estimate of the percentage of sanctions episodes that achieved the goal of compelling a policy change, it would first be necessary to ascertain which of these were actually aiming to bring about such changes. Still, compliance stands out as a goal not because it is meant to be the *primary* goal of sanctions, or even because it is consistently envisaged as such. What makes compliance different from all other goals is that virtually all other functions and goals may be used as means towards its achievement.

In conclusion, an increasingly optimistic trend towards the feasibility of assessing success is apparent in that scholars grew confident that the efficacy of sanctions can be assessed, and conducted some tentative evaluations. Whereas it seems contradictory that the judgements on the outcome of sanctions preceded the development of a discussion on the feasibility of such a judgement, and even of their finality, the rising optimism regarding the feasibility of such assessments encourages further deliberation about the methods of evaluating the efficacy of sanctions.

Developing a methodology for measuring efficacy

The negative assessment of the efficacy of sanctions is partly due to a selection bias emanating from the predominance of case studies over large-N analyses in the literature. As noted by Drezner (1999:20), this has resulted in an overconcentration of scholarly attention on 'difficult' cases rather than on the 'broader picture'. Studies entailing and assessing comprehensive databases are rare. It is problematic, protracted and ultimately unsuccessful sanctions episodes that normally constitute the object of these investigations, contributing to a distorted picture of the relative efficacy of sanctions. The inclusion in large-N analyses of cases that were hardly publicised – if at all – due to the scarce significance of the target, or that have been forgotten in the collective memory, can help to control for the overemphasis on failures.

Distinguishing 'economic' from 'political' effectiveness

Before proceeding with our analysis, a central conceptual clarification is in order. A distinction should be drawn between the notions of effectiveness in inflicting disutility on the target and of efficacy in compelling policy changes. There is no unified terminology, as authors use different terms to describe these notions. Van Bergeijk distinguishes 'effectiveness' from 'success' (van Bergeijk 1994:23), whereas Cortright and Lopez speak of 'economic' and 'political' success (Cortright and Lopez 2000:3). While de Jonge Oudraat distinguishes between 'effectiveness in terms of economic impact' and 'effectiveness from a political point of view' (de Jonge Oudraat 2001:328), Kirshner refers to 'effectiveness' at a 'first' and 'second' stage (Kirshner 2002:171). Brzoska assesses the aim of the sanctions regime (*Sanktionsziel*) separately from the political aim (*Politikziel*) (Brzoska 2005). This distinction is sometimes ignored, and economic effectiveness is confused with political efficacy in studies whose definition of success suggests that their aim is not primarily to investigate the economic impact of sanctions, but their efficacy in inducing concessions by the target. In the interests of clarity, the present study will refer to 'disutility' to describe the damage produced by sanctions, and 'efficacy' to characterise their impact on the conduct of leaders. The synonymous terms 'effectiveness' and 'efficacy' are used interchangeably.

Ascertaining the goals of sanctions

'Success' is routinely judged on the basis of whether or not sanctions contribute to the achievement of stated policy objectives. The yardstick of a successful sanctions regime is an 'observable change in behaviour' (de Jonge Oudraat 2001:325). When determining the success of a sanctions episode, others confine their analysis to 'changes in policies'. Policy outcomes are judged 'against the stated policy goal of the sender country' (Hufbauer et al. 1985:32).

The measurement of changes in behaviour against stated policy goals is fraught with difficulties. Sender countries do not always announce their goals in a clear manner (Hufbauer et al. 1985:31). Until the late 1990s, EU sanctions were imposed without spelling out the policy goals pursued. Indeed, imposing documents typically include a *description* of the situation giving rise to the imposition of sanctions, while remaining silent on the policy changes that are expected from the target. Arguably, the condemnation of certain policies can also be interpreted as the demand to reverse such policies. If sanctions were triggered by the imprisonment of political opponents, it can be presumed that the policy goal pursued by the sender is their release. However, it is often hard to ascertain exactly what the sender expects of the target. EU sanctions against the Transnistrian leadership were imposed due to its 'obstructionism of the peace process' (Council of the European Union 2003a). From this formulation, we can infer that the sender's intention is to compel the target to cooperate in the peace process; however, no concrete output is specified.

From the sender's point of view, vague or indeterminate objectives can have major political advantages, since they dispose of considerable leeway to decide when objectives are met. In the case of concessions by the target, the sender alone determines whether and when these are sufficient to warrant the lifting of sanctions. When sanctions are imposed by international organisations, this problem can be exacerbated by the fact that the language of the imposing documents is often the result of hard-won compromises, where ambiguous formulations become necessary to obtain the agreement of all senders. The fact that goals are not explicitly spelled out as such makes it difficult to ascertain if and when goals have been accomplished. Public statements of officials from the sender country, supplemented by the assessment of historians, are often used as an indicator (Hufbauer et al. 1985:2). Statements by decision makers cannot be considered completely reliable sources, as both sides may have an interest in delivering a politically convenient version of events or even in distorting data (Harris 1968:5–20). Nevertheless, they must be taken into account in the absence of any further evidence.

The single standard for success

Modifying the conduct of the target state's leadership is not always the *main* purpose of sanctions. Some sanctions may never even have intended to produce a change in the target's behaviour (Elliot 1998:52). In fact, while the existence of a multiplicity of functions of sanctions is generally acknowledged, their success is only measured against one single standard, namely, whether they accomplish their coercive aim. This state of affairs risks the paradoxical situation where some sanctions regimes are judged as failed for not having yielded a result they were never meant to deliver. The rationale for this single standard of success can be largely ascribed to the fact that the coercive effect of sanctions is the only one which is clearly measurable. The success of sanctions is thus normally measured in a 'visible change of behaviour'. In contrast, the success of the other functions fulfilled by sanctions cannot be easily assessed. Barber expressed pessimism regarding the feasibility of their measurement: 'Judgments on the success or failure of sanctions in achieving their secondary aims are difficult to reach … In the case of tertiary objectives there are even greater problems of evaluation than there were for the secondary' (Barber 1979:381–83).

It is indeed extremely difficult to recognise when a sanctions regime has deterred a third party from engaging in objectionable behaviour. Equally, some sanctions can be held to have realised their functions, such as punishment or the satisfaction of public opinion, by their very imposition. While some observers have pointed out that this exclusive focus creates a misleading impression of ineffectiveness (Cortright and Lopez 2000:15), it is nevertheless striking that none of the many critics of the single standard of success (Elliot 1998, Mack and Khan 2000) has attempted to measure other effects.

The oversimplifying dichotomy 'success and failure'

Another question that merits consideration regarding the standard of success concerns the method of assessment. Some of the methodological choices made by analysts can be partly blamed for the overall conclusion that sanctions are ineffective instruments of influence. This regards two main aspects. One concerns the implicit assumption that the objective of sanctions is to 'return to the status quo that prevailed prior to the act … which brought the sanctions about' (Daoudi and Dajani 1983:2). Since the goals of sanctions regimes are often vague, it is presumed that they are imposed for the purpose of reversing policies with a view to re-establishing the preceding status quo. Drezner criticises this approach as a 'wrong counterfactual':

> The hypothetical alternative is the outcome if coercion was not attempted in the first place. If the targeted country does not change its policies at all, then the event should be judged as a failure. If there is some compromise, however, and the value of the concession outweighs the sender's costs of coercion, then the episode counts as a partial success.
>
> (Drezner 1999:18)

This contention highlights a central methodological challenge in the evaluation of sanctions. The dichotomous values *success* and *failure* are insufficient to accommodate middle-range outcomes that fall short of the accomplishment of the stated goals, or the re-establishment of the status quo, but which nevertheless represent an improvement with respect to the situation prior to the imposition of sanctions. The omission of intermediate values can distort the results of the evaluation, as they fail to distinguish between limited concessions made by the target and none at all.

A second consideration relates to the fact that sanctions regimes often pursue a multiplicity of goals which often remain unaccounted for in the analyses. In their research design, Hufbauer, Schott and Elliot classify episodes of sanctions regimes with more than one objective according to the purportedly most difficult: 'when another goal underlies or accompanies a destabilisation case, we have generally listed these cases only in the destabilisation group' (Hufbauer et al. 1985:29, 43). This approach overlooks the attainment of secondary or minor goals, which constitute successes in their own right.

The case of Iraq can serve as an illustration for both preceding points. Cortright and Lopez argue that sanctions have led to the partial or complete fulfilment of as many as seven of the eight objectives spelled out in UNSC Resolution 687 (Cortright and Lopez 2000:37, 55). However, despite this partial success, where success is defined as a dichotomous variable and the performance of sanctions is judged only against the most difficult objective, the Iraqi case will be coded as a failure.

Determining the 'sanctions contribution'

Once the goals of sanctions have been identified, and the goal they were designed for has been attained, how can we tell that sanctions actually contributed to that outcome? The most fundamental problem faced in sanctions research consists in ascertaining whether sanctions contribute to the expected result, and to what extent they do so. This is especially difficult in view of the fact that sanctions are often embedded in wider coercive strategies where other elements are at play. Aware of this problem, Hufbauer, Schott and Elliot dissociated the variable 'policy result' from the variable 'sanctions contribution'. The *policy result* is defined as the extent to which the sanctions objectives were achieved, while the *sanctions contribution* is defined as the degree to which sanctions contribute to this outcome. The dependent variable, the success of a sanctions episode, results from a combination of both variables. Each of these elements is ranked on a scale from 1 (lowest) to 4 (highest), and then multiplied. The resulting figure, the *success score*, will qualify as a success if it is 9 or higher. For the policy result, the scores are: (1) failed outcome, (2) unclear but possibly positive outcome, (3) positive outcome, (4) successful outcome. For the sanctions contribution, scores feature: (1) zero or negative contribution, (2) minor contribution, (3) modest contribution, (4) significant contribution (Hufbauer et al. 1985:32–33).

Yet, Hufbauer, Schott and Elliot do not explain precisely how they evaluate the contribution made by sanctions to a particular policy outcome. A glance at the dataset reveals that the figures for sanctions contribution tend to reflect the figures for policy results. While a case-by-case reassessment of the whole dataset would be necessary in order to ascertain any bias, there seems to be a correlation between the overall outcome and the sanctions contribution: the higher the score for outcome, the higher the score for sanction contribution. Thus, the reader gains the impression that whenever a coercive strategy is crowned with success, sanctions have made a substantial contribution to that outcome.

Controlling for 'concomitant policies' and the use of force

Hufbauer, Schott and Elliot also provide for a variable in their dataset accounting for the existence of what they call 'companion policy measures', which include 'covert action', 'quasi-military action' and 'regular military action' (Hufbauer et al. 1985:34). However, this enumeration presents problems because the kinds of coercive measures dubbed 'companion policies' are far more compelling than economic sanctions, as they indeed recognise: 'Sanctions frequently serve as a junior weapon in a battery of diplomatic artillery aimed at the antagonistic state' (Hufbauer et al. 1985:33). It would be more accurate to label sanctions the *companion policy*, since what they call *concomitant policies* constitute the principal coercive action. In this sense, this variable is the most important control variable for the dependent variable *sanctions success.*[3] Therefore, the inclusion of a variable merely indicating the presence of companion policies is insufficient to control for other factors leading to the outcome. Hufbauer, Schott and Elliot fail to clarify the relationship between the variable *companion policies* and the variable *sanctions contribution*.

The failure to control for the use of force is one of Pape's main criticisms of the study by Hufbauer, Schott and Elliot. He claims that 18 of the 40 cases of alleged sanctions success are miscoded as they were actually determined by force (Pape 1997:99). How much credit should be assigned to economic sanctions in cases where they were imposed alongside the use of force? This question is especially relevant since Hufbauer, Schott and Elliot's aim is to analyse the independent efficacy of sanctions (1990). A possible way of overcoming this problem is to credit sanctions with success only in those cases where force is not employed. However, Pape expresses reservations: 'given that sanctions are often used in conjunction with diplomacy and military pressures, this approach would unfairly stack the deck against sanctions' (Pape 1998:70). He therefore suggests three criteria to credit sanctions with success even in the presence of military force (Pape 1998:97):

1. the target state concedes to a significant part of the coercer's demands
2. economic sanctions are threatened or actually applied before the target changes its behaviour, and
3. no more-credible explanation exists for the target's change of behaviour.

The third point is further specified by the *timing of concessions* in relation to specific military threats or economic sanctions, and the *statements by the target state's* decision makers (Pape 1998:98). If economic and military threats are made simultaneously, and statements by target-state decision makers are unavailable, then the case should be coded as indeterminate.

The present investigation is bound to face the challenge of dissociating the contributions made by sanctions, since targeted sanctions are invariably conceived by policy makers as a complementary measure within a broader strategy. This is consistently recognised by policy makers and officials. For instance, the former director of the Security Council Affairs Division at the UN Secretariat asserts that 'smart sanctions alone might not be sufficient to induce compliance by the target with the Council's resolution. For this reason, they must be integrated into an overall conflict resolution strategy and be complemented by other … measures' (Stephanides 2002). The present investigation adopts Pape's criteria for the determination of the variable *sanctions contribution*, adapted to the specificity of the type of sanctions studied here.

The use of political statements as evidence

Pape refers to statements by the decision makers of the *target* state as a source for ascertaining whether or not sanctions should be credited for a policy change. Regrettably, statements by neither targets nor senders constitute totally reliable sources. They are both susceptible to distorting events in order to present their decisions in a politically favourable light: 'both sides may have an interest in distorting and/or incompletely supplying data' (Harris 1968:8). According to Baldry and Dollery, data were purposefully distorted by South African authorities at the time of UN sanctions: 'apart from the suppression of disaggregated trade and investment statistics by the South African authorities, nations, firms and individuals engaging in economic relationships with South Africa tend to disguise or understate the extent of their transactions' (1992:1–2, quoted in van Bergeijk 1994:22). Van Bergeijk himself notes that Saudi Arabia reported its full compliance with the UN oil embargo on South Africa, while the Shipping Research Bureau established that 76 oil tankers departing from Saudi Arabia delivered oil to South Africa in an eight-year period while the sanctions were in force (van Bergeijk 1994:22).

Nevertheless, from a methodological point of view, the validity of the claim that sanctions were responsible for the leadership's change of behaviour would be substantially enhanced if some evidence from the target side were available. Assessments of the efficacy of sanctions commonly stem from the sender's rather than the target's side, partly due to the fact that statements by the target are often unavailable in the international press. When evaluating the success of UN sanctions against Yugoslavia, Cortright and Lopez quote the official UN report as well as statements by the US ambassador and chief US negotiator as evidence that sanctions compelled the Belgrade leadership to sever links with the Bosnian Serb party (Cortright and Lopez 2000:68). Thus, maximum use of the available statements by decision makers should be made.

Targets are reluctant to concede openly that they are ready to capitulate to pressure, even if they eventually yield. In response to the aid freeze imposed on Turkey following the coup d'état of September 1980 and the subsequent suspension of civil liberties, Turkish authorities protested that blocking aid was 'an attempt to interfere in domestic Turkish politics', while General Evren is reported to have claimed that Turkey would 'not be hurried by foreign opinion into a premature move towards parliamentary democracy' (Keesing quoted in Hufbauer et al. 1985). Yet, less than one year later, the military regime gave assurances that it would soon take steps towards the restoration of democracy, and in 1983 the Turkish leadership legalised political parties and announced parliamentary elections (Hufbauer et al. 1985:712). Public statements by targeted authorities following the imposition of sanctions are invariably negative, and sometimes even aggressive. Following the imposition of a ban on the import of Argentinean products by the European Community, Minister Alemann claimed: 'The Community is mistaken if it thinks it can persuade the president or the military junta … we are prepared to hold out as many months as necessary until our sovereignty is recognized' (Hufbauer et al. 1985:718). When the US decided to subscribe to the embargo, the Foreign Minister stated: 'the Argentine people will never forget that in a critical hour of their history … the US sided with an aggressor' (Hufbauer et al. 1985:719). Equally, China does not openly concede that it has improved its human rights record in response to international pressure: 'they present their decisions as motivated by their commitment to human rights' (interview 2005). In the present study, statements by both senders and targets will be used whenever available, while bearing the caveats mentioned in mind.

2 EU sanctions

Evolution, legal framework and policy

From the early 1980s, the EC – later EU – established the practice of imposing sanctions on third countries in the absence of United Nations Security Council (UNSC) mandates. The following presents a general overview of the development, as well as the legal framework of this aspect of European foreign policy. The aim of this background chapter on the evolution and complex legal configuration of EU sanctions is to facilitate the understanding of this practice, illuminating both the political impulses that shaped the existing procedure and its impact on policy output.

Understanding the institutional configuration of EU decision-making process on sanctions is useful because it has a direct impact on their outcome. Ultimately, the institutional set-up for the adoption of sanctions also has an impact on efficacy. The flexibility with which the sanctions instrument can be wielded significantly affects its efficacy. Scholars emphasise the use of sanctions as part of a bargaining process, highlighting that the ability to reciprocate concessions made by the target is essential for success. In fact, those who have analysed EU sanctions policy have partly blamed complicated EU decision-making procedures for the inefficacy of their sanctions (de Wilde d'Estmael 1998, Buchet de Neuilly 2003). Also, the institutional and legal set up of sanctions instruments reflects the significance that the EU attaches to this instrument, and how it conceives of its utility.

Origins and evolution of EU sanctions practice

EU sanctions practice has two strands. On the one hand, the EU adopts measures to implement sanctions imposed by a United Nations Security Council (UNSC) Resolution.[1] On the other hand, the EU may impose measures in the absence of a Security Council Resolution, which can be described as the 'autonomous' (Koutrakos 2001) or 'independent' (Wessel 1999) practice of sanctions. In order to understand how this practice came about, it is first necessary to look at the EU's role in implementing the UNSC measures. Until the end of the Cold War, the UNSC only imposed sanctions on two occasions: against Rhodesia in the mid-1960s, and against South Africa in the mid-1970s.

When the UNSC mandated sanctions against Rhodesia between 1965 and 1968, EC member states decided to implement them individually with national measures rather than through a Community instrument. However, the national measures implementing the UNSC Resolution differed in content and were implemented at different times, which significantly hindered the effectiveness of the sanctions regime. Homogeneity considerations thus compelled member states to shift from this original method towards the implementation of sanctions through the Community, i.e. by having recourse to the Common Commercial Policy set out in Art. 133 EC. The new method consisted in agreeing on the imposition of measures within the intergovernmental framework of European Political Cooperation (EPC), and subsequently adopting a Community Regulation for their implementation. The first sanctions regimes implemented through a Community instrument were imposed against the USSR in 1980 following the Soviet invasion of Afghanistan, and again in 1981 as a response to the imposition of martial law in Poland (Council of the European Communities 1982a). A further instance followed in 1982 with the invasion of the Falkland Islands by Argentina.[2]

This autonomous EU practice was facilitated by the progressive enhancement of foreign policy coordination amongst member states, signalled by the evolution of the EPC into the CFSP. In parallel with this development, the decision-making process for the establishment of EC sanctions was formalised in subsequent Treaty revisions. In its present form, it still retains its peculiar two-phased character. The political decision to impose sanctions is first taken in the framework of the CFSP in a Common Position. Depending on the nature of the sanctions, the second phase can take two possible forms. Arms embargoes, diplomatic sanctions and visa bans are implemented directly by member states, as they concern national competencies. In contrast, the implementation of financial sanctions, partial trade measures and flight bans require the adoption of a Council Regulation as they involve Community competences.[3]

EU autonomous sanctions have always coexisted with the implementation of UN sanctions. Both practices are closely intertwined. Sanctions regimes originally imposed by the EU have been superseded by UNSC sanctions, as in the cases of Ethiopia/Eritrea, Yugoslavia, Iraq and Libya. This is hardly surprising, given the overlapping membership of the UK and France in both organisations, and often results from the EU's policy to promote the adoption of its sanctions regimes by the UNSC (Bohr 1993). Finally, the EU has also imposed additional sanctions on countries already subject to UNSC sanctions. However, in these cases it is not always easy to distinguish whether EU sanctions are supplementarily imposed by the EU or whether they represent the specification of the often vaguely formulated UNSC Resolutions.

The legal framework of EU sanctions

The international legal framework

The term 'sanctions' does not have any fixed definition under international law; i.e. no authoritative legal source contains a universally accepted definition of the term (Partsch 1994). In order to avoid this legal imprecision the EU refers to this instrument as 'restrictive measures' (*mesures négatives*) in its legal acts.

Since positive international law does not provide any definition, its meaning must be inferred from the practice of states. The concept of sanctions encompasses a wide array of legal figures. Among them, the category that seems to conform best to the usage attached to the practice in international relations scholarship is defined as 'measures taken by a state acting alone or jointly with others in reply to the behaviour of another state, which, it maintains, is contrary to the international law' (Combacau 1992:313). From a legal point of view, this concept overlaps with the notions of 'reprisals' and 'retorsion'. However, in practice, sanctions are imposed in reaction to forms of behaviour that the sender considers objectionable, even if they do not constitute a breach of codified norms. They are not intended to be repressive or punitive, but rather 'coercive' (Combacau 1992:314). The sender does not primarily intend to punish the state for a wrongful act already completed, but to coerce it into putting an end to the continuing situation resulting from the initial action. Most often, these measures are applied in situations where the offending state can still renounce its unlawful conduct and cease to produce the continuing damage flowing from it.

In the doctrine, the definition of economic sanctions appears to be better established than that of 'sanctions' in general. Bohr defines economic sanctions as a 'government initiated ban on trade with another state in reaction to illegal or politically undesirable acts of that state' (Bohr 1993). Koutrakos describes sanctions as measures that 'connote the exercise of pressure by one state or coalition of states to produce a change in the political behaviour of another state or group of states' (Koutrakos 2001:49). Lukaschek offers a more complete definition: 'trade restricting discriminatory measures imposed by one authority against another subject of international law in pursuance of a foreign policy objective, namely to alter the conduct of the target state' (Lukaschek 2002). Leaving aside the fact that all these definitions deal exclusively with economic sanctions, they entail some elements that are essentially constitutive of the concept of sanctions. They are geared to 'exercising pressure' with a view to 'producing a change in the political behaviour of another actor'. Importantly, they are imposed 'in reaction to illegal or politically undesirable acts'. From an international legal point of view, the notion of sanctions effectively encompasses three categories of measures: the withdrawal of unilaterally given benefits, the suspension of international agreements, and bans. Each rests on a different legal basis, which means that they are susceptible to use under different circumstances. The first category, unilaterally given benefits, encompasses financial or technical assistance, development aid and trade benefits like the Generalized System of Preferences (GSP). The suspension of international agreements concluded by the Community with third countries constitutes a second, separate category. Finally, the category 'bans' is in itself broad, as it entails embargoes on particular commodities, such as arms or oil, bans on financial services and investment, as well as air transportation bans.

Under what circumstances can the EU wield each of these types of sanctions? When the EU acts to implement mandatory sanctions imposed by the UNSC, measures override any other legal obligations.[4] However, these kinds of measures do not form part of the present analysis, which is concerned with the imposition of EU autonomous sanctions where the EU is acting unilaterally. The imposition of each of the above categories of measures gives rise to different legal situations. What is commonly known as sanctions actually encompass two different notions: 'retorsions' and 'countermeasures' or 'reprisals'.

Unilaterally given benefits

In the case of benefits unilaterally given to third countries, the EU is empowered to withdraw these at will, since it is under no legal obligation to provide them. The measures applied here qualify as 'retorsions', defined as 'measures that do not conflict with any international obligations' (Paasivirta and Rosas 2002). The withdrawal of GSP is the example *par excellence* here, since the EU is under no contractual obligation to apply them. The EU is free to determine the circumstances under which it wishes to interrupt the application of such tariff preferences. According to present EU rules, GSP can be withdrawn on the grounds of slavery, forced labour, shortcomings in customs controls, fraud and unfair trading practices.

Suspension of international agreements

A different situation arises in the case of the suspension of international agreements concluded between the Community and third countries. The suspension of agreements often entails the withdrawal of benefits, but in this case, their provision is embedded in a contractual relation. The *lex generalis*, Art. 60 of the Vienna Convention, permits the suspension of treaties if the other party fails to respect an essential element of the agreement. International treaties often contain provisions that govern their suspension, acting thereby as a *lex specialis.* Two areas of *lex specialis* are particularly relevant in this context. As a member of the WTO, the Community resorts to the dispute settlement mechanism in cases of trade agreements with other WTO members. In addition, the EU has included 'human rights clauses' in most of its bilateral agreements with third countries which envisage the suspension of application in the case of the violation of one of its essential elements. The respect of democratic principles, human rights, the rule of law and fundamental freedoms have been established as essential elements in the bulk of agreements concluded between the EU and third countries in the 1990s (Stangos 2000). The EU currently includes support for the fight against international terrorism and the non-proliferation of weapons of mass destruction as essential elements in its treaties with third countries.

Countermeasures

Finally, bans on products or services that do not fall into any of the abovementioned categories must be justified as countermeasures. The notion of countermeasures or reprisals covers 'measures in conflict with other international obligations justifiable as reactions against prior breaches of the other party of its obligations' (Paasivirta and Rosas 2002). In contrast to retorsions, countermeasures 'would be illegal if not for the prior illegal act of the state against which they are directed' (Partsch 1994). The objective of these sanctions is to induce the violating party to restore a lawful state of affairs. Such obligations are not bound to be included in bilateral contractual relations; they are often justified as reactions to so-called *erga omnes* obligations. These are defined as fundamental obligations of international law whose breach can be considered the breach of an obligation towards the international community as whole. Thus, *erga omnes* obligations may be invoked by any member of international society. The main difficulty here is their imprecision. While gross breaches of human rights seem to be covered, the precise kind of actions that qualify as breaches of *erga omnes* obligations is subject to debate.

The community legal framework of EU sanctions

From the 'Rhodesia doctrine' to the 'Malvines doctrine'

When EC member states were first confronted with the requirement to implement UN sanctions – those imposed against Rhodesia in 1965 – they considered themselves free to do so through national legislation. Indeed, a provision had been included in the Treaty creating the European Community (TEC) to expressly allow member states to deviate from the Common Commercial Policy (CCP) in order to comply with other international obligations (Art. 224).[5] The method of implementing UN sanctions through national legislation came to be known as the 'Rhodesia doctrine'. The choice of national measures over the possibility of implementation through Community legislation was motivated by member states' concern not to jeopardise their freedom to determine their foreign policies.

The insight that the Rhodesia doctrine worked to the detriment of the efficacy of the embargo prompted a shift towards a different method which involved the Community. It consisted in the adoption of a Community Regulation under Art. 113 EC (Amst.133), preceded by a decision taken in the framework of consultations held under the auspices of the intergovernmental, extra-communitarian forum of European Political Cooperation (ECP). Although this method first served as a legal basis when sanctions were imposed against the USSR (a cereal embargo in 1980 following the invasion of Afghanistan and some restrictions on imports following the imposition of martial law in Poland in 1982), it was labelled the 'Malvines doctrine' because of its later use in the import ban imposed on Argentina during the Falklands war.

Legal scholarship generally explains the shift from the 'Rhodesia' to the 'Malvines' doctrine primarily by pragmatic considerations. The member states' main concern was to achieve the effectiveness of sanctions through uniformity in their implementation (Koutrakos 2001, Lukaschek 2002). They also point to the fact that reluctance to resort to using the Community during the 1970s was justified by the as yet underdeveloped CCP, and the fact that member states were wary of implementing sanctions through it and thereby broadening its scope. In contrast, the CCP had matured by the early 1980s and its scope was already well established (Koutrakos 2001). Without contending the validity of these claims, it seems apparent that the intention to develop a legal basis for autonomous EU sanctions was also an important factor. The first three instances of application of 113 EC mentioned above occurred in the framework of autonomous EC sanctions (USSR 1980 and 1981, Argentina 1982) rather than UN sanctions.

The post-Maastricht phase

The Maastricht Treaty, signed in 1991, formally codified the abovementioned procedure for the imposition of sanctions, which was already well established at the time. Art. 228a EC (Amst. 301) sets out what has been labelled the 'two-steps procedure' (Bohr 1993). First, member states agree on the imposition of sanctions within the intergovernmental context of the EPC, later the CFSP. They are implemented by Community measures based on Art. 113 EC (Amst.133), or directly by member states when the measures fall outside of Community competences, such as arms embargoes or visa bans. The codification of the inter-pillar procedure for the application of sanctions was a welcome development for legal scholarship, which had resented the inconsistency of the Community implementing decisions that had been taken in an extra-communitarian framework. However, this procedure, which appears as a *sui generis* provision in Community law, is still criticised on both legal and practical grounds.

A practical preoccupation refers to the cumbersome nature of the 'two-steps procedure' resulting from the duplicity of legal acts necessary for the imposition of a sanctions regime – a CFSP act and a Council Regulation. Some expressed anxiety at the amount of time required to produce the two necessary legal acts, considered likely to undermine the EU's capacity to respond quickly to crises. This concern voiced amongst others by the Commission (Commission of the European Communities 1995) is echoed by scholars (de Wilde d'Estmael 1998). Examining the sanctions regimes imposed against Yugoslavia during the Kosovo crisis, Buchet observed how the Regulations required to implement the CFSP decisions on sanctions were the object of long negotiations – which provoked delays that considerably weakened the impact of sanctions (Buchet de Neuilly 2003). The suboptimal character of the EU sanctions strategy in that episode, due to the lengthy decision-making procedure, has been recognised by the Commission itself: 'for the financial sanctions … to have been truly effective in preventing FRY interference in Kosovo … measures should have been targeted swiftly and unambiguously' (Commission of the European Communities 2000:24). The inter-pillar nature of the sanctions imposition mechanism – the two-steps procedure outlined above – has drawn attention to the coordination difficulties that may arise in crafting these measures in the CFSP and Community pillars. Indeed, the field of sanctions was identified as one of the areas where problems of horizontal coherence were likely to arise. The increasing specificity with which the Council has drafted CFSP Common Positions imposing sanctions in the present decade may well be driven by a desire to reduce the breadth of provisions to be negotiated in the Regulation phase (Poeschke 2008). In that sense, the Council seems to be attempting to 'circumvent' the inter-pillar procedure.

While some lawyers conceived of the two-steps procedure as one that preserves member state sovereignty while guaranteeing the uniform application of the law (Bohr 1993, Lukaschek 2002), the idea of creating a single-step mechanism for the imposition of sanctions made its way into the failed Constitutional Treaty.

In the Treaty of Lisbon, Art. 301 has been renamed Art. 215. It reads as follows:

1. 'Where a decision, adopted in accordance with Chapter 2 of Title V of the Treaty on European Union, provides for the interruption or reduction, in part or completely, of economic and financial relations with one or more third countries, the Council, acting by a qualified majority on a joint proposal from the High Representative of the Union for Foreign Affairs and Security Policy and the Commission, shall adopt the necessary measures. It shall inform the European Parliament thereof.
2. Where a decision adopted in accordance with Chapter 2 of Title V of the Treaty on European Union so provides, the Council may adopt restrictive measures under the procedure referred to in paragraph 1 against natural or legal persons and groups or non-State entities.
3. The acts referred to in this Article shall include necessary provisions on legal safeguards.'

All provisions on restrictive measures are now contained in a single article, which extends to 'economic and financial' measures. The main innovation of the article is that it specifies the circle of potential addresses, which expressly includes groups and non-state entities, and provides for the existence of legal safeguards. Under the TEU, the European Court of Justice has jurisdiction to review the legality of sanctions implemented through the first pillar, given that competence for the movement of capital and trade matters corresponds to the Community. The Lisbon Treaty makes it possible for natural or legal persons to seek redress through the Court in respect of restrictive measures affecting them under the CFSP. This innovation has been welcomed, as it strengthens the protection of the rights of persons who are blacklisted in CFSP anti-terrorist measures (House of Lords 2008:185).

Political conditionality and sanctions

At this point, it is necessary to clarify how sanctions relate to another instrument also in use in the EU since the early 1990s, namely political conditionality.

According to Smith, political conditionality 'entails the linking, by a state or an international organisation, or perceived benefits to another state (such as aid, trade concessions, cooperation agreements, political contacts, or international organisation membership), to the fulfilment of conditions relating to the protection of human rights and the advancement of democratic principles' (Smith 1997). A central distinction must be made between positive and negative conditionality. Positive conditionality is defined as the promise of benefits to a state in exchange for the fulfilment of certain conditions, while negative conditionality involves reducing, suspending or terminating those benefits if the state in question violates the conditions (Smith 1997).

In the context of the EU external relations, political conditionality emerged within the framework of development cooperation after the end of the Cold War. Following the landmark 1991 Luxembourg Declaration by the European Council announcing that development aid would be linked to human rights and democratic standards, EU political conditionality achieved its most perfect form in the human rights clauses, which permit the suspension of agreements in the event of 'grave and persisting human rights violations or serious interruptions of democratic processes' (Council of the European Communities 1991). The title of 'human rights clause' is misleading, as these clauses entail obligations to respect not only human rights, but also democratic standards. They were incorporated in the Lomé Agreement, and quickly spread to the association agreements with Eastern European countries. Nowadays, almost all general agreements concluded by the EU with third countries encompass a human rights clause. In addition, some unilateral acts, such as technical cooperation programmes, provide for suspension in case of breaches of human rights obligations and democratic principles.

The present GSP scheme is also embedded in a conditionality framework, generally referred to as the 'social clause', since it links labour standards to trade relations. From the outset, the social conditionality scheme featured carrots and sticks. According to the first scheme (1995–2004), GSP preferences would be withdrawn where countries used forced or prison labour, while additional trade preferences would be granted to countries complying with certain labour standards, such as the freedom of association, the right to organise, collective bargaining and the abolition of child labour. In contrast to that first scheme, which required the application of four principles enshrined in six International Labour Organisation (ILO) conventions, the reformed 2006–14 GSP regulation requires the ratification and application of all eight conventions (Orbie et al. 2005).

An important aspect to bear in mind here is the distinction between suspensions of development aid designed to compel a change in the behaviour of the leadership targeted, and the suspension of development aid with the aim of preventing the diversion of EU funds for belligerent purposes. The outbreak of conflict constitutes a situation in which the suspension of aid is possible on both grounds. In 1999, the Commission suggested that the suspension of aid should be contemplated for countries involved in armed conflicts where the possibility of the diversion of resources for belligerent purposes arises (Commission of the European Communities 1999). In the first case, the aim consists in putting pressure on the leadership(s) involved in the conflict, while in the second case, the measure is geared towards reducing the availability of arms.

Decision making and legal bases for EU sanctions: a catalogue

The first distinction to be made here is between sanctions that can be decided exclusively by the Community because they fall entirely within its competence, and sanctions that need to be agreed within the CFSP first. The second distinction concerns the implementation of sanctions decided within the CFSP. Some pertain to the Community, while others fall to the member states.

Sanctions decided and implemented by the Community

Most sanctions that can be decided by the Community correspond to the notion of retorsions. They typically include the withdrawal of GSP benefits, the interruption of financial and technical assistance, and development aid cut-offs. In the case of the withdrawal of aid, before 1996 decisions were taken informally by the Commission without any Council involvement – e.g. aid to Equatorial Guinea was suspended in 1992 by a letter from the Commissioner without formal approval from the Council (Hazelzet 2005). A second possibility is the suspension of trade and cooperation agreements, a procedure set out in Art. 300(2), whereby the Council decides unanimously. Under the Cotonou Convention, the Council acts by qualified majority when deciding on partial suspensions, while unanimity is required for a full suspension. The suspension of agreements has a double character. It represents a legal precondition for the imposition of economic sanctions, since otherwise the adoption of trade restrictions would contravene Community obligations under the agreement. As a first reaction to misbehaviour, it constitutes a sanction in itself which normally entails a suspension of the benefits provided for in the agreement.

Sanctions agreed by the CFSP and implemented by the Community

This procedure corresponds with the inter-pillar mechanism described above. The first phase consists of an agreement in the framework of the CFSP, resulting in a legal act (a Common Position or a Joint Action), followed by a second phase in which a Community Regulation is adopted to give effect to the CFSP act. While the first phase is invariably based on Art. 15 TEU, the legal basis used to provide for the implementation of the CFSP act varies according to the nature of the measure. Trade embargoes are agreed by the Council on the basis of Art. 301 EC, which was created to encompass comprehensive economic sanctions that exceed the Community powers in the CCP, while Art. 60 EC is used for the implementation of financial sanctions. In both cases, the Council decides by qualified majority on the basis of a Commission proposal.

Sanctions agreed under the CFSP and implemented by the member states

Finally, certain sanctions are decided by the member states within the CFSP and subsequently implemented by the member states through national legislation. This is the case for arms embargoes, visa bans and diplomatic and cultural sanctions, since these measures fall outside the realm of Community competences. Table 2.1 summarises the decision-making procedures for the imposition of the range of sanctions at the disposal of the EU.

EU sanctions policy: practice and rhetoric

The Council has never provided an authoritative definition or list of what it considers a sanction. Until the publication of the first programmatic document setting out a strategy for the use of sanctions by the Council in 2003, information on the finality of EU sanctions had been scarce. While the Treaty on European Union details the procedure for the adoption of sanctions, it does not lay out their objectives. 'Sanctions' are mentioned in official documents as an instrument for conflict management and conflict prevention, but no information is given as to how they should be employed (Council of the European Union 1999c, Commission 2003).[6] The European Security Strategy of 2003 did not throw much light on this question, merely acknowledging the use of sanctions as an instrument of security policy (Council of the European Union 2003f). The EU Strategy against the Proliferation of WMD foresees the use of sanctions as a means of combating proliferation, while no such use has occurred so far (Council of the European Union 2003g).[7] This state of affairs leaves Common Positions imposing individual sanctions regimes as the principal source of information. However, these tend to explain the motives for the imposition of sanctions rather than their objectives. This situation of uncertainty was partly corrected with the adoption of two core documents on sanctions in the period 2003/04, the *Guidelines on the Implementation and Evaluation of Restrictive Measures (Sanctions)* of December 2003 (Council of the European Union 2003e), and the *Basic Principles of the Use of Restrictive Measures (Sanctions)* of June 2004 (Council of the European Union 2004c). The documents are complementary. The *Guidelines* suggest that the wording and design of EU legal instruments imposing sanctions be standardised and their implementation strengthened, while the *Principles* set out the objectives of EU sanctions: the promotion of human rights, democracy, the rule of law and good governance, as well as the fight against terrorism and the prevention of the proliferation of weapons of mass destruction.

Sanctions as a last resort

While the Principles contain scarce information on the EU's approach to sanctions, it is possible to ascertain some features of a distinctive EU sanctions policy from complementary sources. The EU displays a preference for positive

Table 2.1 Decision-making procedures for the imposition of sanctions

Type of sanction	*Legal nature*	*Decision-making body*	*Procedure*	*Implementation body*	*Termination*
Visa ban	CFSP Common Position	Council	unanimity	member states	by unanimity
Arms embargo	CFSP Common Position	Council	unanimity	member states	by unanimity
Embargo on commodities	a) CFSP Common Position b) EC Council Regulation	Council	a)Unanimity b)Majority	Community	by unanimity
Suspension of agreements with third countries	International treaty; Art. 300(2) EC	Council	unanimity	Community	by unanimity
Partial suspension of agreements under Cotonou Convention, including: • reduction of cultural, scientific, or technical co-operation programmes; • suspension of cooperation • suspension of development aid	International treaty; Art. 96 Cotonou Convention	Council	majority	Community	by QMV
Full suspension of agreements under Cotonou Convention	International treaty; Art. 96 Cotonou Convention	Council	unanimity	Community	by unanimity
Diplomatic Sanctions (interruption of cultural and scientific contacts)	CFSP Common Position	Council	unanimity	member states	by unanimity
Freezing assets and investment ban	a) CFSP Common Position b) EC Council Regulation	Council	a) Unanimity b) Majority	Community	by unanimity

(Continued on next page)

Table 2.1 (continued)

Type of sanction	*Legal nature*	*Decision-making body*	*Procedure*	*Implementation body*	*Termination*
Flight ban	a) CFSP Common Position b) EC Council Regulation	Council	a) Unanimity b) Majority	Community	by unanimity
• postponement of new projects, • deferral of the signature or decisions to implement cooperation, • change of contents or channels of cooperation partners	EC Council Decision, or European Council (Commission decision)	Council, Sometimes the assent of the EP is required (Commission)	majority	Community (sometimes only Commission)	diverse procedures apply
Suspension of Generalized System of Preferences (GSP)	EC Council Regulation	Council	majority	Community	by QMV

conditionality over negative measures. A Commission Communication of 1992 restates the policy already announced in the 1991 Luxembourg Council Declaration that 'the Community approach ... must focus especially on positive measures providing incentives for the promotion of democracy and human rights; the use of sanctions should be considered only if all other means have failed' (Commission of the European Communities 1992:11). This is consistent with the principle that the EU 'aims to be a "convincing" rather than an "imposing power" with engagement and dialogue as the preferred means of interaction with third states', as stated in the Council's 2005 Annual Report on Human Rights (Council of the European Union 2005d:36). At first glance this document gives the impression that the Council has become more resolute about the employment of negative measures: 'the EU has to seek a balance between persuasion and critical action' (Council of the European Union 2005d:35). Newspaper reports highlight that member states often oppose the imposition of sanctions in favour of their economic interests (EU Business 2007). Commissioners are most vocal in their dislike for sanctions. Trade Commissioner Mandelson claimed: 'the EU has always rejected a sanctions-based approach to labour standards – and that will continue' (Mandelson 2006). The cancellation of summits with regional groups – such as that planned with Africa in 2003 – is particularly resented, as these provide fundamental impulses to bolster cooperation. In the run-up to the EU–Africa Summit of December 2007, Commissioner for External Relations Ferrero suggested that Zimbabwe should be represented by a high-ranking government minister instead of President Mugabe, in order to allow the Summit to take place in spite of the EU visa ban in place against the Zimbabwean Head of State: 'I understand that the British naturally have a big problem ... but we should not let our political relationship with Africa fall apart because of Mugabe' (Reuters 2007b). Development Commissioner Michel advocated the lifting of diplomatic sanctions against Cuba, and was reportedly 'convinced that a situation of political immobility by the European Union ... would be a big mistake' (Boadle 2008).

The 'double-track' strategy

In parallel to the gradual perfection of CFSP sanctions instruments, the EU has progressively evolved its own, distinctive approach to sanctions. An 'EU-way' of sanctions has taken shape, particularly visible in the most sophisticated strategies. The EU follows a 'double-track' approach, respecting a distinction between those responsible for the violation of electoral standards and human rights, and the population at large, which benefits from strong EU support.

The justification for the sanctions imposed in the aftermath of the flawed elections in Belarus in 2006 offers a perfect illustration of this double-track approach. On the one hand, the EU deployed restrictive measures, which constitute the negative side of its strategy. EU sanctions are not directed simply at the 'leadership', but at those persons bearing direct responsibility for the objectionable behaviour. Commissioner Ferrero pointed out that: 'It is important that sanctions be clearly focused, targeting precisely the individuals – including Mr. Lukashenko – responsible for the fraudulent elections' (Ferrero-Waldner 2006b). Through their inclusion in public blacklists attached to documents imposing asset freezes and visa bans, the EU earmarks individuals responsible for wrongdoing as *personae non gratae*. Considerable attention is devoted to the precise targeting (and de-targeting) of officials, in accordance with their individual responsibility for the condemned actions. Coupled with the condemnation of the suppression of civil liberties, the EU also highlights its preoccupation with the protection of detainees. Again in the Belarus statement, Ferrero expresses concern for the safety of political opponents detained in the wake of elections: 'We must continue to apply pressure; demand the release of all those held for political reasons.'

The legitimacy of EU goals is enhanced by the fact that its sanctions often support demands by international organisations: the Council of Europe, the OSCE and ILO. The disappearance of three opposition leaders and a journalist in Belarus was the subject of a report of the Parliamentary Assembly of the Council of Europe (the 2003 Pourgourides Report) demanding an independent enquiry. Elections were deemed flawed after the Belarusian authorities failed to meet OSCE commitments. Accordingly, the EU pledged to review its position 'in the light of reforms made to the Electoral Code to bring it into line with OSCE commitments' and actions 'to respect human rights with regard to peaceful demonstrations', such as the 'release and rehabilitation of political detainees'.

In its sanctions approach, the EU follows a logic of incrementalism. The idea that sanctions should be applied incrementally in response to developments in the conduct of those targeted leaders is not specific to the EU. Scholars studying the efficacy of economic sanctions advocate the use of full embargoes imposed in one go because of their abrupt impact on the target economy. However, this logic is less relevant in the case of targeted sanctions of such a diverse nature. Incrementalism suits the objective of exerting only limited pressure on leaderships in order to bring about a bargaining process leading to (some) accommodation of EU demands. The EU's preference for incrementalist strategies appears to be connected to its readiness to enter into dialogue with the target, as these measures can create the expectation that the EU will shift its position in line with the leadership's future choices. Most EU sanctions are managed depending on the conduct of the targeted leaders, with sanctions tightened in response to deterioration (Belarus, Burma), and eased where the leadership proves responsive (Uzbekistan). An identifiable sequence has emerged over the years. The first reaction of the EU to what it regards as worrying signs – often the restriction of civil liberties, or unconstitutional reforms – is the so-called 'limitation of contacts'. This measure, nominally not a CFSP sanction, consists in the reduction of diplomatic contacts between the EU/member state officials and the governmental elite. Sometimes, the first step already entails CFSP measures such as the imposition of a visa ban, accompanied by other measures such as the partial suspension of bilateral agreements (as with Zimbabwe or Uzbekistan). Wherever the targeted leadership further deviates from EU demands, the EU reciprocates by tightening sanctions, normally by extending the blacklists to cover larger numbers of individuals, or imposing a new ban such as an asset freeze. Following the same logic, once the objectionable action has been redressed, the responsible individual is de-listed. This was the case after the school crisis in Transnistria. Development aid suspensions follow a rationale of condemnation of leaderships similar to that of blacklist-based bans. Rather than being meant to cut off funds, EU aid sanctions are designed to circumvent official authorities. Following the Hamas victory in the 2006 Palestinian elections, Commissioner Ferrero justified the EU's suspension of funding to the Palestinian Authority as 'a precautionary measure taken to ensure that no Community funds pass into the hands of Hamas' (Ferrero-Waldner 2006c). The wielding of negative measures is accompanied by a set of actions which entail the disbursement of aid, although they challenge their legitimacy or that of their policies. The Cuban leadership protested against the EU Common Position on Cuba (Council of the European Union 1996d), which pledges to support democratisation efforts on the island although it does not encompass any ban (Ahora 2007). EU assistance measures accompanying targeted sanctions can be of diverse character. A first group consists of the establishment of contacts with high-ranking civil servants at technical or 'directors' level. This measure is added on to the abovementioned limitation of contacts: while dialogue with officials at the political level is interrupted, the EU maintains interaction with civil servants. Ferrero announced: 'We will combine contacts with middle-range officials to reduce Belarus' self-isolation with NGO cooperation.' This is viewed by the EU as part of a broad effort geared towards facilitating democratic transition in the middle to long term, while explicitly distancing itself from the notion of forcible regime change: 'We work with civil society groups, parliamentarians, government officials and others to foster as broad a basis as possible for democratic practice – changing mindsets, not regimes' (Ferrero-Waldner 2006a). Other actions aimed at remedying the objectionable policies consist in the provision of funding for democratisation through tools such as the support of free media projects and civil society.

Concurrently, the EU continues actions for the development of the economy and in support of the population. In the April 2006 statement, Ferrero claims: 'We must avoid sanctions which harm the wider population.' She speaks of 'continuing to support the needs of the population through social and economic development under our future European Neighbourhood Partnership Instrument', as well as of providing 'support which directly benefits the population such as health, the environment or in the Chernobyl-affected area'. This is complemented by an attempt to increase dialogue with the non-governmental sections of the Belarusian population: 'throughout our assistance, we are keen to foster people-to-people contacts'.

The EU's humanitarian preoccupation for sparing the population from deprivation becomes particularly evident when sanctions are applied to developing countries or crisis areas. In the case of development aid suspensions, a similar logic is followed. While no further commitments are made in the form of budget support, funds are redirected to NGO-based development projects, and special programmes are put in place to support the most vulnerable sections of the population. Humanitarian aid remains untouched, and in the event of crises such as in Zimbabwe, aid may even increase. Following Hamas's victory in the 2006 Palestinian elections, Commissioner Ferrero claimed: 'We have suspended payments going to the Palestinian government, but we have not suspended aid to the Palestinian people. On the contrary: since the beginning of this year, we have stepped up our aid to the Palestinians' (Ferrero-Waldner 2006c).

The EU has provided substantial assistance for refugees from Burma/Myanmar in neighbouring countries such as Thailand and Bangladesh. In the years 2004–5, 11.5 million euros were allocated to uprooted populations, with projects focusing on return and reintegration (European Commission 2007c:12). The most illustrative case showing the EU's preoccupation with the protection of civilian populations is that of Burundi. In the period between 1996 and 1999 this country was subject to a full economic blockade by its neighbours, which caused severe hardship for the Burundian population. Although the embargo was eventually sanctioned by the UNSC, it was terminated at the instigation of the EU, which was concerned about humanitarian consequences. The EU threatened Burundi's neighbours with suspension from the ACP Partnership Agreement if they persisted with the economic embargo (Wohlgemuth 2005).

The EU invariably accompanies declarations outlining its double-track strategy with a 'disclaimer' on its efficacy – it states that the ultimate responsibility for bringing about democratic change lies with the autochthonous population: 'We understand that democracy can never be imposed from outside: genuine democratic transition must always come from within' (Ferrero-Waldner 2006a). The role of the EU is presented as one of support: 'We must … show Belarus and its people that an alternative – a democratic, open future – is possible. The EU will support them all the way' (Ferrero-Waldner 2006b).

3 What determines the efficacy of EU sanctions?

This chapter explores the factors that may contribute to the policy changes the EU wishes to bring about, with a view to ascertaining the determinants of sanctions success and failure. The choice of variables is critical. The following paragraphs discuss the variables that will be employed in the investigation, and how they are presumed to affect efficacy. A discussion of those variables that has been traditionally dealt with in the literature is then updated with contributions from more recent research. In the course of the review, the errors frequently incurred in their operationalisation of variables are corrected. Particular attention is devoted to the adaptation of these variables, with the specific aim of analysing EU sanctions. The discussion thus focuses on new variables which take into account the specificity of targeted sanctions – measures tailored to maximise the target regime's cost of non-compliance while minimising the target population's suffering – as well as those accounting for the character of the sender entity, the EU.

General sanctions theory, and consequently the variables which it has operationalised for measurement, is unsatisfactory. In order to enlarge the theoretical foundations of the investigation, the following section borrows elements from a number of theories exploring the operation of comparable foreign policy instruments which also have the objective of compelling a policy change in the leadership of a target country. While the tools analysed, which range from conditionality to military force, diverge greatly from one another in terms of their character and coercive capacity, this section will pay attention to the similarities they display in terms of the mechanisms through which they aim to bring about the desired results, as well as to their applicability to the operation of sanctions. The hope is that general sanctions theory will be improved by complementing its existing basis with elements from other approaches which draw attention to unexplored aspects.

Reviewing and adapting the variables to EU sanctions

From 'economic disruption' to 'economic' and 'non-economic disutility'

Basing its analysis on Galtung's naïve theory of sanctions, a substantial strand of the literature quantifies the damage sanctions inflict on their targets in economic terms: the greater the damage to the economy of the target, the higher the chances of success of sanctions. Following this logic, several indicators are employed in order to determine the harm caused to the target in economic terms. Hufbauer et al. (1985) look at the following factors:

1. the cost imposed on the target country as a percentage of its gross national product (GNP) and the cost to the sender country
2. the level of trade between sender and target countries as a percentage of the target country's total trade
3. the economic size of the countries, measured by the ratio of their GNP values
4. the type of sanctions – namely export ban, import ban or interruption of finance (Hufbauer et al. 1985:31–32).

Although all of these indicators are subsumed under the rubric 'economic variables', they are in fact very diverse. The economic losses suffered by the target, quantified in terms of GNP, are the classical indicator expressing the economic disutility caused to the target. The percentage of the target's total trade with the sender prior to the imposition of sanctions is also telling, insofar as it indicates the relative importance of the interruption of commercial relations. In contrast, the comparison of the economic sizes of the countries, measured by the ratio of their GNP, simply expresses the imbalance of their economic power. Little has changed in the analyses of economic impact by later authors, who adopt the first two indicators without any alterations (Rogers 1996, Cortright and Lopez 2000). The extent of disutility caused to the target is traditionally related to two factors: the vulnerability of the target to the particular measure, and the degree of effectiveness with which it is implemented. These two components are interrelated. If the target is vulnerable but the measures are not implemented properly, little effect can be expected. Conversely, if the target is not vulnerable to the particular measure, it will not perceive any disutility even if enforcement is optimal.

The question now is whether this still applies to EU sanctions. With the emergence of targeted sanctions, the types of measures employed have changed considerably. Many do not have any direct economic implications. Since targeted sanctions are designed to raise the target regime's costs of non-compliance in non-economic terms, the variable 'extent of economic disruption' could be replaced by the 'extent of disutility' caused to the target.

Assessing the disutility caused by sanctions is more complicated than it may appear, as it should be measured differently depending on whether sanctions have an economic component or not. EU practice features a number of *selective sanctions*, which affect not only certain individuals, but also broader sectors of society. Certain selective sanctions, such aid cut-offs, the withdrawal of trade preferences and investment bans, while designed to target responsible elites, also have repercussions for the rest of society. This applies to some of the sanctions applied to the Federal Republic of Yugoslavia during the Kosovo crisis: flight bans, oil embargoes, the freezing of federal assets held abroad, and the prohibition of payments to state-owned enterprises. Such sanctions rely to some extent on the 'societal transmission belt'. Thus, while the EU has shifted away from comprehensive measures causing hardship among the broader population, the logic of the naïve theory is still present.

In the cases of interruptions of development aid or partial embargoes, measuring the disruption caused is more difficult than evaluating the impact of comprehensive sanctions. Because they do not affect the economy as a whole, indicators are less straightforward. Many apparently economic measures such as aid sanctions are in reality more about circumventing state authorities than about cutting off funds. Yet, where sanctions have an economic dimension, a central factor is the EU's importance as a trading partner and aid donor to the target country, because EU sanctions with an economic component consist of the suspension of agreements or unilateral regimes providing development aid and/or trade preferences, often of key importance to developing countries.

In the case of *personal sanctions*, the assessment of the disutility inflicted on targets is even more challenging. These measures are blacklist-based, i.e. visa bans and the freezing of assets. They are designed to channel pressure directly to individuals, while other measures have foreseeable repercussions for the population. Ascertaining the degree to which a travel ban disrupts the routine of Zimbabwean or Transnistrian leaders is difficult, because neither the Commission nor individual member states compile information to that effect (interviews 2007). Even with the freezing of financial assets, where financial institutions and the member states have an obligation to report to the Commission about frozen assets, it is uncertain whether or not this duty is complied with. This investigation relies on accounts from EU officials and diplomats, as well as on scholarly assessments and media reports. In any case, the parameters for measuring different types of sanctions are not unitary; they need to be adapted to each instrument.

Measuring the non-economic disutility of EU sanctions also entails a psychological element – not least the stigmatisation that the target suffers in terms of its loss of prestige. The analysis of the psychological aspects of sanctions remains underdeveloped, as the operationalisation of psychological concepts such as 'prestige' remains elusive. The variable 'warmth of prior relations' also has some psychological content. Drezner's (1999) 'sanctions paradox' also contains a strong psychological component. His argument that targets are more likely to capitulate to friendly senders, but that senders are less likely to impose sanctions against friends, recognises that sanctions dynamics are not exclusively about power and economics. Other authors have included psychological factors in their analyses of the mechanisms underlying the operation of sanctions. Van Bergeijk (1999) mentions 'reputation' as one of the political factors accounting for efficacy, while Morgan and Schwebach (1997) mention the role of 'resolve' in both the sender and the target in sanctions dynamics. This set of variables intends to capture, to some degree, the psychological aspect of sanctions interactions. Many of the factors discussed previously present a psychological dimension, such as the target's perception of the importance of the goals pursued by sanctions, or the alleged efficacy of mixed strategies. Mitchell (1997) has tentatively explored how social psychology approaches could help in explaining the effects of coercion in the specific case of nuclear proliferation. Cosgrove (2005) has also made a modest attempt to look into the psychological impact of targeted sanctions on the individuals concerned.

Looking at psychological variables in investigating the efficacy of sanctions is indispensable, since the picture of sanctions dynamics is incomplete without them. The stigmatising of targets constitutes a central component of the impact of CFSP sanctions. According to Chinese officials, the stigma of being subject to international sanctions is a cause of embarrassment to them. Indeed, China undertook an active campaign to have the EU arms embargo lifted. Cosgrove has pointed to the noticeable effects of targeted sanctions on blacklisted individuals (2005). Given that the material disutility inflicted by many of the sanctions levied by the EU is often limited, their psychological impact acquires an enhanced significance. All in all, the difficulty with psychological variables remains their operationalisation. In his measurement of 'reputation', it remains doubtful whether van Bergeijk chose an appropriate indicator. He measures the variable 'reputation as an executioner of sanction threats' via the number of sanctions that were implemented by the sender after the Second World War (van Bergeijk 1999:102). This measurement would probably be more suitable for assessing the deterrent effects of sanctions threats rather than their efficacy. By the time sanctions are in place, the threat has already materialised; therefore, the deterrent potential of the threat has already failed. In addition, this indicator fails to capture the target's specific perception of the sender. Morgan and Schwebach identify 'resolve' as a determining factor. However, they omit it from their investigation, claiming that 'no appropriate indicators exist' (Morgan and Schwebach 1997). In view of the difficulty of capturing and operationalising the psychological impact of sanctions, the present study excludes this factor from the dataset.

From factors 'subservient to economic disruption' to the 'management of the sanctions strategy'

A number of well-established variables in sanctions research are closely related to the abovementioned economic indicators: the duration of sanctions on the one hand, and the strategy for imposing sanctions (incrementalist v. comprehensive) on the other. These variables were first examined because of their significance for the economic impact of embargoes. Hufbauer, Schott and Elliot discovered that the length of the time that sanctions are in force is statistically correlated with efficacy, implying that sanctions that remain in place for several years become less effective. The explanation for the decreasing efficacy of sanctions is that the target's economy gradually adjusts to the new circumstances (van Bergeijk 1999). This is also linked to the debate of incrementalism versus the immediate imposition of harsh sanctions. Those who make the case for comprehensive sanctions imposed 'at one go' rather than incrementalist approaches argue that the abrupt economic disruption of trade leads to the success of sanctions (Cortright and Lopez 2000). Another disagreement refers to the opposition between unilateral and multilateral sanctions. While a majority of scholarship holds the view that sanctions enforced multilaterally are less effective than unilateral sanctions, largely due to public goods problems, coupled with the ability of targets to manipulate coalitions, recent research concludes that multilateral sanctions outperform unilateral measures (Bapat and Morgan 2009:1092). Perhaps the factor most clearly connected to the level of economic disruption is the degree of effectiveness with which measures are implemented. This is the single factor whose weakness or outright absence is most often blamed for the failure of sanctions. Sanctions cannot be expected to work if they are not properly implemented in the first place, be this due to lack of institutional capacity to implement them or to weak commitment of states.

However, the relevance of factors related to the management of sanctions strategies is not completely exhausted in considering their contribution to economic impact, as discussed for the previous variable. The literature has emphasised the effects of a number of factors directly related to the political interaction between sender and target. Scholars have started to devote increasing attention to the analysis of the management of sanctions during the implementation phase (Haass and O'Sullivan 2000). One of the aspects explored is the sender's readiness to reciprocate concessions made by the target. Cortright and Lopez (2000) argue that a 'partial easing of pressure in response to steps toward compliance by the target regime can induce additional gestures of co-operation'. Thus, 'failure to reciprocate concessions may squander opportunities for additional compliance'. This is exemplified by the case of Iraq, which did not receive any sanctions relief when it made partial concessions to UN demands in the mid-1990s: 'if these concessions had been met with a partial easing of sanctions pressure, the Baghdad regime might have responded with further measures towards compliance' (Cortright and Lopez 2000:31).

Several authors contend that the responsive adjustment of sanctions to reflect steps taken by the target can reassure the sender's intention to lift measures once demands have been met, insisting that the conditions under which sanctions can be lifted must be clearly identified (de Jonge Oudraat 2000, Haass and O'Sullivan 2000). George points to the clarity of both the objective and the precise terms for ending the crisis as variables affecting the performance of coercive diplomacy (1991), while other scholars claim that targets who believe that sanctions will not be lifted, regardless of whether they comply with demands or not, can be induced to yield if the sender announces that sanctions may be removed (Hovi et al. 2005:489). Still, senders are not always consistent in their management of sanctions. After the Libyan leadership complied with US and British demands to extradite suspects of the Lockerbie bombing and started to dismantle its WMD arsenal, senior US officials vehemently opposed the lifting of sanctions (Jentleson and Whytock 2005). De Waal has reported the existence of this situation in the case of the leadership of Sudan (de Waal 2008).

The management of sanctions strategies is very relevant to EU practice. The alleged inefficacy of EU sanctions was ascribed to the absence, until very recently, of the option to resort to force. But one of the main criticisms directed at the EU as a sender of sanctions concerns precisely those shortcomings related to strategy, namely the inability to react quickly to unfolding developments, due to the unanimity requirement of the CFSP (de Wilde d'Estmael 1998). Thus, in the present investigation, the exploration of sanctions strategies takes these aspects into account. In order to do so, modifications in sanctions regimes and their rationale are used as an indicator. The variable 'coherence in the management of the sanctions strategy' examines whether modifications in a sanctions regime by the EU were made in response to changes in the target country or in the behaviour of the leadership. Target-motivated modifications include both the easing of sanctions to reciprocate concessions by the target, and the opposite. Conversely, the absence of changes in a sanctions regime despite progress by the target towards compliance is also considered.

From the 'nature of the target society' to the 'impact on target's grip on power'

Having realised that economic impact alone cannot account for the success of sanctions, scholars turned to the political characteristics of the targeted society. This variable has increased in sophistication, developing from the original dichotomy that looked only at regime type, to include a number of characteristics of the target society. Certain authors posit that the societal transmission belt can operate as predicted by the naïve theory in cases where the target country presents some enabling features, such as the democratic nature of the regime, a certain degree of industrialisation, and a relatively ethnically homogeneous society (de Jonge Oudraat 2000). Van Bergeijk suggests that the relationship between success and the presence of democratic rule in the target is significant at the 88 per cent confidence level (1999:106). Cortright and Lopez (2000) qualify this idea, positing that sanctions are more likely to succeed in societies where there is some degree of democratic freedom than in rigidly totalitarian states (2000:22). Grünfeld (1999) elaborates a model detailing four categories of targets according to the degree of permeability of decision making to domestic and foreign pressure (1999:121). Haass and O'Sullivan contradict this idea, suggesting that attempts at external influence work best where decision-making power is highly concentrated and the leadership exerts effective control over its territory (2000). From this perspective, authoritarian regimes often constitute better targets than regimes with more complex domestic situations. Kaempfer and Lowenberg (1999) conclude that sanctions only display their desired effects on policy making where a reasonably well-organised opposition group exists, whose political effectiveness can potentially be enhanced as a consequence of sanctions. In the absence of such a situation, sanctions may display the opposite effect, strengthening the existing regime by helping to rally public opinion around the government (Kaempfer and Lowenberg 1999:52).

Sanctions produce political effects by altering the abilities of domestic interest groups to overcome collective-action problems in the exertion of political influence (Kaempfer and Lowenberg 1999:55). Despite the increasing elaboration of this insight, it has not yet been translated into variables.

It has also been posited that leaders operate in a political environment, and publicity matters to leaders in a way that does not apply to other individuals (Blanchard and Ripsman 2002). This aspect had been underlined by Olson (1979) and Weintraub (1982), who argue that coercive uses of aid are more likely to succeed than economic sanctions because they tend to generate lower levels of publicity. In the same way that senders have an interest in attaining a particular goal, target decision makers have a stake in not appearing to yield to foreign pressure. As Lindsay puts it,

> even if sanctions hurt the target, it has strong incentives not to comply.... Compliance may damage the target leadership's world prestige or diminish its domestic support.... Even if the target decides to comply it wants to avoid appearing to capitulate to the initiator.
>
> (Lindsay 1986:160)

This insight leads Lindsay to formulate what could be termed the 'publicity paradox': 'the publicity needed to make sanctions successful as international and domestic symbols undercuts their success in attaining the goals of compliance and subversion. Since sanctions are highly visible external threats, they tend to increase political cohesion in the target and to restrict the target leadership's ability and willingness to modify its policies' (Lindsay 1986:170).

While democratically elected governments are arguably more responsive to sanctions because they can be held accountable by their constituencies, hardly any variation exists in the present investigation. EU sanctions have almost invariably been imposed against regimes which lack democratic legitimacy, do not exert effective power over the totality of their state's territory, or are engaged in armed conflict. The EU predominantly imposes autonomous sanctions in reaction to the interruption of democratic processes or violent state repression (Portela 2005). Indeed, the dataset collected for the present investigation features very few cases where the target is a democratic regime. In other words, it would make little sense to examine the variable of 'democratic/undemocratic rule' for a dataset overwhelmingly composed of sanctions imposed with a view to promoting the restoration of democracy.

The present study also rejects the idea of ranking goals in 'order of importance'. Hufbauer, Schott and Elliot classify the goals of sanctions regimes according to their alleged importance, or degree of ambition. This classification presents severe problems, as argued in the previous chapter. Quite apart from arguments about the inappropriateness of assessing the utility of sanctions in such terms (Baldwin 1999), any classification of goals as 'minor' or 'major' is subjective. Their categorisation is an exemplary illustration of this. The category 'modest goals' encompasses changes in the target country's policies related to human rights, terrorism, and nuclear proliferation. On the other hand, the reversal of Nepal's pro-China foreign policy is considered to be a major goal equal to that of ending apartheid in South Africa. The disruption of small-scale military ventures constitutes a separate category. However, there is no evidence that these categories coincide with the targets' perceptions, as acknowledged in the authors' own comment that modest policy changes 'are often of burning importance to participants in the episodes' (Hufbauer et al. 1985:38). Thus, the proposition by Hufbauer and his collaborators that sanctions work best for the attainment of modest policy objectives, as later adopted by others (Cortright and Lopez 2000, Rogers 1996), is based on a categorisation lacking any connection with targets' perceptions.

In his work on coercive diplomacy, George presents a useful reinterpretation of the gradation of objectives. He specifies the meaning of 'modest objectives' as labelled by Hufbauer, Schott and Elliot, namely, they are limited in the sense that they do threaten what the opponent perceives to be 'vital interests' (George 1991). This especially concerns the extent to which the measures affect the regime's control, or 'grip on power'. This point reappears in the literature on the provision of incentives to achieve foreign policy goals: 'any … incentive will be insufficient to coerce regimes to take actions that amount to suicide' (Haass and O'Sullivan 2000:167). George postulates that demands are more likely to be met if they do not affect what are perceived to be the 'vital interests' of the opponents.

This insight is also reflected in the work of Schimmelfennig and Sedelmeier on Europeanisation in candidate countries for accession to the EU (2005). In their exploration of why EU conditionality is not equally effective across issue areas and countries, they discovered that conditionality proved less effective where employed to consolidate democracy than where it was used to export the *acquis communautaire*. This is partly explained by the fact that, for reluctant democratisers, compliance would have meant giving up the very instruments of the preservation of their political power (Schimmelfennig and Sedelmeier 2005:213). In contrast, 'as acquis conditionality does not concern the political system and the bases of political power as such, governments generally do not have to fear that the costs of rule adoption … will lead to a loss of office' (2005:215).

Rather than examining the nature of the targeted regime, the present investigation considers how the aims of the sanctions affect the leadership's grip on power, in an attempt to correct for the unsatisfactory manner in which goals were analysed in the study by Hufbauer et al. (1990). In order to adjust the objectives to the purposes of the present investigation, categories are not only renamed, but also reduced. In contrast to Hufbauer et al's study, only one goal of sanctions is considered here, namely that of compliance. The 'destabilisation of a government' and the 'impairment of the military potential of the target' are dismissed as superfluous.

As a result of the rise of the concept of crisis management in the 1990s, and especially in view of the UNSC's increasing readiness to use sanctions in internal conflicts, attention has turned to the use of sanctions for crisis management

(Rogers 1996, Brzoska 2005, Jentleson 2000, de Jonge Oudraat 2000). This strand emanates from an increasing bent in the literature towards evaluating sanctions efficacy depending on specific aims, a trend also visible in the field of non-proliferation (Foran and Spector 1997, Mitchell 1997). Insights from this field can contribute valuable updates to the definition of this variable, since the *Economic Sanctions Reconsidered* dataset that has served as a point of reference for most studies since the late 1980s includes few post-Cold War episodes. Thus, the rise of sanctions wielded in conflict situations barely registers in the generalisations that the authors (and their followers) derive from their dataset. Research on sanctions as a crisis management tool is not entirely limited to the 1990s, though. While crisis management was not reflected in the categories of *Economic Sanctions Reconsidered*, the 'disruption of military ventures' could be seen as an equivalent to crisis management.

The general assumption shared by most authors is that situations of violent conflict considerably distort the operation of sanctions, thereby hindering their efficacy. Some researchers have expressed optimism regarding the expected efficacy of measures when applied skilfully. Both Rogers and Foran and Spector posit that sanctions are more likely to succeed when imposed early on in the crisis (Rogers 1996:429) and that they should make use of the full range of economic instruments available, rather than take an incremental approach. Still, knowledge about the efficacy of sanctions when applied in situations of violent conflict, especially in internal situations, is still very scarce (Niño-Perez 2005). Although Rogers advocates the use of sanctions in internal conflicts, she acknowledges that their effects in a conflict situation are less predictable, and that a good understanding of the roots of the conflict is therefore required for the design of the sanctions (1996).

As suggested by George, goals are ordered according to the extent to which their objectives endanger the leadership's permanence in power. To this effect, four categories are defined. One concerns objectives which have little or no relevance for the leadership's grip on power. Examples here include the accession to the NPT by Pakistan after its nuclear tests. The next category includes the demand to conduct enquiries into the violent repression of demonstrations, such as the Andijan episode in Uzbekistan, or to release imprisoned political dissidents. Since the repression of demonstrations is related to the granting of political freedoms, they are seen by leaders as attempts to overthrow their rule. The highest category is the demand to hold elections following interruptions in democratic rule, as in Fiji and the Central African Republic (CAR). Finally, the last category encompasses situations of armed conflict in which the official government is engaged in fighting. Each of these categories represents different stages of George's 'grip on power'.

This variable attempts to approximate the psychological impact of sanctions on the target, depending on its domestic and international situations. Given that the EU has sometimes employed sanctions for crisis management, this factor refers specifically to whether measures are applied in situations where violent conflict is ongoing (and at which stage of the conflict), or whether they are wielded against the leaderships of stable countries. Since knowledge on this question is still very scarce, EU sanctions can be used as an example from which some initial insights can be drawn. The assumption here is that targets are less likely to yield when they are engaged in conflicts that challenge their exercise of authority over a territory under their jurisdiction.

The classification of goals according to a single criterion, namely impact on the leadership's permanence in power, admittedly leaves out some substantial information on the nature of the goals pursued. The solution chosen allows us to differentiate between dissimilar sender demands in comparable situations: similar acts of state repression against civilians in Tiananmen Square and Andijan were met with different demands by the EU, a circumstance which is captured by the present classification. The use of goal categories does not, alas, capture the possible modification of goals in the course of the sanctions episode.

International isolation of the target

One of the classical variables which quickly became outdated after the end of the Cold War was what Hufbauer, Schott and Elliot labelled 'international cooperation'. During the Cold War, competition for world hegemony compelled the superpowers to support states that the other had subjected to sanctions in order to offset their effects. After 1989, this pattern disappeared from the global scene.

However, it remains relevant how third countries position themselves in the sender–target dispute, particularly in the case of unilateral sanctions such as those wielded by the EU. The oil embargo against the FRY crumbled following Romanian and Bulgarian refusals to continue its implementation after military operations in Kosovo ceased. Zimbabwe counts not only on the symbolic support of its neighbours, but also on their material help. For example, Zimbabwe obtains its energy supplies from South Africa, despite its inability to pay for them. China, India and, to a lesser extent, Thailand have consistently shielded Burma from UNSC sanctions, most recently in February 2007, while extensively profiting from Burma's natural resources. This highlights that material and symbolic support are often intertwined in undermining the efficacy of sanctions. By the same token, the EU's stance is also strengthened by the support of other third states that adopt similar positions. The first reaction of the Uzbek leadership following the wielding of EU sanctions after the Andijan events was to claim that the EU was isolated because it was the only entity to have imposed such measures.

The extent to which the target of EU sanctions enjoys international support, especially when backed by a powerful neighbour, is captured in variable 4. This variable also takes into account how other third countries position themselves vis-à-vis the matter under dispute. Due to the importance of the states immediately neighbouring the target country, particular importance is attached to the attitudes of countries in the same region in the measurement of this variable. Table 3.1 summarises the adapted variables and indicates the 'equivalences'.

Hypotheses, methodology and qualitative comparative analysis of the dataset

The research question the present study intends to address is: under which circumstances do sanctions imposed by the European Union contribute to bringing about the target's compliance with the sender's aims?

Definition of the dependent variable

The dependent variable in this investigation is not the success of sanctions. Unlike the approach followed by Hufbauer, Schott and Elliot, which looks at 'sanctions success' and 'sanctions contribution' as two separate variables, the contribution made by sanctions constitutes the independent variable here. The implicit assumption behind this choice is that sanctions alone rarely, if ever, account for target compliance. The present study considers the overall outcome of the strategy employed by the sender only insofar as it is relevant for measuring the contribution made by sanctions to the stated policy goals of the sender. Whenever the outcome is nil, there is no contribution to measure. Only in cases where strategies have some degree of success can the contribution made by sanctions be rated. As long as EU sanctions can be credited with some contribution towards the accomplishment of the goals – even if it is not the principal force – the contribution will be recorded with the value of '1'.

Table 3.1 Variable equivalences

Classical research on economic sanctions	*Present Investigation*
economic disruption caused to the target (HSE) • level of trade; economic losses • relative economic power of disputants • effectiveness of implementation	economic or non-economic disutility caused to the target (variable 1)
goals classified according to level of ambition (HSE)	only compliance goals (excluding destabilisation of state and economic warfare) classified according to degree to which they endanger the leadership's permanence in power (variable 2)
sanctions strategy (Cortright and Lopez, de Wilde) incrementalism vs. total sanctions multilateral vs. unilateral	sanctions strategy modifications in sanctions regimes in reaction to steps taken by leaderships? (variable 3)
sender- target relationship international support of target (HSE) economic size of the target (HSE) relative military capabilities of disputants (van Bergeijk) reputation of the sender in imposing sanctions (van Bergeijk)	international support of the target (variable 4) level of international support or isolation of target/ support from powerful neighbours

The present investigation deliberately omits the assessment of the efficacy of sanctions in achieving objectives other than target compliance, such as appeasing domestic audiences, weakening the target, or upholding international norms. It is presumed that other goals exist alongside that of compliance, but they are of interest in this study only to the extent that they can contribute to compelling a behavioural change in the target.

Other reasons also justify the definition of the dependent variable. 'Success' remains an elusive notion in attempts to influence in which sanctions is only one among various elements at work. Whenever the goal stated by sanctions was accomplished, the output is best defined as 'success of the influence attempt' or 'success of the strategy'. In this respect, the study is interested only in the extent to which sanctions contributed to success, rather than in whether the final output was positive or otherwise.

Hypotheses

1. The more harm sanctions inflict on the economy of the target state, the more likely they are to be effective

This variable indicates whether the economic harm that sanctions inflict, or threaten to inflict, on the target is economic in nature (or not). Since the EU does not impose comprehensive trade embargoes, the types of sanctions expected to harm the economy are the freezing of state assets (as performed in the FRY during the Kosovo crisis), commodity embargoes, suspension of trade preferences and aid sanctions. In contrast, this variable hardly captures the effects of blacklist-based sanctions regimes.

2. The less threatening the goals of the sanctions are to the leadership's permanence in power, the more likely they are to be effective

Regardless of how the specific objectives of the sanctions are defined, targets are more likely to comply with EU demands if these do not jeopardise their position as leaders. Thus, a gradation is used to classify objectives. Demands which do not directly threaten the leadership's position in power, but only discredit them domestically (such as a demand for an investigation as seen in the cases of Belarus and Uzbekistan, or the demand for cooperation in the extradition of alleged war criminals as seen in the Serbian case) belong at the lower end of the spectrum. Demands for the restoration of democratic rule are at the opposite end of the spectrum, as they fundamentally challenge the leaders' grip on power.

3. The more responsive sanctions regimes are to the target's behaviour, the more likely they are to be effective

This hypothesis is based on the observation by some authors that inability to reciprocate concessions by the target impinges on the success of sanctions

(Cortright and Lopez 2000). It is particularly relevant to the EU, where procedural rigidity in decision making is held responsible for the inflexible management of sanctions, and consequently for their limited success (de Wilde d'Estmael 1998).

4. The more internationally isolated the target is, the more likely are sanctions to be effective

This variable is included in the Hufbauer, Schott and Elliot study. However, it is slightly redefined in the present study. Here, the variable considers only the degree of international support it enjoys, in terms of both diplomatic contestation of the sanctions and economic support. It is assumed that the presence of international support from powerful neighbours renders the target more resistant to EU influence attempts.

Contribution to the refinement of sanctions theory

What contribution can this collection of hypotheses, derived from previous scholarship, make to the refinement of sanctions theory? The variables explored can provide insights that will help to resolve a number of aspects of sanctions theory.

One pertains to the mode of operation of targeted sanctions. According to the naïve theory, economic pressure should translate into political pressure aimed at compelling the target to yield to the sender's demands, where a roughly proportional relationship between economic disutility and political pressure is foreseen. As explained earlier, targeted sanctions are expected to operate in a similar fashion to that posited by the naïve theory of sanctions. Targeted sanctions simply transpose the naïve theory to the individual or group level. However, targeted sanctions theory has left unspecified what exactly is meant to compel the targeted individuals to capitulate: the obstacles they confront in their routine activities as a result of the personal sanctions – in their private capacity or as businessmen – or the stigma that being blacklisted places upon them? The present investigation should shed some light on this question.

Secondly, EU sanctions practice features both non-economic and economic measures. While the EU has subscribed to the concept of targeting in its *Principles* (Council of the European Union 2004c), distancing itself from blanket embargoes, it still applies sanctions which have repercussions for the economy of the target country. It has wielded selective commodity embargoes, such as the oil embargo against the FRY, and the gems ban on Burma. Measures such as the flight ban and the prohibition of payments levied against the FRY had noticeable effects on the economy of the target. The EU also wields measures with economic impact outside the context of the CFSP. Trade preferences may be suspended under Art. 96 of the Cotonou Convention or through the withdrawal of the GSP, and aid may be frozen either informally or under Art. 96 of Cotonou. Thus, the present exploration allows for a comparison of the efficacy of both sorts of measures.

The use of qualitative comparative analysis (QCA)

The principal method employed here is the qualitative investigation of sanctions episodes. This will be preceded by a Qualitative Comparative Analysis (QCA). QCA is not a statistical method. It falsifies or validates the relevance of variables for particular outcomes. This technique is able to identify necessary and sufficient causal conditions – which are embodied in the independent variables discussed above. Necessary causal conditions are independent variables requiring the presence of other conditions in order to produce a particular outcome, without which the outcome will not be seen. Sufficient causal conditions are those whose presence *alone* accounts for a particular outcome.

Why is QCA adequate to the conduct of this study, and what constitutes its added value? The investigation does not expect to uncover any single variable with explanatory power sufficient to account for successful sanctions. It expects, rather, to ascertain a combination of factors which is associated with a result in particular, either positive or negative. QCA's capacity to identify combinations of variables appears appropriate for this purpose, as it can point to specific combinations of variables whose relevance can be validated in the qualitative discussion that follows. Moreover, QCA allows the identification of not one, but several possible combinations of variables leading to a particular outcome. This qualitative technique is routinely employed for the generation of hypotheses. In the present investigation, it will serve as a preliminary test whose results are subsequently confirmed or invalidated by the qualitative study of individual episodes.

The technical requirements of QCA bear certain implications for the operationalisation of the variables. The fact that the method does not admit nominal variables has led to the choice of binary variables. QCA works best where variation exists between the values of the variables. Due to these constraints, variables have been formulated in such a way as to provide for variation. These requirements obviously reduce the flexibility in formulating variables, putting a considerable constraint on breadth width of the aspects that QCA can explore. It also limits the exploration of the goals to their expected consequences for the leaders' permanence in office, while neglecting aspects of the nature of the goals potentially central to the efficacy of sanctions. In order to compensate for these shortcomings, these questions will receive particular attention in the concluding chapter.

Definition of the dataset

On the basis of the above discussion, the present enquiry has been designed in accordance with the following definitions and methodological choices.

Object of analysis

The object of analysis is the universe of autonomous sanctions imposed by the European Union against third states since 1992, when the Treaty on European

Union was signed. Autonomous sanctions regimes are defined as those agreed by the EU in the absence of a mandate issued by the UNSC or by any other international organisation such as the OSCE. Sanctions adopted under four legal frameworks are considered:

- sanctions agreed in the framework of the Common Foreign and Security Policy, created by the Treaty on European Union
- development aid suspensions in the framework of Art. 96 of the Partnership Agreement between the European Union and the group of African, Caribbean and Pacific countries (ACP)
- the withdrawal of trade preferences accorded under the Generalized System of Preferences (GSP) scheme
- other sanctions adopted outside the abovementioned regimes, albeit typically not always reflected in Presidency statements and Council Conclusions, and termed 'informal sanctions' in the present study.

The database encompasses only those sanctions falling outside the realm of trade; notably, it excludes commercial defence measures taken by the Commission, such as anti-dumping measures. In addition, the array of attempts by the EU to influence accession candidates during the process of enlargement of the Union is excluded, given that the EU operates accession conditionality, a particularly powerful incentive (Schimmelfennig and Sedelmeier 2005, Noutcheva 2007). Two accession candidates feature in this dataset; yet, EU demands were not framed as accession criteria defined at Copenhagen in 1993 or as an integral part of the *acquis communautaire* in the episodes explored. Anti-terrorism blacklists are left out of the dataset because they target individuals unconnected with state power, while sanctions analysed here attempt to influence individuals in their capacity as government leaders. Further, rather than an influence attempt, these blacklists fulfil a preventive purpose as they are intended to prevent suspected terrorists from operating in Europe (interview 2007).

Although an effort has been made to compile information exhaustively, there is no guarantee that the dataset comprises the entire universe of cases in the period studied. Legal documents exist for cases of CFSP and GSP sanctions which make these episodes traceable. However, a mechanism allowing the suspension of development aid was only introduced in the ACP-EU agreement with the 1995 revision of Lomé IV-*bis*. Before that date, aid cut-offs took place either as part of CFSP sanctions packages (as with Nigeria) or informally (as with Equatorial Guinea). In the case of the last group, sanctions are often not reflected because there was never any formally agreed decision to impose sanctions as such (as with Turkey or Peru). As a result, not all instances are documented.

Sanctions regimes imposed by member states before the creation of the EU and later formalised as CFSP sanctions (as with Burma) are classed as CFSP sanctions. Sanctions to which not all EU members agreed are excluded from the dataset. This was the case, e.g., with a visa ban imposed against Belarusian leaders, to which Portugal did not subscribe. After Portugal's veto prevented the adoption of a CFSP Common Position, member states adopted the proposed ban individually. Instances where sanctions were considered or threatened by the EU but were never imposed, which could be referred to as 'non-cases' are excluded from the investigation for reasons of methodological purity. Sanctions packages originally imposed by one member state and later transposed to the EU level still count as EU sanctions.

The unit of analysis is the sanctions episode. An episode is defined by the imposition of sanctions by the EU in pursuance of an objective. As long as the aim remains unchanged, the episode remains the same, irrespective of easing or tightening. Renewals of existing sanctions regimes and extensions of the blacklists of individuals to which they applied are not reflected. Every new episode against a recurrent target is recorded with a Roman numeral (I, II, etc.). Upgrades of a sanctions package which entail the imposition of a new sanctions tool are reflected in the dataset with a letter (a, b, c, etc.). The sanctions episode is terminated when sanctions are suspended or lifted. Whenever EU sanctions were superseded by UNSC mandatory sanctions (as with Ethiopia, Eritrea, DRC and the Darfur region in Sudan), the episode is considered as concluded. If, after the lifting of a sanctions regime, it is reimposed on identical grounds – as happened with Togo and Fiji – it is considered as a new episode. Several episodes may take place at the same time: this was the case with the Transnistrian leadership in Moldova, where sanctions imposed due to breaches of the peace process were supplemented with separate blacklists during the 'schools crisis'. The dataset does not feature episodes which were initiated after 2008.

By way of general disclaimer, it should be noted that the empirical study does not intend to assess the pertinence of the use of sanctions by the EU or the consistency with which it selects its targets. It aims, rather, to assess the capacity of the measures actually deployed to bring about compliance among targets. The term 'coherence' used in variable 3 does not refer to the wider debate on coherence in EU foreign policy, a question stemming primarily from the inter-pillar nature of the EU's external relations.[1] Here, the term 'coherence' is specifically and uniquely applied to the management of the sanctions tools once they have been deployed. The dataset created for the investigation includes a total of 62 sanctions episodes.

Sources

The sources employed to obtain the information are the EU documents imposing/lifting the sanctions, and a qualitative investigation consisting of an analysis of reports and articles published by experts, interviews with officials from the EU and member states' bureaucracies, diplomats from non-EU countries and the ACP Secretariat, and experts from the academic and think-tank community. Officials from all of the EU institutions (Council, Commission, Parliament) and diplomats from the Permanent Representations of the member states to the EU were interviewed. Interviews were conducted in Brussels in 2005 and 2007, Berlin in 2007, Singapore and Hamburg in 2008 and Madrid and Canberra in 2009.

Methodological problems

A number of methodological problems associated with the study of EU sanctions pertain to the collection of evidence and the determination of objectives.

Difficulties in the collection of evidence

Given the low media profile of EU sanctions and the marginal attention they have received in International Relations scholarship, the present investigation relies heavily on interviews. Legal scholarship focuses on the specific problems sanctions create for the EC legal order, while ignoring the question of impact. Studies of target countries hardly mention the existence of EU sanctions or their impact.

Previous chapters criticised the fact that sanctions impact assessments are characterised by their reliance on statements by decision makers from sender entities. Officials from the sender country may overstate the importance of sanctions in decisions by targeted leaders, either because of imperfect information on leaders' calculations, or because they deliberately try to present their actions in a positive light in order to justify their policies. Given that sanctions research tries to ascertain the impact of sanctions on the targeted leaderships' decisions, assessments by those concerned can provide a balance to the sender's perception. Yet statements by targeted leaders were often unavailable or heavily biased, either magnifying or dismissing their effects. Thus, the onus was placed on officials from the sender side: interviews were conducted with officials from the EU institutions involved with the sanctions, most of them desk officers dealing with sanctions as an issue area, or in charge of monitoring the countries concerned. The centrality of interviews for the collection of data on EU sanctions has been acknowledged by Hazelzet, who notes that cases of aid freezes agreed before 1996, which were not published in the Official Journal of the EC, are 'traceable only through interviews and reviews of secondary literature' (Hazelzet 2005:4).

Obtaining data through interviews with EU officials entailed serious difficulties, mainly due to the system of continuous rotation existing in both the member states' diplomatic services and the EU bureaucracy, whereby staff are transferred to new posts every four years. As a result of the constant turnover of personnel, the collection of information on episodes prior to 2003 proved extremely difficult. Current desk officers did not hold relevant records on sanctions episodes transferred from their predecessors, and were often uninformed of concluded episodes. Some officials went so far as to deny the existence of past aid suspensions, even though these were referenced in several academic studies. No record of posts held by officials in the past is available to those who do not work for the EU, and contact details for retired EU officials are unavailable. It often proved impossible to trace the identity of officials in charge of a particular country at a specific point in time, as current desk officers were often unaware of the identity or whereabouts of their predecessors. When it proved possible to locate former desk officers, they were often unprepared to talk about questions for which they were no longer responsible. Finally, EU officials generally refrained from commenting on the conflicting positions of different member states in the context of Council discussions. In order to guarantee the anonymity of officials, the identity of all interviewees remains strictly confidential.

Neither the Council nor the Commission conducts any systematic assessment of the impact of sanctions on the targeted leaderships or countries/entities. When agreeing on the renewal of CFSP sanctions, those member states with diplomatic representations in the target countries use reports from their Head of Mission. Member states which do not have embassies sometimes rely on NGO reports for their assessments. The Directorate General External Relations keeps an archive, but this is accessible only to officials.

Difficulties with the determination of goals

CFSP sanctions instruments have been considerably improved since the inception of the practice, and especially since the late 1990s (Poeschke 2008). One of the most noticeable improvements is the progressive specification of the goals sanctions intend to achieve. While early sanctions regimes merely spelled out the breach that triggered sanctions, since the late 1990s Common Positions have stipulated increasingly specific conditions for the lifting of measures. In some early examples, the goal of the sanctions regimes must be presumed to be the termination or reversal of the objectionable behaviour, but even so, this creates a problem of imprecision. The 2005 Uzbek sanctions stipulated that sanctions would be lifted if an international enquiry into the Andijan events was allowed. By contrast, the sanctions against China, imposed prior to the signature of the Maastricht Treaty, spelled out vague conditions. In its statement of June 1989, the European Council requested 'the Chinese authorities to respect human rights and to take into account the hopes for freedom and democracy deeply felt by the population' (European Council 1989).

This formulation leaves ample room for interpretation as regards what exactly the EU expected China to do. How was progress in human rights to be assessed, and in which ways were the authorities being encouraged to 'take into account' the hopes for freedom and democracy of the population? Some observers have criticised the fact that the EU defined the conditions for lifting the China sanctions *ex post facto* (Austin 2005). The CFSP act imposing an arms embargo on Sudan in 1994 following the bombing of civilians in the South does not spell out conditions for lifting. In the case of the *de facto* aid blockade on Turkey, EU goals evolved, becoming increasingly demanding over the years. This circumstance poses obvious problems for the comparability of different cases over time.

Coding and allocation of values

The coding of the episodes is determined by the requirements of the technique employed, Qualitative Comparative Analysis (QCA). The criteria followed in calculating the values allocated to each of them are indicated in Table 3.2.

Results of the qualitative comparative analysis (QCA)

In order to explore the relevance of the variables, a truth table analysis and a truth table algorithm have been performed on the dataset with the help of QCA. The truth table analysis did yield three combinations of variables that bring about success; each of them features a consistency value superior to 0.8:

Table 3.2 Criteria for calculating the values of variables

Variable 1	*(anticipated) economic harm to the target* The measurement of economic harm follows the classical indicators used in the field, on the basis of available evidence. Where evaluations are not available, predictions by experts are employed.
Variable 2	*Extent to which sanctions endanger the leadership's permanence in power* The value 0 is allocated where the demands do not directly threaten the targeted leadership's permanence in office, such as the treatment of diplomats or WMD proliferation. Demands directly connected with the re-establishment of democratic rule, such as call for new elections, are coded 1 as it poses a direct threat to the leader's permanence in power. The demand to end bellicosities is also coded with 1.
Variable 3	*Coherence in the EU's management of the sanctions tool* The degree of coherence of each EU sanctions strategy is measured by assessing the links between modifications made to the sanctions regime and steps taken by the target towards compliance. The tightening or easing of sanctions is a sign of inconsistency unless they are directly connected to changes in the behaviour of the target. Actions by members which contradict the sanctions count as inconsistencies, including exceptions made within the limits of legality of CFSP Common Positions.
Variable 4	*Intentional Support for EU demands* The presence of a powerful neighbour ready to back the target both in economic and symbolic terms in defiance of the EU stance is coded with 0. If the EU stance is supported by major powers in the vicinity of the target, support is coded with 1.
Outcome	*Contribution of sanctions towards a positive outcome* The variable 'outcome' does not refer to compliance by the target, but to the contribution made by EU sanctions towards compliance. Thus, if the target made no progress towards compliance, the contribution of EU sanctions cannot be but 0. When the target takes steps towards compliance, the value expresses whether there was a contribution made by EU sanctions towards that goal. The lifting or easing of measures by the EU predominantly coincides with compliance by the target.

- ~eco*~grip*respon
- ~eco*~grip*support
- ~grip*respon*support

According to this result, three possible combinations allow EU sanctions to contribute towards a successful outcome:

1. Sanctions which do not threaten the permanence in office of the leadership, do not threaten to cause economic disruption and are managed responsively.
2. Sanctions which do not threaten the permanence in office of the leadership, do not threaten to cause economic disruption and enjoy widespread international support.
3. Sanctions which do not threaten the permanence in office of the leadership, are managed responsively and enjoy widespread international support.[2]

The results confirm that no single variable can account for a positive – there is no 'sufficient' condition. This not only validates an idea that emanates from the literature review, but encourages closer investigation of the determinants. These combinations point to the centrality of the variable 'grip', corroborating that the formulation of demands which do not directly threaten the permanence in office of the targeted leadership is necessary for success. The absence of an economic aspect in the sanctions measures is more surprising, as it is disconfirmed by the later analysis. The presence of this variable can be interpreted as indicating the irrelevance of an economic aspect in the sanctions for the exertion of coercion on the target. The remaining variables confirm the relevance of the lack of support granted by other international actors to the target, as well as the responsiveness of the target, although their effect only accounts for positive results when they accompany sanctions whose goals do not threaten to unseat the leaders they try to influence.

To conclude, the QCA analysis indicates that none of the variables formulated in the study accounts on its own for any particular outcome. Nevertheless, according to the results, in successful sanctions episodes we can expect to find measures which have been managed coherently and responsively. In contrast, we cannot expect to find any general pattern as far as the economic disutility inflicted on the target by the sanctions is concerned. On the basis of the qualitative examination of the cases which follow, these claims will be confirmed or invalidated.

4 The efficacy of sanctions imposed under the Common Foreign and Security Policy

Sanctions imposed under the Common Foreign and Security Policy (CFSP) are the EU's sanctions *par excellence.* While the legal documents through which they are imposed refer to them as 'restrictive measures' (French: *mesures négatives*), and the official discourse tends to avoid the term, they are the only measures for which the label 'sanctions' is admitted. Prior to the creation of the CFSP under the Treaty of Maastricht, sanctions were normally announced in Presidency Statements or Council Conclusions. However, sanctions regimes adopted by the EU prior to the conclusion of the Maastricht Treaty and that remained in place after 1993 were formalised in CFSP Common Positions. For instance, the arms embargo originally imposed on Sudan in 1994 (Council of the European Union 1994a) was the object of two consecutive Common Positions in 2004 prior to the Darfur crisis. The only purpose of these documents was to consolidate measures related to the sanctions regime in a single instrument, specifying the scope of the embargo and providing for exemptions (Council of the European Union 2004a, Council of the European Union 2004d). The only exception to the rule of reformulation and consolidation of sanctions regimes in a single document is the case of the arms embargo on China, whose informal legal basis was never transformed in a Common Position. Table 4.1 presents an overview of high-profile CFSP sanctions cases.

CFSP sanctions: what kind of sanctions?

If anything characterises the group of sanctions gathered under this heading, it is their diversity. The types of sanctions contemplated in the context of the CFSP are the following:

Arms embargoes

The arms embargo is the most frequent form of EU sanction. Arms embargoes typically forbid the 'supply or sale of arms and related material of all types including weapons and ammunition, military vehicles and equipment paramilitary equipment, and spare parts of the aforementioned' (e.g. Council of the European Union 2002b). They also prohibit the provision of technical training

Table 4.1 CFSP sanctions

	Measure	*Time Period*	*Main Goal*	*Outcome*
Belarus	Visa ban, freezing of assets	2000-ongoing	Reverse illegal constitutional change Free elections	limited compliance
Burma	Development aid suspension; diplomatic sanctions; arms embargo; visa ban; freezing of assets; investment ban	1991-ongoing	Recognition of 1989 elections results, democratisation process, national reconciliation, respect for human rights	no compliance
FYR	Arms embargo, investment ban, oil embargo, flight ban	1998-2000	Terminate military operation in Kosovo	no compliance
Indonesia	Arms embargo	1999	Cease state-sponsored violence, Allow UN force into East Timor	compliance
Transnistria (Moldova)	Visa ban	2003-ongoing	Co-operation in peace process	no compliance
Nigeria	Arms embargo, aid suspension	1993-1999	Free elections	compliance
DRC	Arms embargo	1993	Cease armed conflict	no compliance
Sudan	Aid suspension; arms embargo	1994- ongoing	Co-operation of peace process; Cease state-sponsored violence	no compliance
Uzbekistan	Arms embargo; visa ban	2005- 2009	Allow international inquiry into Andijan events	compliance
Zimbabwe	Arms embargo; visa ban; assets freeze	2002 – ongoing	Free elections, reverse expropriations	no compliance
Guinea- Conakry	Arms embargo; visa ban	2009- ongoing	Free elections	no compliance

or assistance related to the manufacture or use of these items. Military cooperation is generally interrupted alongside the supply of arms. The imposing instruments exempt the provision of 'equipment intended solely for humanitarian or protective use'.

Visa bans

Visa bans comprise the prohibition of entry into, or transit through, the territories of the member states for certain individuals. The blacklist featuring the names and positions of these individuals is generally annexed to the documents detailing the ban, often accompanied by available identifiers such as dates of birth. The Common Positions contain some provisions that warrant exemptions and detail the procedure for granting them. Exemptions may be conceded 'on the grounds of humanitarian need, including religious obligations, or on grounds of attending meetings of international bodies for the purpose of conducting political dialogue that promote democracy, human rights and the rule of law' (Council of the European Union 2002b). Member states wishing to grant exemptions must notify the Council in writing, and the exemption is considered to be granted unless one of the other member states raises an objection within 48 hours of receiving notification.

Financial sanctions

The heading of 'financial sanctions' comprises a wide variety of measures. The most frequently applied financial sanction is the freezing of assets of individuals included in blacklists. EU blacklists for asset freezes are the same as visa blacklists. Other types of financial sanctions are rarely used by the EU. Investment bans, for example, have only been applied for the FRY and Burma. There is only one case of a ban on export credits, again against the FRY in 1998, which was then extended to the provision of export finance by the private sector the following year.

Flight ban

There has been only one instance of an EU flight ban: that imposed on Yugoslavia in 1998. The legal difficulties encountered in this episode appear to have made the use of this measure undesirable. The UK failed to enforce the ban on Yugoslav commercial flights, with the justification that existing air services agreements with Yugoslavia took precedence over EC law (Buchet de Neuilly 2003:97), which led to the suspension of this measure in early 2000.

Embargoes on specific commodities

This type of embargo is considered a targeted sanction because it applies on a product of special importance for the continuation of the activities of the party judged to be at fault. Embargoes on specific commodities have been imposed by the UNSC, the most notable example being the ban on diamonds whose sale provided funding for rebel groups involved in African conflicts. Only two embargoes of this sort have ever been employed by the EU: the ban on the supply and sale of petroleum and petroleum products to the FRY in 1999, and the partial embargo on the import of timber, precious and semi-precious gems and the export of technology related to these industries in imposed on Burma in 2007.

Diplomatic, cultural and sports sanctions

This heterogeneous group encompasses measures such as the limitation of contacts, the invitation of political dissidents to national celebrations at embassies abroad, the suspension of scientific cooperation or bans on participation in international cricket tournaments. The scarce attention received by such measures in discussions on targeted sanctions is due to their low profile. Visa bans, one of the main CFSP sanctions tools, indirectly bans participation by the leaders concerned in high-level meetings between the EU and regional groupings. This includes summits and inter-parliamentary meetings between the EU and the ASEAN or ACP group, where the participation of Burmese or Zimbabwean leaders has proved controversial.

In early sanctions regimes, documents imposing the measures tended to group together sanctions of all kinds, from sports sanctions to arms embargoes (see Council Conclusion, 27 June 1989, Doc Nr 89/180 imposing the arms embargo on China).[1] Over time, a pattern of the increasing differentiation of legal bases emerged. The use of diplomatic sanctions has subsided and shifted to a more informal framework. The most common combination of measures consists of an arms embargo and a visa ban, subsequently complemented by the freezing of assets. At later stages, the lists of individuals affected by visa bans and asset freezes is often expanded in response to a deterioration in the situation.

Considerable improvements have been made in terms of transparency and specificity. Council Common Positions have replaced Presidency statements as the instruments for imposing sanctions. They indicate the motives for the imposition of sanctions with increasing precision. In recent years, the blacklists of targeted persons have been appended to documents imposing visa bans and asset freezes, while arms embargoes are accompanied by lists of items covered. Improvements in the design of EU sanctions regimes have been most obvious in the inclusion of provisions for exemptions, and of mechanisms for review or expiry. Exemptions on humanitarian grounds are routinely incorporated into trade restriction regimes, allowing medical products, foodstuffs and supplies for essential civilian needs to enter the country. In some cases, the release of funds or other financial assets has also been authorised; provided they are used 'solely for projects in support of democratisation, humanitarian and educational activities and independent media' (e.g. Council of the European Union 1998c prohibiting new investment in Serbia, Art. 2).

In recent years, legal instruments have also been endowed with provisions for the termination of the sanctions regime or sunset clause. Arms embargoes tend to include review clauses, while visa bans or asset freezes normally have expiry dates. This mechanism enables the Council to review measures regularly, and provides some flexibility with regard to the decision to renew, modify or lift sanctions.

CFSP sanctions practice

The following selection of cases encompasses all instances of CFSP sanctions, i.e. sanctions regimes adopted after the Maastricht Treaty entered into force in 1993 or regimes imposed before that date but subsequently formalised in CFSP Common Positions and EC Regulations. Only sanctions against states are considered. The visa ban against leaders of the Transnistrian Republic in Moldova – a state-like entity – is included in the investigation.

EU sanctions as conflict management: Yugoslavia and Africa

Over the past few years, attention has focused to the specific effects of sanctions in situations of armed conflict (Jentleson 2000, Brzoska 2005, Rotschild 1997, Rogers 1996). This reflects the increased use of multilateral sanctions against countries engaged in internal armed conflict in the post Cold-War era. Two types of targeted sanctions take on particular importance in conflict situations: arms and commodity embargoes. Selective embargoes can disrupt the operation of one of the parties if they affect the commodity that constitutes their main source of funding, while arms embargoes can militarily disadvantage contending groups. While there is no agreement on how sanctions affect conflict situations, some authors have pointed to certain factors believed to facilitate their efficacy. Authors agree that effective implementation is a precondition for success (Rogers 1996, Brzoska 2005). In an examination of African conflicts, Brzoska observes that sanctions were most efficacious when senders wielded a combination of several types of targeted sanctions or a comprehensive trade embargo. By contrast, arms embargoes levied without other measures had no effect on the political situation, despite the fact that their effectiveness gradually improved in terms of reducing the supply of light weapons (Brzoska 2005:214). Rogers posits that sanctions wielded in the early stages of conflict are more likely to succeed (Rogers 1996:428). Some scholars postulate that sanctions are most effective when embedded in strategies which combine them with positive incentives (Rotschild 1997:255), and that targets are more likely to resist sanctions imposed for crisis management because of the high stakes involved for parties at war, which often concern their very survival (Rogers 1996:418).

The few programmatic documents on the use of sanctions by the EU remain silent on the role of sanctions in crisis management. The *Principles* merely refer to sanctions as 'an important way to maintain international peace and security'. The enumeration of goals later in the document does not explicitly mention conflict management or prevention, and refers instead to the fight against terrorism and weapons of mass destruction, respect for human rights, democracy, the rule of law and good governance (Council of the European Union 2004c:2). Indeed, most cases of EU sanctions were officially justified as reactions to the interruption of democratic processes and human rights violations.

EU sanctions have been imposed on countries in which violent conflict was taking place. Five relevant cases can be identified: two consecutive episodes in the former Yugoslavia (the post-1996 arms embargo and the Kosovo crisis), and three episodes in Africa: Sudan, DRC and Ethiopia/Eritrea.

During the 1990s, the UNSC introduced some new features into its sanctions policies that were relevant to their employment in violent conflicts. It imposed sanctions on only one party of the conflict, a technique which has come to be known as 'asymmetric sanctions', notably targeting non-state entities such as rebel groups. In contrast to the UN, the EU follows a general policy of refraining from supplying arms to non-state actors (Brzoska 2005:211). Non-state actors are thus subject to a 'perpetual' EU arms embargo.

Federal Republic of Yugoslavia

The sanctions regime imposed on the former Yugoslavia is one of the best known EU sanctions episodes, perhaps a close second to the 1989 arms embargo on China. The EU imposed sanctions several times during the course of the Yugoslav conflict; however, only the third phase is considered here, as early episodes were soon superseded by the UNSC.

ANTECEDENTS OF THE KOSOVO OPERATION

Three sanctions phases can be distinguished: the first phase (1991–96) took place during the hostilities that followed the disintegration of Yugoslavia. It consisted of two kinds of measures: an arms embargo on all the former republics of the Yugoslav Federation, at first imposed by the EU and the US but soon superseded by the UN, followed by a comprehensive trade embargo imposed by the UN against the republics of Serbia and Montenegro. In the early months of the conflict, the EC member states attempted to bring about a resolution to the conflict by threatening the suspension of the bilateral trade and cooperation agreement (de Wilde d'Estmael 2004). However, these attempts resulted in a short-lived diplomatic solution which was soon superseded by the UNSC measures. The second phase (1996–98) refers to the period following the signing of the Dayton Agreements, when both the EU and the US decided to maintain an 'outer wall' of sanctions after the UN had lifted its measures. The transatlantic partners acted in concert, but did not impose identical measures. The US chose to continue financial sanctions barring Belgrade from membership in international financial institutions, while the EU maintained a bilateral arms embargo on all the former Yugoslav republics.

The permanence of the EU arms embargo followed a double justification: the need to protect the security of international forces deployed in Croatia and in Bosnia Herzegovina, and the need to 'establish peace and stability for the people of the region'. Export licence applications from Slovenia and Macedonia were considered on a case by case basis. The embargo was thus geared towards reducing the availability of arms in a post-conflict situation. While it is acknowledged that 'little is known about which impact, if any, the embargo had on the transfer of arms and military equipment to the conflict parties in the inter-war period' (Paes 2009:71), the sanctions failed to prevent the recurrence of conflict in the region, given that violent conflict erupted in Kosovo just two years later and in Macedonia in 2001. The explanation for this failure is straightforward. The weaponry used by the Kosovo insurgents originally came from Albania, where the regional arms market had benefited from the extensive looting of government armouries and police stations following the breakdown of state authority in December 1996. As for the Serbian side, the security forces continued to be supplied by the local defence industry, which had retained a substantial capacity throughout the conflicts, due to its strategic location in the heart of the republic. The EU arms embargo in this case illustrates the use of a tool for an end it is ill-suited to accomplish. Given that the Serbian defence industry remained active throughout the period, and various suppliers shipping arms into the remaining republics were unconstrained by any multilateral UN embargo, the EU embargo could not have any real effect.

EU SANCTIONS DURING THE KOSOVO CRISIS

The third phase of EU sanctions against Yugoslavia took place during the Kosovo conflict, when a UN arms embargo was supplemented with targeted financial sanctions and travel bans for key members of the Milosevic regime imposed by the EU and the US. In addition, the EU levied a number of autonomous targeted measures which constituted its most sophisticated use of this tool to date. It encompassed following elements:

1. Visa Ban. A visa ban prohibiting entry to the EU to senior FRY representatives was first adopted in March 1998. It was progressively expanded to encompass almost 800 names, thus becoming the largest EU blacklist ever. Originally targeted at officials identified as responsible for repressive action in Kosovo, it came to list individuals connected to the curtailing of independent media, as well as members of the security forces and the judiciary.
2. Financial Sanctions. Several types of financial sanctions were applied during the Kosovo conflict. They included a ban on official financial support for trade, investment or the privatisation of state-owned enterprises, a freezing

of federal and Serbian assets held abroad, and a ban on new investments in the Republic of Serbia. Again, sanctions were tightened progressively. The scope of Serbian assets frozen was expanded one year after imposition, while the investment ban was strengthened by prohibiting participation in any company controlled by the federal or Serbian government.

3. Flight Ban. A ban on all flights by Yugoslav carriers between the Federal Republic of Yugoslavia and the EU, agreed in June 1998, was primarily intended to deprive the FRY regime of the revenue obtained from the state-owned carrier, JAT. The flight ban was extended to cover all flights between the EU and Yugoslavia when NATO began its military intervention.
4. Ban on Petroleum and Petroleum Products. Once military action between NATO and FRY was under way, an oil embargo was imposed in order to deprive the federal army of essential supplies of petroleum and derived products.

The sanctions sequence consisted of several waves, from the lightest to the most forceful measures. The first package, rolled out in March 1998, featured a moratorium on export credit support for trade and investment and a visa ban for senior officials, along with an arms embargo that was soon superseded by a UN embargo. These measures were supplemented by the freezing of federal and Serbian funds held overseas, closely followed by an extension of the visa ban. As the situation on the ground deteriorated, the sanctions campaign intensified, with the inclusion of a ban on Yugoslav carrier flights between the FRY and the EU which was later upgraded to a comprehensive flight ban. Besides the expansion and tightening of existing measures, the final phase of the sanctions regime also included an embargo on oil and petroleum products.

The EU sanctions strategy displayed a series of unique features, with some unprecedented innovations in the field of international sanctions. The EU measures against Yugoslavia were unusually far-reaching, and included a number of sanctions that are only rarely employed by the EU (Portela 2007a). Visa bans on high-ranking officials are routine CFSP sanctions, often complemented by the freezing of personal assets of those individuals affected by the visa ban. Yet, in the case of the Kosovo sanctions, state assets held overseas were frozen. The abundance of selective economic sanctions constituted a departure from mainstream EU practice. The investment ban is an extremely infrequent measure which has been imposed on only one other occasion, against Burma. Furthermore, two of the measures employed in the Kosovo operation are unique. The autonomous flight ban and the ban on payments were wielded for the first time, and to date they have not been applied again.

Equally peculiar was the practice of targeting through the use of exemptions. A typical feature of EU sanctions practice, the use of exemptions followed both geographic and thematic criteria. The Republic of Montenegro was exempted from all measures. Kosovo was excluded from the flight ban, and companies based in that province were exempted from the asset freeze. Exemptions reflect the EU's humanitarian goal of avoiding harm to individuals not targeted, as proclaimed some years later in the *Basic Principles*: 'targeting should reduce to the maximum extent possible any adverse humanitarian effects or unintended consequences for persons not targeted or neighbouring countries' (Council of the European Union 2004c:2). It also embodies the EU's traditional approach of combining the threat of sanctions (sticks) with the offer of incentives (carrots). The EU's concern for geographical differentiation between (sub-)entities within the same legal subject finds a precedent in earlier EU efforts at crisis management in the initial phases of the Yugoslav conflicts.[2] The EU excluded not only Montenegro from the measures, but also sub-entities such as Kosovo, the province at stake. The most innovative feature is that under the so-called *Energy for Democracy* programme, the oil embargo did not apply to municipalities controlled by the Serbian opposition. Differentiation also followed non-geographical criteria. The EU excluded all those Yugoslav enterprises not linked to the Yugoslav state and leadership from its asset freeze and ban on payments. In order to achieve this, it devised an innovative approach. Rather than creating blacklists, it produced 'white lists' of enterprises whose lack of connections with the government could be demonstrated. This procedure allowed European enterprises to continue trade with some Yugoslav partners. The transfer of funds for projects supporting democratisation, education and an independent media was also exempted from these measures.

IMPACT AND EFFICACY

Several difficulties mar the assessment of the impact of measures. The main difficulty in assessing the impact of these sanctions is that the operation was interrupted by NATO's military intervention in Kosovo. As a result, the EU measures could not fully develop in terms of their effects. Following the end of hostilities, most measures were left in place in an attempt to exert pressure on the Milosevic regime and in order to prevent the Serbian military from re-arming. The fact that the objectives of the sanctions shifted after the end of the air strikes further complicates the assessment of their efficacy: 'initially, the goal was ending the use of force against ... the Albanian population in Kosovo. Later the goal was to convince the FRY to negotiate a political solution' (Blockmans 2007:156). Finally, evidence on whether these measures denied the targets the fulfilment of essential needs is admittedly meagre (de Vries 2002). Despite these difficulties, the sanctions episode has been described as a 'relative success' (Blockmans 2007:171), and some authors have ventured to offer some tentative evaluations of the efficacy of these sanctions.

The visa ban did not compel the targeted individuals to change their behaviour (de Vries 2002). However, two other measures appear to have had some noticeable impact. The oil embargo is held to have contributed to constraining the behaviour of the Yugoslav army and to have prompted Belgrade's decision to withdraw from Kosovo. Equally important, the exemptions to the oil embargo under the *Energy for Democracy* programme succeeded in bringing fuel to democratically controlled municipalities of Serbia to which Milosevic had denied oil supplies for homes and public buildings (Patten 2005:171). Following the military intervention, the implementation of the embargo was weakened, as non-EU neighbours of Serbia who had previously enforced the embargo proceeded to provide oil and gas. In contrast, it has been suggested that some financial sanctions, such as the freezing of funds, contributed significantly to the massive protests that followed the elections of September 2000. The investment ban has been praised for its potential to harm the regime rather than the private sector, as the most powerful companies in Serbia were state owned or controlled: 'the investment ban deprived those companies of access to new capital, debt relief, capital goods and patents. As a result, those companies could not transfer funds to the FRY or Serbian governments' (Blockmans 2007:171). Yet, it has also been posited that the investment ban may have been superfluous, given that the poor state of the Yugoslav economy provided a disincentive to new investments or the provision of loans by outside parties. The flight ban is reported to have inflicted substantial damage on the state carrier company, and consequently on the federal government. The strong resistance shown by the federal government to this measure, including the wielding of retaliatory measures, suggests that it was sensitive to its effects. However, Yugoslav opposition groups claimed that this measure hit the ordinary population harder than the regime. As a result, these sanctions did not fully reveal their potential.

With the exception of the oil embargo, the bans on payments and investments and the flight ban, the damage inflicted was modest. The flight ban was suspended, and the oil embargo ceased to be implemented properly after NATO ended its air campaign. It has also been argued that EU sanctions during this period were weakened by inconsistencies created by member states' behaviour in the EU decision-making process. Buchet has documented how measures first decided within the second-pillar were subsequently watered down in the implementing Regulations (Buchet de Neuilly 2003). An illustrative indication of this problem is the time interval that elapsed between the publication of the Common Position and the adoption of the Regulations, which was longer than 40 days in all cases, reaching a total of 83 days in the case of the flight ban, a conspicuous abnormality 'given that there was already unanimity of votes for the Common Position and that the EC Regulations needed only majority consent' (Buchet de Neuilly 2003:95).

Two other factors diminished the impact of the measures. The first was the gradualist approach followed by the EU, consisting in initiating minimal sanctions that were expanded only slowly. The investment ban and financial sanctions were at first imposed in their mildest form and narrowly defined, and the first visa-ban blacklist featured only ten people and excluded Serbian President Milosevic. Measures were later upgraded after the only marginal degree of discomfort they caused had become evident (de Vries 2002), thus approximating a 'trial and error' logic. When upgrading the measures, extreme care was taken to avoid damaging non-targeted persons and entities along the lines stated above. Gradualism made the sanctions appear weak when they were meant to redress a situation with a sense of urgency. Indeed, the gradual tightening of EU sanctions was a response to the realisation that they were not inflicting any noticeable damage in their original form. Gradualism negatively affected efficacy. The second factor was the EU's preoccupation with avoiding humanitarian consequences. The EU's timid management of the new tool of targeted sanctions reveals its preoccupation with avoiding indiscriminate effects, while exempting the Republic of Montenegro and non-state-controlled companies. These concerns seem to have taken precedence over efficacy or expediency in the design of sanctions (de Vries 2002, Buchet de Neuilly 2003), which suggests that the goal of appeasing domestic public opinion carried more weight than that of affecting the targets' choices. For the EU, the sanctions sequence constituted a successful learning exercise in crafting targeted sanctions. Yet, its experimental character prevented it from fulfilling its aims.

Some contextual factors also come into play. The EU was operating in an environment in which the leaders and the population of the target country built on their previous record of antagonism towards the EU as one of the external powers involved in earlier interventions, which included a military operation, and the enforcement of a comprehensive UN trade embargo. This experience strengthened Milosevic's regime, which skilfully presented Western policies as unfairly disadvantaging the Serbs (Dragovic 2003). The EU also acted against the background of an existing UN arms embargo. In the midst of the sanctions episode, NATO conducted a bombing campaign that eventually put an end to the fighting. Military action probably obscured the already scarce visibility of EU measures. In view of this record of antagonism and parallel military action, the population was hardly sensitive to the EU's precautions to avoid indiscriminate effects and its offer of incentives such as the *Energy for Democracy* programme.

A final consideration concerns the consistency with which the sanctions strategy was managed. In the Kosovo sanctions episode, implementation and enforcement by the member states was mostly satisfactory, the most notorious problem being the initial reluctance by Greece and the UK to enforce the flight ban, with the justification that bilateral air services agreements took precedence over EU law.[3] A number of measures were not implemented satisfactorily: 'most EU member states continued to permit payments into accounts of Yugoslav banks and companies. The competent authorities of the member states did not devote sufficient resources to determining which companies were to be sanctioned' (Blockmans 2007:171). These failures can be ascribed to the technical difficulty of implementing targeted financial sanctions, in particular in view of their innovative character.

At first glance there is little novelty in the claim that EU sanctions had modest effects for the end of the Kosovo conflict and the destabilisation of the Milosevic regime in Yugoslavia, given that sanctions are generally believed to be ineffective tools in conflict management. Still, despite the incomplete information on the actual damage they caused to their targets, the examination of the EU measures applied to the Yugoslav case offers useful insights.

The EU sanctions exercise in Kosovo remains an exceptional example of the EU's effort to manage a conflict by means of this tool. The Yugoslav experience contrasts with other examples of CFSP sanctions for crisis management, such as Sudan and the DRC. While in the Kosovo episode the EU amply experimented with gradualism and targeting, the African sanctions were characterised by stalemate and a lack of inventiveness. The arms embargoes, accompanied only by a visa ban in the case of the DRC at the time of imposition, remained unmodified during the ensuing decade and eventually proved futile. In contrast, in the handling of the Kosovo crisis, the EU constituted a reasonably 'unified front' which wielded sanctions with resolve. This 'sanctions operation' thus reveals a genuine intention to stem the Kosovo conflict by affecting the capabilities of one of the sides in the conflict, the Republic of Serbia and the federal forces. The background to the conflict explains this determination: the EU had matured as a result of the frustrating experience of the Bosnian wars. The EU's capacity to formulate a sanctions strategy for this crisis was also motivated by the proximity of the conflict, and the extent to which it was affected by its consequences, notably refugee flows.

CODING SUMMARY

The goals of the sanctions were not achieved; therefore, the EU cannot be credited for any contribution (contr 0). The measures were both economic and non-economic in character, and their combined impact was noticeable, especially some of the financial measures, the embargo on petrol products and the flight ban (eco 1 and 0). They threatened the leader's permanence in power (grip 1). The measures were managed coherently, despite some problems (coh 1). The EU's stance found considerable international support, although mainly from Western countries (int 1).

Sanctions for crisis management in Africa: Sudan, DRC, Ethiopia and Eritrea

The suspension of development aid is a sanction of particular relevance in the African context. In the framework of the EU-ACP Partnership Agreement, which applies to sub-Saharan Africa, the Caribbean and the Pacific, as will be shown in a later chapter, the EU designs aid freezes with care, in an attempt to spare the population from deprivation, whereby humanitarian aid is maintained.

The development aid cut-offs studied here were decided at a time when the mechanism for suspension under Lomé/Cotonou was not yet in place. However, the record shows that the EU tends to avoid invoking Art. 96 in cases of armed conflict. The effective control by the government over the territory of the country (or most thereof) seems to be a precondition for the opening of consultations. The EU refrained from invoking Art. 96 in situations of violent conflict, such as 'during a civil war, or when a country was on the verge of a peace agreement' (Hazelzet 2005:12). For the EU, the involvement of other organisations, notably the UN, in many of the countries involved in conflict makes Art. 96 consultations redundant (García-Pérez 2007:4). The Council was most explicit about its reluctance to invoke Art. 96 in the case of the Ivory Coast. Consultations with this country were proposed by the Commission in 2004, following the intensification of fighting in the north of the country, which had begun in 2002. However, the Council rejected the proposal, arguing that the threat of civil war would render Art. 96 consultations ineffective (Laakso et al. 2006).

The Commission has outlined its approach to the suspension of development aid to ACP countries involved in armed conflict, motivated by the concern about the diversion of community funds for belligerent purposes following the escalation of the conflict in the DRC into a regional war (Commission of the European Communities 1999). The Commission refers to aid suspensions for countries involved in armed conflicts as having a double goal. The first is to avert the misuse of funds for military purposes: 'the continuation of co-operation programmes ... to countries involved in armed conflicts ... involves the risk of a diversion of funds for belligerent purposes'. The second rationale is to foster the resolution of the conflict: 'where armed conflicts are accompanied by violations of the essential elements of the Lomé Convention, a partial or total suspension of aid should be set in motion to encourage a cessation of hostilities and political dialogue' (Commission of the European Communities 1999:5). By the same token, the document states that 'to make peace more attractive, the international community, and notably the EU should offer assistance to those working towards peace' (Commission of the European Communities 1999:15). The EU policy is to freeze those lines of aid which can be easily diverted for war-fighting purposes (Commission of the European Communities 1999:11). In contrast, funds devoted to decentralised cooperation and projects directly administered by NGOs are difficult to divert, while their suspension may 'put implementing NGOs in dire financial straits' (Commission of the European Communities 1999:12).

Sudan

The case of Sudan presents a complicated interplay between sanctions imposed by the EU and the UN. The EU suspended development aid to Sudan in 1990 and imposed an arms embargo in 1994. The UN imposed a series of sanctions between 1996 and 2001; however, this regime did not include an arms embargo. Only in 2004 was the EU arms embargo partly superseded by a UNSC arms embargo on the southern region of Darfur in reaction to the crisis of summer 2004 (UNSC Res. 1554 (2004)). The following year, the UNSC complemented this measure with a visa ban (UNSC Res. 1591 (2005)). Therefore the following analysis considers only those sanctions imposed by the EU, namely the cutting of development aid and the arms embargo.

Sudan has experienced decades of protracted civil war over divisions between the north and the south. Despite strong military rule, its fundamentalist government only controls part of the country's territory, northern Sudan, while power in the south is divided amongst several rebel groups. Until the late 1980s, when a coup d'état brought President Al Bashir to power, Sudan enjoyed significant levels of official development assistance. The situation in the country under Al Bashir's rule, in particular with respect to human rights violations, bombings of civilians in the south, slavery and support for international terrorism, provoked a radical shift in the support provided by the international community, which redirected more than 80 per cent of donor resources to humanitarian objectives. The EU unilaterally suspended cooperation under the Lomé Convention in 1990, due to breaches of human rights and democracy. Subsequently, Sudan was the recipient of humanitarian assistance only. However, this suspension took place outside of the ACP framework, given that no specific procedure existed at the time. In addition to the suspension of aid, the Council imposed an arms embargo on Sudan in March 1994 in the aftermath of the government-led bombings on civilians in the south (Council of the European Union 1994a). The arms embargo is generally held to have had no effect, as arms were supplied to the country by other actors (interview 2007).

The Sudan episode has been described as illustrative of the fact that the EU is ill-suited to dealing with complex situations in fragile states (Lehtinen 2001). Over time, the EU increasingly recognised that short-term humanitarian aid not only failed to assist in the capacity building of local actors, but also had perverse effects. It is widely documented that the war economy has profited from humanitarian aid, especially in the south: 'the provision of humanitarian assistance over the long term creates economic and political dependence, fuels the war economy and conflicts through spin-off effects and undermines local capacities' (Lehtinen 2001). This recognition prompted an evolution towards a development-oriented cooperation that enables local communities to become self-reliant.

In November 1999, the EU resumed political dialogue with Sudan. In this context, the EU made the resumption of development cooperation conditional on the Sudanese government's progress on human rights, democratisation and its efforts to find a peaceful solution to the war. In a background note on Sudan published in 2000, the Commission claimed that the decision to resume dialogue was taken 'on the basis of tangible, though still insufficient improvements in the performance of the Sudanese government in the areas that had been particularly criticised in the past, i.e. respect for human rights, democracy and freedom of the press and religion'. The same note asserts that 'the continuation of the EU–Sudan dialogue is the only way through which influence can be exercised over Sudan, especially in the areas of human rights and democratisation' (quoted in Lehtinen 2001). Parallel discussions were held in 2002 and 2003 with the Sudan People's Liberation Movement (SPLM), the south's main rebel group.

One year after the re-establishment of dialogue, the EU agreed the 'Humanitarian Plus' programme, which provides a grant of some 15 million euros from the sixth European Development Fund's balance of uncommitted funds.

The programme aimed at 'improving the living conditions of the distressed civilian population by establishing a minimum capacity for self-reliance in the sectors of food security, water and health' (Commission of the European Communities 2000). The implementation of the programme was linked to progress in political dialogue, and the decision was only taken after a troika mission dispatched to Sudan in November 2000 gave a positive assessment. The setting up of this special programme instead of the partial resumption of cooperation under the ACP partnership was due to some member states' resistance to the use EDF funds for Sudan, because they were afraid of sending 'the wrong political signal to the Sudanese government' (Lehtinen 2001). For some time, the Commission considered the opening of consultations under the current Art. 96 of the Cotonou Agreement, given that the decision to suspend cooperation under Lomé was taken before the non-execution clause was in place. This measure would allow the EU to legalise the situation *ex-post facto*, to re-examine the suspension, and to eventually resume aid (Lehtinen 2001).

However, the approach eventually adopted to resume aid was a different one. The re-establishment of the previously suspended dialogue and the resumption of aid took place within the framework of a rather delicate peace process in which the EU played a minor role (Gibert 2006). The EU used political dialogue to address the issues of the peace process, democracy, the rule of law, human rights and terrorism. The eruption of the crisis in Darfur complicated the situation. Although the UNSC had threatened the Sudanese government with sanctions, it refrained from imposing any in order to encourage its cooperation in the finalisation of the agreement (Tull 2005:5). The concurrence of the peace process and the Darfur crisis partly accounts for the lack of coercive measures levied in the face of this grave humanitarian situation.

The resumption of development aid was offered as an incentive for the parties to participate in the peace process and sign the Comprehensive Peace Agreement (CPA). This incentive worked well with the SPLM, given that it foresaw the allocation of funds to the prospective government of South Sudan (interview 2007). Following the signing of the CPA between the central government and South Sudan in January 2005, political dialogue centred on its implementation, as well as on the Darfur crisis and the human rights situation (interview 2007).

As is generally the practice with the re-establishment of cooperation with ACP countries, the EU adopted a gradual strategy on the resumption of aid to Sudan, making it conditional on progress in the political domain. The Commission has consistently indicated that the resumption of cooperation with Sudan is linked to the evolution of the situation in Darfur (Commission of the European Communities 2005) and progress in the implementation of the CPA. Currently, the EU is supporting the negotiation process in Darfur and the African Union's Mission in Sudan (AMIS). While political dialogue is ongoing, it is conducted irregularly and no high-level troika meeting has taken place since 2005 (interview 2007).

IMPACT AND EFFICACY

The assessment that the EU lacks an appropriate legal framework and operational instruments to deal with the complex political emergency in Sudan appears to be accurate. The EU's approach suffers from the fact that it has to deal with Sudan within a framework that was designed for 'regular' settings, i.e. situations where there is no conflict, or where the government has effective control over the entire territory of the state. In Sudan, the EU encountered abnormal circumstances, with part of the territory under the control of rebel forces, and where the ECHO ceased operations for some years before the eruption of the Darfur crisis in 2004. The refusal to sell arms to non-state actors equates to an arms embargo on the south, while political dialogue was originally conducted only with the north. This left the EU in the paradoxical situation of limited development cooperation activities and dialogue first being resumed with the government-controlled north, the same entity subjected to CFSP sanctions as a result of its attacks on the civilian population in the south. Rapprochement with the north has been criticised for reinforcing the position of the Sudanese government despite the lack of progress in peace negotiations, and the Humanitarian Plus programme as a reward that the government could interpret as a disincentive for peace.

The EU's re-engagement with Sudan is illuminating in two respects. First, it exemplifies how sanctions fatigue sets in where they fail to produce results for a long period of time (in this case a decade). An exceptional device was found in order to provide development-oriented aid outside the 'orthodox' EDF framework in the form of the 'Humanitarian Plus' programme, which funds reconstruction and capacity-building actions that go *beyond* humanitarian aid. In order to justify such a programme, the Commission indicated that some improvements in human rights conditions had been observed. Still, the importance of the country in the African context and the wish to promote the government's cooperation in the peace process also had some bearing on the decision to re-engage. In addition, re-engagement was encouraged by the fact that the suspension of aid was not only failing to deliver the right results, but was actually aggravating the situation by fuelling the war economy.

As with all EU arms embargoes in Africa, member state compliance has been satisfactory. Yet the measure still failed to have any effect. Countries like China, Iran and Iraq amply supplied Sudan with arms.

Democratic Republic of Congo

Until the early 1990s, Zaire was ruled by a one-party system led by President Mobutu. In 1990, Mobutu initiated a transition period which was to be supervised by a Zaire National Conference (ZNC). However, this process was suspended by Mobutu shortly after it began, and a period of crisis characterised by violent clashes between opposition groups and the armed forces set in. The Commission suspended development aid to the country in 1992. The ZNC and Mobutu finally appointed the moderate opposition leader Tshisekedi as Prime Minister. Following Mobutu's dissolution of Tshisekedi's government in 1993, the EU requested that Tshisekedi be reinstalled, and imposed an arms embargo, along with travel restrictions on senior officials loyal to the regime. The crisis was aggravated by the arrival of large numbers of refugees from Rwanda and Burundi in 1994. Mobutu was ousted by rebel forces led by Laurent Kabila, who renamed the country Democratic Republic of Congo (DRC) in 1997. Following the assassination of Laurent Kabila in 2001, his son Joseph Kabila took power. During the 1980s, the country became a base for armed opposition groups fighting neighbouring governments. In the late 1990s, the DRC became a battleground for seven different African countries. The civil war that started in the early 1990s lasted until the signing of a peace agreement in 2002. Following signs of a resumption in the fighting, the EU arms embargo was superseded by a UN arms embargo in 2003 (UNSC Res 1493 (2003)).

The DRC is one of the most troubled countries of the African continent. The economy is in an advanced state of collapse, and due to its lack of financial resources is reliant on international support. Because of the poor results of aid in the past, donors have long been reluctant to increase it. In 1990, the World Bank and the IMF suspended their aid to Zaire, and between 1991 and 1993 other donors followed suit, due to human rights violations and the prevailing insecurity.

In reality, donors continued to provide aid under a humanitarian label – similarly to the 'humanitarian plus' programme for Sudan. Despite cutting off aid in 1992, the EU has remained one of the country's most important donor agencies since 1993. In 1995, it reoriented part of its aid to two programmes focusing on roads and the health sector, although with funding at less than 60 per cent of pre-1993 levels. The replacement of Mobutu by Laurent Kabila saw the resumption of development aid from some Western donors, including the EU, which, however, proved to be short lived. Still, during the last year of Laurent Kabila's rule, the EU launched a process of programme formulation to utilise outstanding EDF funds. The replacement of Laurent Kabila by Joseph Kabila in 2001, which was followed by rapid progress on several fronts, once again encouraged donors to resume aid.

On the diplomatic front, the EU appointed a Special Envoy to the Great Lakes region in 1996. However, a lack of agreement between EU member states limited the Special Envoy's capacity to formulate a common line (Bourque and Sampson 2001:8). In its interventions in areas under rebel control, the EU endeavoured to preserve a certain 'parity of power between actors so one can increase the willingness of the parties to seek peace' (Bourque and Sampson 2001:8). In the framework of the Lusaka Accords, the EU has also tried to make use of the resumption of aid as an incentive to encourage agreement among inter-Congolese negotiators, linking increased aid in the east of the country to the positive outcome of the negotiations. However, the lack of success of such initiatives may be related to the volatility of the situation. As

Bourque and Sampson claim, in order to introduce reforms, the state needs a minimum operating budget; however, it is difficult to prevent funds from being used directly or indirectly for the war effort in a country actively involved in conflict. It was the risk of the diversion of funds in the DRC that compelled the Commission to create mechanisms to reduce the fungibility of funds for belligerent purposes.

IMPACT AND EFFICACY

The EU imposed an arms embargo and a visa ban on Zaire in April 1993 as a result of the violation of the process of democratic transition. The refusal to hand over power to a newly elected government constitutes a typical breach of the human rights and democracy element of the Cotonou Agreement that the EU usually addresses through consultations. However, since this option was not available at the time, it reacted with a suspension under the second pillar. As with most stand-alone EU arms embargoes in Africa, the effect of the measures was non-existent. The flow of arms continued through smuggling along the porous borders and trade with alternative suppliers (von Bömcken 2009).

Ethiopia/ Eritrea

The EU imposed an arms embargo on Ethiopia and Eritrea in March 1999 following a recommendation by the UNSC, after the escalation of clashes between the armies of the two countries over a border dispute. The persistence of conflict and the failure of mediation attempts by the Organisation of African Unity (OAU) prompted the imposition of a UN mandatory embargo in May 2000. Soon thereafter, negotiations leading to an OAU-brokered peace agreement were initiated, culminating in its signature in December of the same year (Kreutz 2004). The UN subsequently lifted its embargo in 2001.

IMPACT AND EFFICACY

The short-lived EU embargo, superseded by UN measures less than a year after its start, does not appear to have exerted any independent effect on any of the parties involved in the conflict. It thus follows the pattern that characterises stand-alone EU arms embargoes in Africa (Brzoska 2005).

African episodes: evaluation of strategy and context

The EU proceeded similarly in all African cases (Sudan, DRC and Ethiopia/ Eritrea). Consultations under Art. 96 of the Cotonou Agreement were never convened. Instead, the EU first reacted by imposing arms embargoes and suspending aid. Following the imposition of these measures, the situations were characterised by stagnation. No further sanctions were threatened, and none of the parties appears to have taken any steps towards lifting the measures until they were partially or totally superseded by UNSC measures.

The fact that consultations were never called can be linked to the fact that in all of these cases state authority had either collapsed, or had ceased to cover the entire territory of the state. These cases of CFSP sanctions correspond to the notion of 'failed state', identified as one of the main security risks in the European Security Strategy. These episodes confirm that the Council does not want to use Art. 96 to deal with armed conflict and state collapse and prefers to address such situations through the UNSC, probably because it does not expect to exert any influence. The Commission seems to diverge somewhat from this idea, having considered consultations with Sudan following the suspension of aid as a way of legalising the latter. Divergences between EU member states concerning the line to take in these situations, and the degree of legitimacy to confer on each party to the conflict, may have contributed to the Council's decision to reject the Commission's proposal to call consultations.

The Sudan experience is unique. Development cooperation was resumed in the absence of Art. 96 consultations. The EU's behaviour in the Sudanese case reveals how it considered a country involved in a protracted armed conflict to deserve exceptional treatment. This case also highlights an interesting finding. While the arms embargo, as a CFSP measure, had more visibility and resonance than any aid sanction, it was aid conditionality that displayed some impact. In sub-Saharan Africa, which is characterised by informal trade and porous borders, a stand-alone EU arms embargo is bound to have little effect. The only possible impact of an EU arms embargo – the lack of access to sophisticated weapons technology – is irrelevant for countries that cannot afford them. In contrast, the provision of aid can have some impact on leaders in these countries, even if in the case of oil-rich states, such as a Sudan, it is less important.

It appears paradoxical that the entity the EU contributed to influencing was a non-state actor. The prospect of benefiting from a share of development aid was an incentive for the SPLM to engage in the peace process. Aid is attractive to these groups precisely because it cannot reach them outside the framework of a formal peace agreement. Both in Sudan and DRC, humanitarian aid only was delivered to areas outside governmental control, and not even this reached the entire rebel-controlled territory. In addition, the ECHO withdrew from southern Sudan once the emergency situation had ended, due to adverse conditions. Security considerations are often compounded by political sensitivities, as donors do not want to be viewed as supporting the legitimacy of rebel groups. This was observed in the east of the DRC, where most donors halted aid programmes after 1988, including humanitarian ones. The fact that some multilateral donors and the EC maintained aid in that area suggests that the refusal to work in the east was due more to a lack of political will than to insurmountable obstacles (Bourque and Sampson 2001:18).

At the same time, the EU's willingness to resume development aid was not without an element of self-interest. After years of providing exclusively humanitarian aid, it set up some development-type interventions in the hope that they would eventually result in the sustainability of some communities, thereby releasing the ECHO from its duties. The creation of development-oriented actions under the 'humanitarian plus' label in Sudan and DRC proves this agenda.

CODING SUMMARY

The embargoes against Zaire, Ethiopia/Eritrea and Sudan failed to accomplish any behavioural changes in the concerned leaders; therefore the EU cannot be credited for any contribution (contr 0). The measures were economic and non-economic in character and their impact was not felt (eco 1). They did pose a threat to the leaders' permanence in power (grip 1). The measures were managed coherently (coh 1). The EU's stance found a high degree of international support (int 1).

Indonesia

The arms embargo on Indonesia was connected to the conflict in the separatist region of East Timor. Of all the conflicts that destabilised Indonesia in the mid-1990s, the East Timor issue bore particular significance for the EU, given that the UN considered the area as being under the jurisdiction of its former colonial power, Portugal (Kreutz 2006:36). Following Indonesian consent in May 1999, an UN-sponsored referendum on independence was organised in East Timor for late August 1999. However, in the lead-up to the vote, both the UN election mission and independence supporters were attacked by army-backed paramilitaries. After the announcement of results overwhelmingly in favour of independence, the violence escalated and several hundred thousand East Timorese were compelled to seek refuge abroad. In response, the EU imposed a ban on economic aid (Kreutz 2006:36) and an arms embargo (Council of the European Union 1999b). The ban was imposed due to 'serious violations of human rights and International Humanitarian Law', in order to prevent 'the supply of equipment which might be used for internal repression or terrorism' (Council of the European Union 1999b). Although the embargo was only imposed for a period of four months, its extension became unnecessary as military forces were once more under democratic control when the embargo was due to expire.

IMPACT AND EFFICACY

It has been suggested that the EU/US arms embargo against Indonesia was important in forcing Indonesia to accept a UN-led peace-keeping force in East Timor: 'in an effort to force Indonesia into agreeing to an international peace-keeping force, the EU, along with the US, cut off its arms exports. The pressure worked. The military pulled out of East Timor, the peacekeepers went in and peace was restored' (Parry 2000). However, available accounts ascribe far more centrality to the role of the US. Against the background of an embargo on arms sales and military cooperation which had started in 1992 and would remain in force until 2005 (Taylor 2009:195–98), President Clinton issued a longer list of demands than the EU. The fact that Indonesian President Habibie – who had opened up the option of East Timorese independence in the first place – eventually complied with US demands suggests that the EU's role was simply one of support (interview 2009). Rather than the EU arms embargo, what appears to have influenced the calculations of Indonesia was the need for credits from the international financial institutions to relaunch its economy, which was in dire straits at the time. As put by White, 'East Timor was a problem for Indonesia internationally. In the United States and Europe, concern about East Timor limited Indonesia's ability to get a hearing for its concerns and interests. Especially after Indonesia's economic collapse in the financial crisis of 1997–98, Jakarta needed all the friends it could get' (White 2008:70).

CODING SUMMARY

The goals of the sanctions were achieved, but the EU has to share the credit with other actors, especially the US (contr 1). The measure was not economic in character and its impact was negligible (eco 0). It did not pose a threat to the leader's permanence in power (grip 0). The measure was managed coherently (coh 1). The EU's stance was internationally supported (int 1), although in this case the EU itself did not play a principal role.

Nigeria

The emergence of the Nigerian crisis does not, at first sight, differ much from the situations that led to the call for Art. 336a/96 consultations in ACP countries described in a later section. When the EU imposed its measures, the country was in the midst of a protracted, problematic transition to democratic rule which had provoked a political crisis. The results of the June 1993 presidential elections that took place as part of the transition to democracy were cancelled by its ruler, General Babarngida, which provoked the imposition of sanctions by the EU and other donors. The political crisis that followed resulted in the seizure of power in November 1993 by General Abacha, who then proceeded to dissolve the transitional institutions and forbid all political parties. The following month, the EU imposed new sanctions on Nigeria, namely:

- the suspension of military cooperation
- visa restrictions for members of the military and the security forces and their families
- the suspension of visits of members of the military
- the restriction of movement of all military personnel of Nigerian diplomatic missions

- the cancellation of training courses for all Nigerian military personnel
- the suspension of all high-level visits that were not indispensable to and from Nigeria (mentioned in Council of the European Union 1995).

Concerning restrictions on arms exports, new licences for defence equipment were to be examined, with an automatic presumption of refusal by member states (Kreutz 2006:32). Further CFSP sanctions were imposed in response to the execution of nine human rights activists, including the prominent minority-rights campaigner Ken Saro-Wiwa, in November 1995. The measures included visa restrictions on military leaders and their families, an embargo on arms, munitions and military equipment, and the suspension of development cooperation (Council of the European Union 1995). In parallel, the US barred all military sales to Nigeria and broadened an existing visa ban for junta members and supporters (Cortright and Lopez 1996:1).

At the same time, the Commonwealth suspended Nigeria's membership, and requested the dispatch of a delegation to the country in order to conduct an investigation into the events. The Nigerian government refused to allow such a visit, making its authorisation conditional on a commitment from the Commonwealth to conduct an investigation into human rights violations perpetrated by other countries. However, in November 1996 a Commonwealth delegation was finally allowed to visit the country. Still, the government made no progress in the transition to democratic rule. Only parties favourable to the ruler were allowed to participate in the local and legislative elections organised in 1997/98 as part of a simulated 'transitional process'. Throughout the period, the country was in deep economic crisis, marred by corruption and terrorist attacks in the oil-rich delta region.

The end of the Nigerian crisis was prompted by a rather fortuitous circumstance. Two months after being officially appointed the only candidate in the upcoming presidential elections, Abacha died of a heart attack. His successor, General Abubakar, accomplished the transition towards democratic rule through the implementation of a programme of democratisation which included amnesty for Nigerians in exile, and which culminated in presidential elections in February 1999, supervised by an EU observer mission (Council of the European Union 1998c). CFSP sanctions were first eased (Council of the European Union 1999d) and then lifted after the formal end to military rule in May 1999 (Council of the European Union 1999d).

IMPACT AND EFFICACY

The fact that the EU did not interrupt aid to Nigeria in 1993, when presidential elections were annulled, but did so only following the international outrage over the execution of human rights activists, is partly responsible for the inefficacy of its sanctions: 'The partial nature of EU measures for over two years must have sent a mixed message to the Nigerian military authorities, indicating … opposition to the turn of events but not the unequivocal condemnation and tough punitive action' (Crawford 1997:50). The fortuitous nature of the event that allowed the transition to democratic rule to take place, i.e. the natural death of the autocratic leader Abacha, makes it impossible to credit the CFSP sanctions for the happy conclusion of the Nigerian episode. If anything, concessions from the Nigerian leadership were obtained by the British Commonwealth – not the EU or other donors (Pabst and Klein 2006).

While CFSP sanctions did not compel any behavioural change in the Nigerian leaders, the fluency with which the transition to democratic rule was accomplished by the former defence minister following the death of Abacha is striking. It gives us grounds to believe that the degree of international pressure that had accumulated through the sanctions imposed by a number of donors, including the EU, had created an environment conducive to the re-establishment of democratic rule. The improvement in the Nigerian situation during Abubakar's stint as transitional ruler has been described as being 'beyond all hope' (French: *au-delà de toute espérance*, European Parliament 2006:8). Once the principal ruler was absent from power, the forces anxious to restore democracy, as well as international prestige, were unleashed.

Apart from the personality of Abubakar, who did not entertain any political ambitions (Pabst and Klein 2006:5), several factors can account for Nigeria's smooth transition to democracy following Abacha's death. Despite calls for the imposition of an oil embargo, thereby targeting Nigeria's main source of wealth (Cortright and Lopez 1996), CFSP sanctions were restricted to an arms embargo, a visa ban and diplomatic sanctions. The suspension of development cooperation did not seem to be effective: 'the suspension of development aid had almost no effect on such a rich country. It was peanuts' (interview 2007). The visa ban appears to have significantly affected the wealthy Nigerian leadership, who were used to travelling regularly to European capitals, and were largely British educated. According to an EU official involved in the episode, the visa ban for military leaders and personnel inconvenienced them as 'they all had children studying abroad they could not … visit. Their wives could not take the private jet and go shopping' (interview 2007). With the country's oil wealth and its status as Africa's most populous country, with about 118 million inhabitants, Nigerian elites regarded it not only as a regional power, but as the continent's leader, rivalled only by post-apartheid South Africa. The loss of international prestige associated with the sanctions to which it was subjected had a disruptive effect on Nigerian leaders. However, the involvement of the Commonwealth in the Nigerian episode complicates the assessment of the impact of the EU sanctions, as the membership of its former colonial ruler, the UK, in both organisations makes its influence difficult to ascertain.

CODING SUMMARY

The goals of the sanctions were achieved, yet the EU can be credited for its contribution only to a very limited extent (cont 0). The measure was economic in character but its impact was very modest (eco 1). It did not directly endanger the regime's continuance in office (grip 0). The measure was managed coherently (coh 1). The EU's stance had a high degree of international support (int 1).

Uzbekistan

Uzbekistan is a unique case in CFSP sanctions practice. Never before had a target of EU sanctions made concessions leading to a partial lifting of the measures only a few months after these were first imposed.

The EU decision to apply sanctions here was a result of the use of force by the Uzbek government in response to an uprising that took place in Andijan in May 2005, in which hundreds of civilians were killed. However, the CFSP measures were imposed in reaction not to the use of force against civilians, but to the government's refusal to allow an international independent investigation into the Andijan events, as urged by the UN. After condemning the Uzbek security forces, the Council set a deadline for the end of June, which the Uzbek leadership failed to meet (Council of the European Union 2005c). In November, the Council imposed the following measures (Council of the European Union 2005b):

- an embargo on exports to Uzbekistan of arms, military equipment used for internal repression and other equipment that 'might be used for internal repression'
- a visa ban on individuals 'directly responsible for the indiscriminate and disproportionate use of force in Andijan and for the obstruction of an independent inquiry'
- the suspension of technical meetings in the framework of the Partnership and Cooperation Agreement (PCA).

The Council indicated in the same text that it would review the situation after the one-year period of validity of the Common Position in light of:

- the outcomes of the trials of individuals accused of participating in the disturbances
- the detention and harassment of individuals who questioned the Uzbek authorities' version of the events
- Uzbek cooperation with any international inquiry into the events and the outcome of such an inquiry, and
- 'any action that demonstrates the will by the Uzbek authorities to adhere to the principles of respect for human rights, rule of law and fundamental freedoms'.

From a technical point of view, the Common Position displays several innovations. The Council made explicit the criteria it intended to use when deciding on the renewal of the measures. Instead of merely condemning the events, the sanctions make a demand of the leadership and point to a number of developments that will influence the decision on the continuation of measures. This marks a departure from other cases in which sanctions were imposed to protest irreversible situations (e.g. the 1994 bombings of civilians in Southern Sudan). The *ex ante* character of the demands offers the government extensive information on how to reverse the measures. At the same time, some flexibility is visible in the hierarchy of the demands. Authorising the inquiry is the core demand, while the provision that 'any action' demonstrating the Uzbek leadership's will to 'adhere to the principles of respect for human rights, rule of law and fundamental freedoms', broadens the room for manoeuvre.

The first signs given by the Uzbek leadership following the imposition of the CFSP measures were negative and left little hope for compliance with the conditions. EU sanctions were not accompanied by equivalent measures from any other entity. While the US had contemplated imposing sanctions jointly with the EU, it eventually failed to do so. This situation permitted the Uzbek side to claim that it was the EU, and not Uzbekistan, that was isolated. In the political realm, the Uzbek shift towards Russia was noticeable, for example in the conclusion of a mutual defence agreement (Blagov 2005).

Following the EU's realisation that the sanctions were having the undesirable effect of reorienting the policies of a major regional power in Central Asia towards Russia, some member states adopted a proactive stance aimed at persuading Uzbekistan to comply with the demands. In the run-up to the Council meeting that was to decide on the renewal of the sanctions in mid-November, a total of four official visits to Tashkent were conducted by both the Presidency holders (Finland and Germany), individually and as a troika, and the Special Representative for Central Asia Mr Pierre Morel. The message conveyed to the Uzbek authorities was that they faced a unique opportunity to have sanctions lifted as a result of the favourable constellation of acting and incoming EU presidencies. The November EU–Uzbek Partnership and Co-operation Council confirmed that an experts' mission ('study group') would be dispatched to Uzbekistan before the end of the year, and that a human rights dialogue would be established. In exchange, the Council unlocked the subcommittees on economic affairs and justice and home affairs under the EU–Uzbek PCA. Within the Council, two main positions needed to be reconciled. One highlighted that there had been a positive gesture from the Uzbek side and argued that sanctions should be lifted in order to encourage the leadership to cooperate further. The other insisted that despite this gesture, no progress had been made concerning the conditions of those detained and indicted as a result of the Andijan events. The Council decided on the innovative formula as a compromise between both views, extending the arms embargo for one year, while the visa ban was renewed only for six months, with a revision after three months, labelled the '12–16–3' formula. The Uzbek leadership was still disappointed at the renewal of sanctions, as its understanding was that concession on its side would lead to a total lifting (Eurasia Insight 2006). The study group was dispatched the following month, as agreed in the Partnership and Co-operation Council.

What followed was a gradual evolution towards full lifting. In the revisions of sanctions of November 2007, the Council decided to renew the arms embargo for another year, but to suspend the application of the visa ban for an initial period of six months, announcing that it would 'review the situation in Uzbekistan and assess progress made by the Uzbek authorities towards ensuring respect for human rights and fundamental freedoms, as well as for the rule of law' before deciding on a new extension (Council of the European Union 2007a). While no information on the contents of the political dialogue was made public, steps taken by Uzbekistan in the following months included the abolition of the death penalty, the introduction of habeas corpus and the ratification of the ILO Convention on the Worst Forms of Child Labour. In February 2008, Uzbek authorities released four human rights defenders and cancelled the probation period of two other human rights defenders, who had been released from prison the previous year. In addition, the Uzbek government agreed to the resumption of visits by the International Committee of the Red Cross (ICRC) to prisons in the country. After deciding on the renewal of the visa ban suspension, the Council called on the Uzbek authorities to 'ensure the early release' of the imprisoned human rights defenders and to cease their harassment, announcing that it would closely monitor the human rights situation in Uzbekistan and might amend the visa restrictions (Council of the European Union 2008b). Sanctions were lifted in October 2009 in a move that was subject to widespread criticism by civil society groups appalled at the poor human rights record of the country. The Council justified its decision on the basis of the positive steps taken in Uzbekistan over the last years, adding to the above list the ratification of conventions against child labour, efforts to improve detention conditions and progress in judicial reform, among others (Council of the European Union 2009c). Replicating the language of its previous position, the Council announced that it would closely observe the human rights situation in Uzbekistan. Significantly, the decision to lift sanctions was warranted in order 'to encourage Uzbek authorities to take further substantive steps to improve the rule of law and the human rights situation'.

IMPACT AND EFFICACY

The partial compliance in the Uzbek case makes it the most successful case of CFSP sanctions. How are we to explain the 'deviant case' of the Uzbek sanctions? The damage inflicted by the sanctions was limited. There were no arms sales to Uzbekistan prior to the sanctions, and the Uzbek authorities indicated that they had no interest in purchasing European military equipment. The targeted authorities expressed indifference towards the ban, albeit according to Council sources 'they were unhappy about them' (interview 2007). From the observations of some experts, one could infer that the success of the episode was due to the intermediate nature of the solution (rather than full compliance), coupled with the perceived stigma resulting from the sanctions. As Olcott has put it,

> The Uzbeks do not want to become any sort of international pariah, or to have the movements and free action of their leaders and their families restrained. … Yet they don't want to have to publicly admit any errors, or ask forgiveness, by, for instance creating an OSCE or EU sponsored formal investigative commission to examine the events in Andijan.
>
> (Olcott 2007:13)

The proactive behaviour of the EU was motivated by 'a sense of impasse' (interview 2007). The fact that the EU was preparing a Common Strategy on Central Asia geared to a new lease of life for cooperation with this region is likely to have influenced the EU's attitude. The original reaction to the sanctions was negative: in the face of sanctions, the Uzbek regime tended to 'retract rather than entering into interaction'. EU sources explain success as follows: 'sanctions were only successful because they were combined with repeated attempts to put political pressure through four visits in five months conveying the message "it's now or never"' (interview 2007).

On the EU side, two considerations are revealing. Firstly, when deciding on the EU 'study group' rather than an international 'enquiry', the EU settled for less than what it had originally demanded. Similarly, 'progress in the field of human rights' took the form of the establishment of a human rights dialogue. According to EU sources, this compromise formula was 'the only thing they would accept' (interview 2007). Secondly, the proactivity of those EU elements interested in bringing about the lifting of the sanctions was directed not only at the Uzbeks, but also at fellow member states. The original split between delegations for and against the easing of sanctions could be bridged: 'everybody understood that there was a political opportunity' (interview 2007). Beyond the skilfulness of the presidencies involved and their interests in the region, some insights can be obtained from the proactive stance which ultimately brought about the easing of sanctions. Some member states had important security interests in the region: Germany depends upon a military base in Uzbekistan to support NATO's military mission in Afghanistan (Olcott 2007). By the time the EU agreed sanctions against Uzbekistan, there were a total of five autonomous sanctions regimes against state or state-like entities (Belarus, Burma, China, Sudan, the Transnistrian entity and Zimbabwe) in place, of which the most recent dated from 2002. A general 'sanctions fatigue' set in. Fearful of the prospect of adding yet another target to the list of protracted, unfruitful sanctions regimes, some member states worked to avoid such a scenario. The result was the successful reversal of an attitude of increasing antagonism on the Uzbek side.

Nevertheless, this success story of CFSP sanctions is not without critics. Experts accuse the EU of half-heartedness, declaring that sanctions against Uzbekistan were eased because they were detrimental to the security interests of some member states (Olcott 2007), or condemning the fact that 'individual members of the EU just as promptly went about undermining these sanctions and firming up their unilateral relationships with the abusive government'

(Kreikemeyer and Zellner 2007:22). Yet, it is conceded that the EU's 'current strategy' shows 'more promise for modifying the behaviour of the Uzbek state than the previous sanctions regime, although the current level of engagement is limited and the concessions of Tashkent modest by any criteria' (Olcott 2007:13).

CODING SUMMARY

The goals of the sanctions were achieved, for which the EU alone can be credited (contr 1). The measures were not economic in character but their impact was still noticed (eco 0). They did not pose a threat to the leader's permanence in power (grip 0). The measures were managed coherently (coh 1). The EU's stance found little international support (int 0).

Burma

Initiated in 1991, the sanctions against Burma constitute one of the oldest cases of autonomous EU sanctions still in place. They are undoubtedly the EU's most comprehensive, but arguably also one of its most ineffective regimes. The sanctions strategy has been one of incrementalism. Sanctions started with the failure of the ruling military junta, the State Peace and Development Council, to respect the results of the May 1990 elections won by the National League for Democracy (NLD) with an overwhelming majority. All non-humanitarian aid programmes were suspended in 1991, while an arms embargo was imposed, along with a range of diplomatic sanctions, which included the expulsion of military personnel attached to the diplomatic representations of Burma in the member states and the withdrawal of military attachés to diplomatic representations of the member states in Burma (Council of the European Union 1991, see also Council of the European Union 1996c). A visa ban and the suspension of high-level visits were introduced in October 1996 following the failure of attempts at a negotiation with the junta, and on the basis of continuing human rights violations (Council of the European Union 1996c). In 2000, the visa ban was expanded and a freezing of assets was imposed on the blacklisted individuals (Council of the European Union 2000b). Further extensions of the blacklists followed in succeeding years (Council of the European Union 2001b and Council of the European Union 2002a).

In April 2003, the Council also attempted to start using the suspension of sanctions, rather than the sanctions themselves, as a tool to elicit compliance. It suspended extensions of the visa ban, the asset freeze and the prohibition of technical training and assistance until October 2003, pledging that it would refrain from re-imposing the measures if 'substantive progress towards national reconciliation, the restoration of a democratic order and greater respect for human rights' had been made by then (Council of the European Union 2003b). In view of the renewed detention of Aung San Suu Kyi and a crackdown on the opposition in May, the suspension was lifted well before the deadline, in June of the same year (Council of the European Union 2003c).

Again, the Asia–Europe meeting (ASEM) of April 2004 urged the Burmese authorities to release Aung San Suu Kyi from house arrest, to stop the harassment of the National League for Democracy and to allow for genuine open debate at the National Convention. The following September, the EU threatened to impose new measures if the military junta failed to comply with its conditions before the upcoming ASEM summit:

- an expansion of the visa ban to include members of lower military rank not yet included in the black list
- a prohibition on 'EU registered companies and organisations from making financing such as loans and equities available to named Burmese state-owned enterprises'
- a policy of negative votes against extending loans to Burma from international financial institutions to be implemented by the member states.

Notably, the investment ban was not formulated in a Common Position, but only in Council Conclusions. The ban prohibited European companies from investing in certain state-owned enterprises in Burma, but exempted existing investments, which could be prolonged. Before the imposition of the investment ban, member states banned the extension of state export credit guarantees to European enterprises conducting business in or with Burma (Will 2003).

In addition, positively framed measures were also announced: an expansion of assistance programmes to the Burmese people in the domains of health and education, which were to be 'defined in consultation with democratic groups' and implemented by the UN, and a mandate for the Commission to produce proposals 'to address the issue of Burmese illegal logging, including opportunities for decreasing deforestation in and export of teak' from Burma (Council of the European Union 2004f). The blacklist was again expanded in October 2004 (Council of the European Union 2004b).

The Common Position adopted in April 2006 as a result of lack of compliance on the Burmese side constituted the most far-reaching and perfected Common Position containing CFSP restrictive measures of its time, featuring a total of 11 articles (Council of the European Union 2006b). The package encompassed:

- an embargo on arms and military equipment
- the suspension of non-humanitarian aid
- a visa ban and the freezing of assets of members of the junta and high-ranking military officers and authorities in the tourism sector
- an investment and loan ban, including extensions of participation in state-owned enterprises
- the suspension of high-level bilateral governmental visits
- a ban on the attachment of military personnel to the diplomatic representations of Burma in EU member states, as well as on the attachment of military personnel to diplomatic representations of the member states in Burma.

Several features distinguish the sanctions against Burma from other CFSP sanctions regimes, making it the harshest EU autonomous sanctions regime. The investment ban, now formalised in a Common Position including an annex listing those enterprises affected, was strengthened with extensions to participation in state-owned enterprises, although it still exempted agreements concluded prior to October 2004. The blacklist of individuals covered by the visa ban and asset freeze is 13 pages long. It is also virtually the only Common Position in force which has formalised diplomatic sanctions: the prohibition of high-level meetings and the attachment of military officials to representations on either side.

The motives for the imposition of the sanctions are clearly explained: the failure of the authorities to allow a democratic transition to civilian rule, the detention of Aung San Suu Kyi and the harassment of the opposition, human rights violations and restrictions on the operation of international organisations and NGOs. However, the conditions for the lifting or easing of sanctions are not spelled out as such, and are condensed in a broad formulation that allows the Council ample discretion to consider their lifting:

> In the event of a substantial improvement in the overall political situation in Burma/Myanmar, the suspension of these restrictive measures and a gradual resumption of cooperation with Burma/Myanmar will be considered, after the Council has assessed developments.
>
> (Council of the European Union 2006b:2)

A noteworthy aspect of the sanctions design relates to the exceptions permitted to the general suspension of non-humanitarian aid. These affect projects in support of 'human rights, democracy, good governance, conflict prevention and building the capacity of civil society; health and education [and] poverty alleviation, and environmental protection' (Council of the European Union 2006b:2). This selection of goals respects EU priorities in general terms. It is original in that it foresees implementation through UN agencies, NGOs, and local civil administrations *in consultation with civil society and all democratic groups*: 'programmes should … be defined, monitored, run and evaluated in consultation with civil society and all democratic groups, including the National League for Democracy' (Council of the European Union 2006b:2). This constitutes an attempt not only to circumvent governmental authorities, as is common practice in EU sanctions, but to empower the opposition and actors at the local level.

In reaction to the repression of the pro-democracy demonstrations of autumn 2007, the Council further strengthened its sanctions (Council of the European Union 2007b). This time, the EU agreed measures which do not feature in the EU's usual repertoire. This new set of measures specifically targets state-owned industries by prohibiting:

- the export of equipment and technology, and the provision of technical or financial assistance destined for enterprises engaged in logging and timber processing, and the mining of metals, precious and semi-precious stones, and

- the import of round logs, timber products, metals, precious and semi-precious stones.

The investment ban was also complemented with a ban on the creation of joint ventures with blacklisted enterprises or their subsidiaries. The original list includes over 1,200 Burmese enterprises. In the aftermath of the trial of Aung San Suu Kyi by a Burmese court which sentenced her to continued house arrest, the EU extended its blacklists in August 2009 to cover those members of the judiciary responsible for the verdict as well as four state-run media outlets for their involvement in disseminating regime propaganda.

The only field where some flexibility can be discerned in the EU's stance is development aid. Burma is one of the least developed countries in the world. Until 2004, EU interventions in the country were based on ad hoc assessments and financed from a variety of budget lines, with assistance limited to humanitarian aid. However, compelled by the stalemate in the situation, Commissioner Ferrero-Waldner announced in March 2005 that the EU would engage in a critical dialogue with the regime in an attempt to push it to reform. Thus, the current version of the CFSP Common Position acknowledges the possibility of more forms of aid. In 2007, the Commission released its first Country Strategy Paper on Burma, covering the period from 2007 to 2013 and allowing for increased levels of assistance focused on the educational and health sectors.

The EU strategy of incrementalism has not been exclusively determined by the conduct of the Burmese junta. The sanctions dynamics have also been heavily influenced by developments in the EU's relationship with ASEAN. The EU refused to allow Burma to accede to the EC–ASEAN cooperation agreement after the country became a member of this organisation, and launched the Asia–Europe meeting as an alternative framework excluding Burma. Still, a number of 'diplomatic crises' erupted, due to refusals by some ASEAN ministers to participate in summits from which Burma was banned, which led to the EU's eventual acceptance of its presence in 2004, albeit at a lower level than the other delegations (Smith 2006:165). Sanctions were tightened in order to compensate for the *de facto* lifting of the ban on Burmese participation in the EU's dialogue with Asia.

IMPACT AND EFFICACY

If anything characterises the situation in Burma under EU and US sanctions, it is its unchanging nature. The inefficacy of sanctions against Burma is widely recognised. A high-ranking official from the UK Foreign Office acknowledged in a parliamentary hearing at the House of Lords in 2006 that the sanctions against Burma were 'not working very well' and that EU sanctions were 'unlikely to bring about change' (House of Lords 2007:22). A former European diplomat sent to Burma asserts that 'the restrictive measures applied by Britain and the EU since 1988 have had no perceptible effect in persuading the military junta in Burma to moderate its repressive policies' (Tonkin 2006:3).

Compliance with the embargo has been assessed positively, with countries imposing the embargo having halted arms shipments from their own territory. However, the embargo has failed to prevent Burmese government access to arms, as it was able to find alternative suppliers. Although China was the dominant supplier throughout the 1990s, Burma has since been able to diversify its arms imports, purchasing from Ukraine, Russia, Singapore, Bulgaria and North Korea. The effects of the EU arms embargo appear to have been negligible, given that 'even if the EU was ready to sell arms, the Burmese would not have been able to afford but very few items' (interview 2007).

The stalemate in relations with Burma can partly be explained by stagnation in the circumstances in which sanctions operate. Not only was there a lack of progress by the Burmese leadership in meeting EU demands, EU interests in the region have not evolved greatly over the past fifteen years, and the Burmese junta remains as uninterested in developing the country and increasing its international prestige as it was when sanctions were first imposed. Importantly, Burma is far from regionally isolated. It has strengthened its relations not only with China, but also with Russia, India and Thailand. The interest of Burma's neighbours in maintaining access to the country's vast natural resources makes their collaboration in promoting the EU's goals unlikely in the near future. Thailand has a special interest in relations with the regime because of the problems of the cross-border trade in narcotics and ethnic insurgencies. However, the support offered to Burma by its neighbours is less staunch than is often believed. Following the crackdown on the opposition carried out by Burmese security forces in May 2003, ASEAN countries hardened their views on the standards of behaviour expected from members. At EU and US insistence, ASEAN agreed to Burma losing its turn as chair of the Standing Committee in 2005. As some observers have noted, the ASEAN ministers' decision to discuss the situation in Myanmar and urge the country's peaceful transition to democracy marks a 'significant move away from their traditional principle of non-interference' (Hughes 2007:322). In the aftermath of the crackdown of October 2007, the EU and ASEAN agreed a joint statement urging the Burmese government to free all political prisoners (AsiaNews 2007).

As with most EU sanctions cases, the imposition of sanctions for more than a decade brought about a fatigue that resulted in the initiation of contacts which then led to the re-establishment of cooperation in selected fields. This was also the case, for example, with China and Belarus. In the case of Burma, the upgrade in relations with the EU that took place around the year 2000 in the domain of humanitarian assistance, which was reflected in the opening of a Burmese diplomatic representation in Brussels, was a prelude to the resumption of limited development actions in the fields of democratisation aid, poverty alleviation, health and education and the environment. This partial resumption has been criticised as unmerited by the Burmese junta, and as sending a signal that 'a worsening of the political situation is rewarded by the EU' (Smith 2006:159). Following the upgrade in sanctions of 2007, the

EU strategy on Burma unusually combined a partial trade embargo with limited development cooperation.

At the same time, the effects of the harshest EU sanctions regime, still less coercive than US and Canadian measures, are mitigated. With the current Burma sanctions, the EU is bordering on the limits of pressure allowed by the concept of 'targeted sanctions' and by its self-declared policy of 'targeting only responsible individuals'. Before the imposition of the partial trade embargo, European experts lamented the negative impacts of sanctions on the standards of living of the population:

> Those most affected by the sanctions are those inhabitants of Burma who would experience an improvement in their living standard (even if a modest one) through rural development projects, or who remain unemployed as a consequence of the underdevelopment of the public economy sector. In addition, sanctions harm all those interested in closer co-operation with foreign countries: private entrepreneurs ... scholars ... but also forces in government and administration convinced that modernising the country is indispensably linked to intensive exchange with industrialized countries.
> (Will 2003:16–17)

In Will's eyes, at least in the short term, the EU's sanctions play into the hands of the military junta, as they shield the country from external influence while contributing to its underdevelopment and impoverishment. From this perspective, the solution chosen for Burma is in line with the EU's double-track strategy.

CODING SUMMARY

The goals of the sanctions were not achieved; therefore the EU cannot be credited for any contribution (cont 0). The measures were both economic and non-economic in character and have displayed, or are expected to display, some noticeable impact: (eco 1) for all sanctions except for the blacklist-based. They directly threatened the permanence in office of the current regime (grip 1). The measures were managed relatively, although not entirely, coherently: problems of inconsistency affected the blacklist-based sanctions, while other measures remained free of them (coh 1). The EU's stance found considerable support from Western countries, especially from the US and Canada, but not from countries in the region (int 0).

Belarus

The current CFSP sanctions regime against Belarus has two forerunners. The country was first the subject of negative measures in 1996 in response to its constitutional crisis. Restrictions on the freedom to demonstrate and freedom of speech, followed by the enactment of a new constitution concentrating powers in the hands of the President, subsequently confirmed by a flawed referendum, were the reasons for this first wave of EU measures. The irregularities and unconstitutionality of the referendum were corroborated by an EU expert mission dispatched in early 1997 (Toledano 2001:207). In reaction, the Council decided to impose the following measures:

- withdrawal of support for Belarus' application for membership of the Council of Europe
- limitation of political contacts with Belarusian authorities
- freezing of negotiations for a PCA and Interim Agreement, as well as of negotiations for a TACIS indicative and action programme
- a mandate to the Commission to examine ways of associating civil society with the democratisation process.

This was accompanied by a European Parliament declaration announcing its intention to withdraw assent to any bilateral agreement with Belarus (Fierro 2003:369). In implementing the Council's mandate, the Commission proposed a grant of 5 million ECU to Belarus in order to develop its media system. This was facilitated by the presence of a human rights clause in the TACIS Regulation on assistance to Newly Independent States, which foresaw 'appropriate measures concerning assistance to a partner state' in cases of violations of democratic principles and human rights (Council of the European Union 1996b). At this stage, the EU's actions amounted to informal measures, as described in a later chapter of the present study: they consisted of diplomatic sanctions and the redirection of aid, not of the mainstream types of CFSP sanctions (visa bans, asset freezes and arms embargoes). Somewhat ironically, the EU's first reaction to the democratic crisis in Belarus was celebrated in the literature as a precedent for the use of unilateral regulations in order to offer incentives in support of democracy: it represented 'the first time in which a measure was ever decided by the Council, under the human rights clause with the objective of helping restore human rights and democracy in a country in serious constitutional crisis' (Brandtner and Rosas 1998:482). Most of these sanctions were gradually lifted, following recommendations from the OSCE after the establishment of an OSCE Advisory Monitoring Group (AMG) in Minsk in 1999 (Kreutz 2006:38). The second 'forerunner' to the current CFSP sanctions regime was the short-lived crisis which erupted due to the ill-treatment of Western diplomats based in Minsk in the summer of 1998. It was triggered by renovation works in the Drozdy diplomatic compound in Minsk, where some EU ambassadors resided. The Council released a Common Position denouncing the measures affecting the residences of the ambassadors as an 'infringement of the Vienna Convention on Diplomatic Relations' and as 'contrary to the principle of friendly relations among States', and imposing a visa ban on high-ranking officials (Council of the European Union 1998b). The visa ban was lifted following agreement between the EU and Belarusian authorities (Council of the European Union 1999a). A third EU sanctions episode for Belarus was narrowly avoided, due to resistance from one member state, Portugal. In November 2002, the closure of the AMG office in Minsk by Belarusian authorities was followed by the imposition of a visa ban on the officials responsible, by all other member states, on an individual basis (Kreutz 2006:38). These national measures were removed after the opening of a new OSCE office in Minsk in early 2003.

It was in the autumn of 2004 that a series of CFSP sanctions began. The first of these episodes related to the disappearance of four well-known Belarusian citizens. The incident had been the subject of an April 2004 report of the Parliamentary Assembly of the Council of Europe (the Pourgourides Report), which demanded an independent inquiry on the matter. A CFSP Common Position imposed a visa ban on the individuals responsible for failing to initiate the independent investigation and prosecution of the alleged crimes (Council of the European Union 2004e). Barely four months later, the EU imposed a new visa ban on officials directly responsible for the fraudulent parliamentary elections and referendum, and the repression of peaceful demonstrations, in October 2004 (Council of the European Union 2000d). Following the Presidential elections of March 2006, the EU decided to extend its visa ban to those directly responsible for the violation of international electoral standards, and for the crackdown on civil society and democratic opposition (Council of the European Union 2006a). This blacklist included the name of President Lukaschenko for the first time. An asset freeze followed (Council of the European Union 2006d). Conditions for lifting the measures were spelled out as follows:

> Restrictive measures … should be reviewed with a view to the speedy release and rehabilitation of all political detainees, and in the light of reforms made to the Electoral Code to bring it into line with OSCE commitments and other international standards for democratic elections as recommended by the Office for Democratic Institutions and Human Rights of the Organisation for Security and Co-operation in Europe, the conduct of future elections and concrete actions by the authorities to respect democratic values, the rule of law, human rights and fundamental freedoms, including the freedom of expression and of the media, and the freedom of assembly and political association.
>
> (Council of the European Union 2006a:2)

The conditions are broadly defined in the sense that they first establish two conditions central to the eventual lifting of sanctions: the release of political detainees, the reform of the Electoral Code, and the holding of flawless elections. However, the Council also indicates that it will reconsider the measures ‘in the light of … concrete actions by the authorities to respect democratic values, the rule of law, human rights and fundamental freedoms’. This statement leaves the kinds of actions expected from Belarus unspecified. Similarly, the Common Position makes the conditions for re-engagement explicit. It calls on the Belarusian government to ‘embark on fundamental democratic and economic reforms to bring the country closer to European common values … the EU remains open for dialogue with Belarus on gradual development of bilateral relations, as soon as the Belarus authorities demonstrate by concrete actions a sincere willingness to re-engage' (Council of the European Union 2000d:1).

In view of the negative trend in EU–Belarus relations, as reflected in the increasing number of sanctions regimes imposed on Belarusian officials, the Commission undertook a public attempt to improve relations with the country. In late 2006, it presented a 'non-paper' on what it could offer Belarus, in particular through inclusion in the European Neighbourhood Policy (Commission of the European Communities 2006a). This four-page document detailed how the EU could improve the quality of life of the Belarusian people, provide for business opportunities and increase financial assistance to the country. It also spelled out the reforms that would make these benefits available. The list of conditions is longer and much more specific than any of those contained in the CFSP document. It presents most of its demands in the form of rights for Belarusian citizens, namely their right to elect leaders democratically, to independent information and free expression, to an impartial judiciary system, the rights of workers to join a trade union, and even the right of 'entrepreneurs to operate without excessive intervention by the authorities' (Commission of the European Communities 2006a:4). This suggests that whereas all EU institutions – Council, Parliament and Commission – converge in their condemnation of the Belarusian regime, the focus on pro-democratic reforms and the strengthening of the rule of law has recently been supplemented by requirements pertaining to free-market liberties. The Commission document also includes demands absent from the CFSP Common Positions, such as the abolition of the death penalty and the protection of minorities. This initiative was followed up with contacts with the Belarus authorities through a troika visit to Minsk; however, it remained unfruitful (interview 2007).

The 'non-paper' presented a peculiarity: in addition to reiterating the political conditions spelled out in the CFSP legal instruments, it made the offer of inclusion of the European Neighbourhood Policy dependent on the introduction of market-oriented reforms. The EU sanctions strategy against Belarus followed an incremental logic, mirroring the evolution of the Belarusian state towards authoritarianism. Every further step was met by a tightening of EU sanctions, which have come to encompass a visa ban and a freezing of assets on individuals connected with the violations of international electoral standards, the repression of peaceful demonstrators and the obstruction of justice.

The energy crisis of January 2007 marked a reversal in the deterioration of EU–Belarus relations. In early 2007, Russia more than doubled the amount Belarus must pay for Russian natural gas, and forced Belarus to relinquish a 50 per cent stake of its state-owned gas transport company, Beltranshaz, to Russia's state-controlled gas monopoly, Gazprom (Hamilton 2008:18). In the wake of Russia's announcement that it would cut off gas supplies to Belarus,

Minsk interrupted the supply of gas to EU countries. As a political crisis erupted with its principal partner, Belarus showed interest in engaging with the EU, emphasising its importance as a 'transit country' for energy supplies. This led the Commission and Belarus to set up 'structured discussions' on energy – a cooperation framework at expert level falling short of a full dialogue. The Belarusian authorities granted permission for the opening of a European Commission Delegation in Minsk in 2007 (Vysotskaya 2008). In 2008, the Lukaschenko regime initiated a series of policies which departed from practices condemned by the EU. A privatisation programme was launched in April, accompanied by measures destined to attract foreign investment into Belarus. In the political realm, in a move actively promoted by Germany (Lindner 2008:3), the last prominent political detainees were released from prison in August, including leading Lukaschenko opponents such as former presidential candidate Kozulin and the former MP Klimov. The parliamentary elections of September 2008 were supervised by an OSCE delegation numbering 449 international observers, making it the biggest election observation mission allowed into the country in the post-Soviet era. While acknowledging improvements in cooperation with the OSCE and broader access for the opposition to the media, the EU resented that the parliamentary elections failed to meet the OSCE electoral standards. Nevertheless, the Council decided to restore contacts with the Belarusian authorities, while the Commission intensified technical cooperation with Belarus. The Council simultaneously decided to suspend, for a period of three months, the travel restrictions on all members of the blacklist, with the exception of the President of the Central Electoral Commission and those involved in the disappearances which occurred in 1999 and 2000, with the explicit intention of 'encourage(ing) dialogue with the Belarusian authorities and the adoption of positive measures to strengthen democracy and respect for human rights' (Council of the European Union 2008c). The continuation of the suspension was made conditional on progress towards reforms in terms of electoral standards and fundamental freedoms.

In the following months, gestures of rapprochement by the EU succeeded one another, invariably accompanied by messages signalling that further benefits were conditional on continued progress by Belarus. In March, the Council extended the suspension of the visa ban until the end of the year. Notably, the Council explicitly stated its readiness to consider the possibility of lifting the measures 'provided there are further positive developments' (Council of the European Union 2009a). On the institutional side, high-level bilateral contacts in the form of foreign minister troikas resumed, while technical cooperation with the Commission intensified: as of summer 2009, technical dialogues in the fields of environment, agriculture, customs, transport and norms and standards complement the now fully fledged energy dialogue. Most visibly, the EU has included Belarus in the Eastern Partnership, an association scheme reinforcing the links developed in the framework of the ENP and ultimately aiming at the establishment of free trade and visa liberalisation. For the time being, Belarus is already participating in the multilateral track of the Eastern

Partnership, while the bilateral track has not yet been activated. The Commission has allocated an assistance package of 10 million euros towards food safety. In her first visit to Minsk in June 2009, Commissioner for External Relations and ENP Benita Ferrero-Waldner spelled out the conditions for closer cooperation in the following terms:

> We would like to see changes to the electoral process to make it more transparent and fair translated into changes in the legislation. All media should have equal and fair access to information, printing presses and distribution networks. … The people of Belarus should be able to express their views in meetings or at peaceful demonstrations in the street. And civil society and opposition activists should be free to carry out their work without intimidation or fear of arrest.
>
> (Ferrero-Waldner 2009)

In exchange for the fulfilment of these conditions, Ferrero-Waldner mentioned potential benefits in the form of economic support, access to the EU market, lighter visa requirements and opportunities for cultural and educational exchange.

IMPACT AND EFFICACY

The abundance of sanctions regimes against Belarus in the decade that has elapsed since the original constitutional crisis reveals that the EU has become increasingly assertive in its responses to the deterioration of the political situation in Belarus. The illegal change of the constitution, a substantial breach of democratic rule, prompted only a range of 'informal sanctions' at a time when CFSP sanctions instruments were already well developed. Over time, the EU started to employ mainstream CFSP sanctions tools: the visa ban and the freezing of assets. The EU also demonstrated a high sensitivity to developments in Belarus, levying sanctions that were not directly connected to flawed elections, for reasons such as the improper treatment of diplomats. The sanctions regime related to the disappearances of four citizens can be ascribed to the defence of the rule of law.

The failure of EU pro-democracy sanctions for an entire decade can be partly ascribed to domestic dynamics within Belarus. The leadership capitalised on Western condemnation, portraying the country as being 'under siege'. This perception was aided by the fact that the country has been subject to EU sanctions of diverse nature, and by the absence of free media and the severe restrictions on civil society. In economic terms, Belarus is better off than its neighbours Ukraine and Moldova, which have embraced Western-inspired economic reforms (Beichelt 2007). The maintenance of the relative wealth, characterised by sustained economic growth and low unemployment, was made possible by the vast economic benefits resulting from the State Union concluded with Russia in the late 1990s, with an annual equivalent of 11–14% of national GDP (Bosse and Korosteleva-Polglase 2009). Moscow financed the Belarus economy after the collapse of the Soviet Union by providing energy at prices far below market rates (Hamilton 2008:18). Thus, Russian support was critical for the permanence of the Lukaschenko regime, both through the supply of subsidised energy and through political links (Zurawski 2005). It was when the relationship between the two countries came under strain as a result of the energy crisis in 2007 that Belarus was prompted to distance itself politically from Russia and introduce changes that accommodated, at least partially, EU demands (Lindner 2008). In spite of EU efforts to support democratic forces, these were not substantially strengthened (Grant and Leonard 2006).

Following their accession to the EU in May 2004, a number a Central European countries directly neighbouring Belarus introduced a revision of the EU's Belarus policy. Their desire for engagement became particularly evident in their bilateral relations with Minsk (Jarabik and Silitski 2008). Newcomers to the EU such as Lithuania, Poland, Latvia, Slovakia and the Czech Republic, who reportedly opposed the GSP suspension, intensified high-level contacts with Belarusian authorities. Also Germany, Belarus's largest international donor, played a central role in incentivising the release of political opponents (Lindner 2008). Belarus's limited opening to the EU can be ascribed to the efforts of these countries by influencing the EU's position and delivering a signal to Belarusian elites that the EU had a sincere will to accommodate. This was conducive to a climate in which the Belarusian authorities consented to the release of the last prominent political prisoners as a condition of relaxing sanctions. However, the main impulse compelling a change of heart in the Belarusian leadership came from the energy crisis with Russia in January 2007. In its absence, deadlock would have persisted.

There are both internal and external rationales to the Belarusian reorientation. The internal dimension refers to the power base of the Lukaschenko regime. Experts agree on the significance that the comparatively high standard of living had on securing the regime's rule. Jarabik and Silitski claim that 'the stability of the regime has mainly rested on its ability to provide rising living standards for the population' (Jarabik and Silitski 2008). According to Beichelt, economic indicators displaying figures superior to those of Ukraine and Moldova help to explain why Lukaschenko's regime has not been jeopardised, despite its increasingly repressive character (Beichelt 2007). After Russia phased out its energy subsidies, the Belarusian leadership realised that it was unable to maintain the same level of prosperity. This became evident when the government was forced to abolish the wide-scale system of social privileges and subsidies in May 2007. Compelled to attract alternative sources of wealth, the authorities announced a privatisation programme before the last prominent political detainees were released. The Belarusian government set up a Council for Business Co-operation between Belarus and the EU in May 2007 (Bosse and Korosteleva-Polglase 2009). Commenting on the Eastern Partnership, Lukaschenko declared: 'we aim for the free trade zone. If we have a free trade zone with Europe, we will be twice as rich' (National Centre of Legal information of the Republic of Belarus 2009). The external dimension is related to Belarus's relationship with Russia. Whereas official rhetoric appears determined to relax political ties with Russia, economic dependence on the Russian market makes full disengagement impossible. As Jarabik and Silitski put it, Lukaschenko 'needs a friendly European attitude to convince Moscow to pay Belarus' bills and/or attract … Western investment' (Jarabik and Silitski 2008). Both motivations downplay the influence that the EU per se has on the calculations of the leaders. However, the anticipated internal and external repercussions of the energy crisis combined to compel the regime to seek a limited accommodation with the EU. Although initially futile, the Commission's 'non-paper' paved the way for the reversal of the EU–Belarus confrontational course by formulating an offer of cooperation to the authorities, publicly spelling out the conditions for engagement. Despite its informal character, the 'non-paper' was central in marking a departure from previous practice, reassuring the Belarusian authorities of the existence of opportunities for accommodation. Brussels, along with a number of European capitals, had made similar advances to Belarusian authorities; often in response to the latter's attempts at rapprochement. However, these contacts remained invisible to the public eye, while the declassified nature of the 'non-paper' would have made it difficult for the EU to back down on its promises in the event of Belarusian compliance. Most importantly, it did not escape the attention of the Belarusian authorities that the Commission had added the requirement of market reform to the political conditions formulated by the target. Rather than further alienating the targets, the inclusion of an additional requisite in the catalogue helped the elites in identifying a window of opportunity for rapprochement which it successfully managed to exploit.

Belarusian compliance was unequivocally suboptimal. The leadership met EU demands only partially, rather than conforming to their entirety. This constituted a limited re-orientation rather than a U-turn. This might signify prudence on the target's side, aimed at confirming the EU's willingness to reciprocate before proceeding to further concessions. Belarus used a formula which combines the fulfilment of economic conditions with limited concession in the field of political freedoms. This is illustratively reflected in the addressees of these steps: relations were restored first with the Commission rather than the Council. Months before meeting the core precondition of releasing political detainees, Lukaschenko released a decree launching privatisation of state enterprises, a demand formulated by the Commission but not by the Council. This emphasises the central role played by economic interests in the reorientation of Belarusian policies: for one leadership determined to boost the economic standing of the country, the Commission emerges as the obvious partner. At the same time, the fact that the electoral observers were not granted access to the counting of votes indicates the leadership's reluctance to fully conform to democratic standards.

CODING SUMMARY

In the two first sanctions episodes, the goals of the sanctions were achieved, largely due to EU sanctions. In the case of the pro-democracy sanctions, the longest sequence, the goals of the sanctions were achieved largely, but not fully. For the progress made, the EU can be largely credited, bearing in mind that the central factor was Russian withdrawal (cont 1). The measures were not economic in character and had some limited impact (eco 0). The economic incentive to participate in the Eastern partnership was not a CFSP measure proper; thus, it cannot be accommodated in the coding. They posed a direct threat to the leader's permanence in power (grip 1). The measure was managed coherently (coh 1), and the EU's stance found international support only from the West (int 0).

Transnistria

The internal situation in Moldova provides an example of what has been defined as a 'frozen conflict'. In the aftermath of the dissolution of the Soviet Union in the early 1990s, the region of Transnistria declared independence from the Republic of Moldova. Following limited clashes between Transnistrian and troops loyal to Moldova, a cease-fire agreement was signed which stipulated that Transnistria would have a special status within the Moldovan state. Since then, Transnistria has existed as an autonomous entity which has not been formally recognised as a state except by Russia. An OSCE-led peace process has been under way since 1993, but has so far remained fruitless. In conjunction with the US, the EU imposed a visa ban against Transnistrian leaders, alleging a motive so far unique in CFSP sanctions regimes, namely the leadership's 'obstructionism of the peace process' (Council of the European Union 2003a:1). In the summer of 2004, a new visa ban was imposed on officials responsible for what came to be known as the 'school crisis'. This was provoked by the closure of several of only six Romanian-language Latin-script schools in the region, accompanied by the intimidation of children, teachers and parents. The Common Position stipulated that the ban would be reviewed according to an assessment of whether schools had reopened and the intimidation of children, teachers and parents ceased. By December 2005, most of the schools were operating again. In contrast, the ban on the Transnistrian leadership has continued to be renewed. The current version of the Common Position consolidates both visa bans, featuring a list of thirteen individuals in the first list and six in the second (Council of the European Union 2008a).

A peculiarity of the Transnistrian case is that EU policies encompass a variety of accompanying actions with a bearing on the 'status quo'. These actions are based on Community competences and address the economic vulnerability of the region, whose survival is based on trade which benefits from illegal practices. These actions included the establishment of a Border Assistance Mission (EUBAM) in November 2005, whose purpose is to boost the capacities of the Moldovan and Ukrainian border guard and customs services in order to combat trafficking and smuggling. The Commission explicitly stated that it would 'play an important role in building preconditions for seeking a peaceful settlement of the Transnistrian conflict' (Commission of the European Communities

2005). A second, trade-related EU measure consisted in the introduction of a double-checking system for steel exported from Moldova. As a consequence of this measure, steel could no longer be exported to the EU without Moldovan certificates confirming its origin. Considering that steel constitutes one of the main Transnistrian exports to the EU, this measure obliged producers to register legally with Chisinau or to redirect exports towards non-EU countries.

IMPACT AND EFFICACY

The end of the school crisis is attributed to general international condemnation, of which EU sanctions were one manifestation (interview 2007). Nevertheless, it should be noted that the resolution of the crisis was neither immediate, nor total, given that six individuals remain affected by the ban. The visa ban on Transnistrian leaders has proved less effective. Sanctions against the leadership have been criticised as being 'too limited in scope to impose a serious burden on the leadership to make it reverse its policies' and especially for 'the vagueness with which objectives are formulated' (Popescu 2005:33). While the ban 'does not seem to bother Mr Smirnov, he seems to be worried about the next possible steps, such as freezing financial assets' (interview 2007). While the travel restrictions placed on individuals responsible for the school crisis clearly spelled out the developments that would entail a reversal (the end of intimidation and the reopening of the schools), the consolidated Common Position imposing the ban on Transnistrian leaders currently in force does not contain any conditions for its lifting. It simply stipulates that 'the EU considers unacceptable the continued position of the leadership of the Transnistrian region of the Republic of Moldova and its unwillingness to engage fully in efforts to reach a peaceful and comprehensive solution to the Transnistrian conflict', and announces that it will adopt modifications to the blacklists 'as required by political developments in the Republic of Moldova' (Council of the European Union 2008a).

In contrast, actions undertaken by the EU to address the vulnerabilities of the fragile Transnistrian economy are proving more effective. Analysts point to the business community as the most likely catalyst for change in Transnistria. It has been argued that EU actions are already bringing about a change of attitude: 'There are some signs that the Transnistrian business community is gaining influence and beginning to recognise that the breakaway region's unresolved status is bad for profit' (International Crisis Group 2006:21). Indeed, Popescu highlights that one of the factors which undermine the efficacy of the ban is that it does not target 'senior executives of the most important industries or business groups that are key in supporting the regime' (Popescu 2005:6). The functioning of EUBAM is generally assessed positively (Kononenko 2006), in that it has succeeded in countering smuggling and illegal trafficking, and has contributed to a one-third decrease in the Transnistrian budget. The impact of the setting up of both EUBAM (International Crisis Group 2006:6) and the steel regulation was felt immediately (Popescu 2005:32).

The Transnitrian statelet constitutes perhaps the clearest example of an entity chaperoned by an outside patron. Like the Georgian separatist regions Abkhazia and South Ossetia, Transnistria 'would probably have been unable to win, still less to maintain, [its] separate status without the military, economic and political assistance provided by Russia' (Pelczynska-Nalecz et al. 2008:373). Finally, due to Ukraine's reluctance to associate itself with EU sanctions, which it regards as incompatible with its position of neutral mediator in the conflict, the ban does not disrupt the activities of Transnistrian leaders considerably (Popescu 2005:6).

CODING SUMMARY

The goals of the sanctions have not been achieved. Thus, the EU's contribution is nil (cont 0). Only in the school crisis episode were some concessions extracted, but the EU's contribution was modest (cont 1). The sanctions were not economic in character and their impact was negligible (eco 0). They hardly posed a threat to the leader's permanence in power (grip 0). The sanctions have been managed coherently (coh 1), and have found some international support among Western partners, but not in neighbouring Ukraine (int 0).

Evaluating CFSP sanctions

CFSP sanctions: how successful and why?

The success rate of CFSP sanctions remains low, and some of the cases where partial successes were observed cannot be primarily ascribed to EU action. Nigeria's smooth transition to democracy can largely be attributed to the death of its authoritarian ruler. In Indonesia, the EU arms embargo contributed rather marginally to US threats to compel the government's acceptance of the deployment of a UN force in East Timor. In both cases, EU measures can be seen as part of broader international pressure which prompted the leadership's decision to cooperate.

The EU appears to be prepared to settle for less than it originally strives for. In other words, it is ready to lift measures after an only partial fulfilment of the conditions. The 'proclivity' of the Council to ease sanctions is made possible by the discretion it retains regarding the evaluation of progress by the target. Conditions are often spelled out broadly in Common Positions, and no benchmarking for the evaluation of progress has been defined. This contrasts with the ACP agreement's 'appropriate measures' and GSP suspensions, which define measurable benchmarks that facilitate evaluation. The EU's flexibility can have potentially negative effects: it may create a climate of uncertainty in which, rather than assuming that limited compliance will be rewarded with an easing of sanctions, certain targets could believe that the EU will not ease measures anyway.

One of the most remarkable peculiarities of the CFSP regimes is that they do not entirely preclude the establishment of cooperation between the EU and its targets. Engagement can range from regular contacts in selected fields of mutual interest, such as the 'structured discussions' on energy with Belarus (interview 2007), to the 'strategic partnership' with China, which includes the sensitive field of satellite navigation, and whose vitality is superior to the bilateral relations the EU entertains with other partners not subject to sanctions. At the very least, and in accordance with the EU's general humanitarian concern, the EU has established functioning relationships allowing for the dispatch of humanitarian assistance to those CFSP targets that require it, even with most intractable beneficiaries such as Sudan, Zimbabwe or Burma.

From the 'threshold' cases surveyed, it appears that the central element leading to the revision of measures is the fact that some interaction to this end takes place between sender and target. Either of the parties can take the initiative – the attempt can prosper as soon as both actors identify an area of common interest that is unconnected to the motive that triggered sanctions. In the case of Belarus, it is difficult to determine which side took the initiative, and it is unknown whether the removal of sanctions was discussed in bilateral contacts. In any case, some limited cooperation came about despite, and without any consequences for, the sanctions regime.

Under which conditions do these attempts at interaction prosper? The presence of sanctions regimes causes discomfort among leaders and elites. Virtually all cases of sanctions targeted at individuals – visa bans and asset freezes – have caused visible discomfort to the leaderships of Zimbabwe (Eriksson 2007), Belarus, Uzbekistan, Nigeria, and even some elements of the Transnistrian leadership. Not even the Burmese leadership has remained insensitive to the embarrassment produced by their blacklisting (interviews 2007). However, this uneasiness often fails to translate into concessions.

Whenever CFSP sanctions have contributed to positive outcomes, they have done so by depriving the target of international prestige. It was only to the extent that the target wished to maintain their international reputation that the EU was capable of exerting influence. Thus, the extent of the target's concern for its international prestige critically affects the fruitfulness of the rapprochement between both parties. It appears that leaderships will make some effort to bring about the lifting of measures only if they aspire to consolidate themselves as regional powers and care about their international standing, irrespective of the specific type of sanctions imposed. The leadership is likely to show an interest in the removal of sanctions. This factor was certainly present in Uzbekistan, Indonesia and Nigeria – as well as in China, technically a case of 'informal' sanctions. In contrast, it is absent in the cases of Sudan, Belarus, Burma and, more acutely, the Transnitrian leadership. These countries regard themselves as 'associates' of powers that provide for their protection, or their self-understanding is dominated by a sense of threat motivated by the lack of control over their entire territory.

Thus, the extent of support of neighbouring countries appears to affect the susceptibility of targets to EU influence. None of the CFSP targets is entirely isolated internationally, they all find support or to some extent protection from a patron. However, the number of neighbours which support them, and the strength of the link between targets and their protectors, varies. Burma counts on assistance from China and maintains good relations with its neighbours, who in turn rely on its natural resources. Zimbabwe is also supported by its neighbours, notably South Africa. Transnistria is protected by Russia. In contrast, Uzbekistan finds itself competing for regional leadership with its neighbours, leaving it more exposed to influence. Equally, the withdrawal of support from Belarus by its only ally, Russia, immediately prompted the establishment of contacts with the EU.

A further conditioning factor is the extent to which EU demands threaten the leadership's permanence in power. CFSP sanctions regimes aimed at re-establishing democratic rule are unlikely to attain their objectives. Those who remain in power undemocratically are not prepared to trade their grip on power for international prestige. This is evident in the cases of Belarus, Zimbabwe, Burma and even Nigeria at a first stage. Concessions by the target are more likely when demands fall short of a democratic transition, as with the school crisis in Transnistria, the Drozny crisis in Belarus, the Andijan inquiry in Uzbekistan, and even Indonesia.

Targets less likely to acquiesce to the EU's 'standard' sanctions (visa ban, asset freezes and arms embargoes) are those which find themselves involved in armed conflicts (FRY, Sudan, DRC) or non-state entities (Transnistria). Thus, leaderships involved in military operations tend to be insensitive to considerations of prestige, while non-state entities already lack international recognition by virtue of their status. In these cases, pressure needs to be complemented by economic instruments in order to yield results. One of the instances in which the EU made a noticeable impact, thanks to the use of financial and economic instruments, was in the FRY during the Kosovo episode. The most effective measures against the FRY were of an economic nature: the EU bans on investments, export credits, flights and especially on direct payments to state-owned enterprises reduced state revenues. The strategy did not bring about the desired termination of military operations, largely because this was brought about by NATO's bombing campaign. These attempts, experimented with by the EU for the first time in the FRY, were never repeated.

Equally, EU pressure on Transnistria is complemented by measures which have an economic impact, such as the regulation of steel imports and the reduction of illegal trade through EUBAM. Some indications of societal change, especially in the preferences of the business community, make progress towards EU objectives more likely than before. The Transnistrian Republic, is particularly sensitive to economic-related measures, due to its status as a non-state entity deprived of legal personality, and especially the illicit practices that sustain its fragile economy. So far, the EU has managed to make a visible impact on the Transnistrian economy by taking measures that fall within the scope of routine activities – customs assistance and the specification of origins of imported goods. These measures have resulted in a growing recognition amongst the Transnistrian business community that the advantages of operating in an unrecognised entity are bound to disappear. By virtue of this recognition, it is developing into a catalysing force for yielding to the EU's demands. These examples suggest that an enhanced use of EU economic instruments could improve the performance of EU sanctions regimes while continuing to avoid US-type general trade embargoes. In the African conflicts, while the EU imposed arms embargoes, the core of its strategy towards Sudan and the DRC consisted in incentives to induce the parties to respect peace agreements (de Waal 2008), deploying peace-keeping forces and in dispatching election observers.

EU sanctions for crisis management: evaluating the record

A glance at the EU's record of employing sanctions as a conflict management tool suffices to present an evident finding on the subject: it is the exception rather than the norm. While the overwhelming majority of EU sanctions episodes are inspired by interruptions in the democratic process accompanied by human rights violations, the use of sanctions in situations of armed conflict constitute only a small fraction of these. This reveals the preference among EU member states to deal with conflict situations by different means. EU sanctions for crisis management constitute 'anomalies' in EU sanctions practice.

Indeed, the crisis episodes that saw the imposition of sanctions correspond to the types of situations in which the UNSC has become involved throughout the 1990s: internal armed conflicts often accompanied by state collapse. Moreover, the episodes discussed present an unusually high level of convergence with UN sanctions. The DRC arms embargo was superseded by a UN arms embargo ten years after its imposition; the Sudan arms embargo partly overlaps with the UNSC-imposed arms embargo on the Darfur region. The EU arms embargo on the FRY was a unilateral continuation of the UN embargo after this was lifted, which in turn had superseded the original 1991 EC embargo (Bohr 1993). From this perspective, EU sanctions for crisis management can be described as 'substitutes' for UN sanctions.

The EU's interventions in the examples explored could hardly be more diverse. In the handling of the Kosovo crisis, the EU constituted a reasonably 'unified front' which wielded sanctions with resolve. The background to the conflict explains this determination: it came about as a result of the frustrating experience of the Bosnian wars. The EU's capacity to formulate a sanctions strategy for this crisis was also motivated by the proximity of the conflict, and the high degree to which Western Europe was affected by its consequences, notably by refugee flows. The EU responded to the crisis with a sequence of sanctions crafted with an unprecedented degree of creativity. The limited efficacy of these sanctions can be attributed to the experimental character of the exercise – most measures had never been attempted in such forms before – and by the termination of the Federal military operations as a result of NATO's bombing campaign.

In contrast, the African episodes fall at the opposite end of sanctions inventiveness. While in the Kosovo episode the EU experimented widely with gradualism and targeting, the African sanctions were characterised by stalemate. The arms embargoes, accompanied by a visa ban in the case of the DRC, were not modified in any way for the ensuing decade. This stalemate was partly due to the absence of a common political strategy on the part of the Council. This, combined with the ineffective measure that was an arms embargo in Africa, rendered the EU's interventions largely futile. Only in the case of Sudan, and in the context of the peace process, was the EU able to capitalise on one of its measures in order to contribute to success. The prospect of the provision of development aid, as yet unseen in southern Sudan, constituted one of the incentives that encouraged the SPLM to sign the peace agreement. Technically speaking, the offer of development aid is an incentive rather than a sanction – however, it shows how the option of lifting a previously imposed sanction can be used as leverage in support of a desired outcome. Interestingly, it is in the field of development that the EU has displayed some creativity in the protracted African episodes, by devising ways in which development interventions could take place while these countries officially remained subject to an aid suspension.

In sum, the contrast between the Kosovo and African experiences illustrates that the use of sanctions *in conflicts* is not identical to the use of sanctions *for crisis management*. In the Yugoslav case, the EU endeavoured to have an impact on the conflict situation, crafting sanctions carefully and adjusting them in order to increase their effectiveness. In contrast, the African experience shows a largely futile use of sanctions, characterised by the imposition of sanctions doomed to remain without effect where their lifting was not used as a political tool. It is the prospect of a resumption of aid that offers some possibilities for influence in African conflicts.

Conclusions

CFSP sanctions cases constitute a heterogeneous universe from which few generalisations can be drawn. This difficulty is compounded by the low number of episodes available. Yet, it can be concluded that CFSP sanctions are generally ineffective tools for accomplishing the objectives they aim for, which are predominantly related to the protection of human rights and democracy. In these rare instances of success, EU sanctions contribute to a broader effort, as in Nigeria or Indonesia. Limited concessions have also been extracted from a number of leaderships, notably in minor episodes in Belarus and Moldova. Finally, agency by the EU in bringing about compliance has also been fruitful, as in Uzbekistan and Belarus. However, the presence of CFSP sanctions does not entirely preclude collaboration between the EU and some of its targets. In the long term, some accommodation takes place, at the very least in order to facilitate humanitarian and development activities, as in Burma and Sudan, and permit sector-specific cooperation, as in Belarus.

5 The efficacy of 'informal' sanctions

The present chapter brings together sanctions whose common denominator is that they were adopted in the absence of a CFSP act, and outside any contractual bilateral framework. The notion of 'informal sanctions' is neither an established category in sanctions research, nor does it belong to the EU's legal terminology. The present investigation employs this term to describe a heterogeneous group of measures wielded by the EU against third countries in order to place pressure on the leadership targeted, encompassing diplomatic sanctions, the postponement of signing or ratification of agreements and the redirection of aid. What they have in common is that, while they fit into this investigation's definition of 'sanction', they are adopted outside the legal frameworks featured in other sections of this study, namely the CFSP, ACP and GSP Regulations. Some were announced in EU Presidency statements, others appeared in conclusions of the European Council or the General Affairs and External Relations (GAEC) Council; in other cases no evidence of the decision on the measures exists apart from a letter.

Table 5.1 features all cases of informal sanctions identified in the present study. Their common denominator is the absence of a specific label. Unlike CFSP 'restrictive measures' or the ACP's 'appropriate measures', they have not been categorised into any generic group. They are merely referred to as 'measures'. In the very early days of the EPC, 'informal' sanctions were commonplace. As more elaborate legal instruments became available, the EU formalised its ongoing sanctions regimes, transforming them into CFSP Common Positions. The measures discussed in the present chapter have never been the subject of CFSP acts even though many of them were agreed after these instruments became available. Thus, the practice of imposing informal sanctions continued in parallel to the formal practice of the CFSP.

Information sanctions: what kind of sanction?

In contrast to all other cases analysed in the present investigation, the situation of these sanctions episodes is one of legal uncertainty. This applies on two levels. Firstly, procedures permitting member states to deviate from agreements reflected in Council Conclusions or statements are not stipulated. No time

Table 5.1 Informal sanctions

	Measure	*Time Period*	*Goal*	Outcome
Cuba	Diplomatic sanctions	2003–2009	Release of imprisoned dissidents	Limited concessions
China	Arms embargo	1989– ongoing	Improvement of human rights record	Limited concession
Russia	Redirection of aid	1999–2001	Violations of humanitarian law in Chechnya	No compliance
Pakistan	Deferral of signing of agreement	1998	Abandonment of nuclear weapons	No compliance
Peru	Freezing of development aid	2000–2001	Free elections	compliance
Serbia	Suspension of negotiations on EU accession	2006–2007	Co-operation with ICTY	compliance
Guatemala	Suspension of aid	1993	Free elections	compliance
PA	Suspension of aid	2006–2007	Recognition by Hamas of Quartet terms for peace process	No compliance
Turkey	Suspension of aid (and diplomatic sanctions)	1981–1997	Improvement in democratic rule/ human rights record	compliance

frame for their validity is specified, sometimes they are explicitly repealed or revised and sometimes they simply cease to be applied without much ado, or sink into oblivion. This uncertainty also concerns the target: motives are often vaguely formulated, and since no conditions are specified, it is unclear whether and how it can remedy its alleged breach. In the absence of a time frame or renewal date, the target is left in the dark as to whether the measures will be left in place indefinitely, be redressed or simply 'vanish' after some time. The measures featured display different degrees of informality. Those against Guatemala, China, Pakistan, Serbia and Russia were announced by the Council, while no decision on sanctions was taken with regard to Peru or Turkey.

Informal sanctions practice

One of the characteristic features of measures adopted in an informal manner is that they are rarely adopted in isolation. Most cases consist of a mixture of measures. Therefore, the cases discussed below are 'combination cases'. The informal legal bases of these decisions render their identification extremely difficult, to the extent that an exhaustive investigation of cases is unviable. Therefore, the selection of cases simply follows the criterion of the public accessibility of information.

The anomalous embargo: China

The arms embargo on China is described by EU officials as an 'anomaly' (interview 2007). It certainly presents unique characteristics. It is the only EU sanctions regime to have lasted for more than one decade after the introduction of the CFSP without having been transformed into a Common Position. Consequently, in contrast to all other CFSP sanctions, it is the only sanctions regime whose legal basis remains a Presidency statement. It is also the only one of a variety of sanctions imposed in 1989 to have remained in force, while all the others 'died a natural death' (interview 2007). Notably, it is the only stand-alone CFSP arms embargo to have remained in place for over a decade without being either superseded by a UN embargo (as in the case of the 1999 embargoes on Ethiopia and Eritrea) or complemented by other measures. While EU arms embargoes are routinely accompanied by an interruption of military links, military cooperation between EU member states and China coexists with the embargo (Casarini 2006). Far from remaining marginalised in the EU's purview, EU–China relations are flourishing.

The imposition of sanctions by the EU was motivated by the repression of pro-democracy demonstrations that took place in Tiananmen Square in the spring of 1989, and the executions that followed. The measures taken by the Council in June 1989 were as follows:

- arms embargo and interruption in military cooperation
- suspension of bilateral ministerial and high-level contacts

- postponement of new cooperation projects
- reduction of cultural, scientific and technical cooperation programmes
- prolongation of visas for Chinese students in Europe
- postponement of the examination of a new request for credit insurance and new credits from the World Bank.

A number of member states – Belgium, Germany and Italy – supplemented these EU actions with national measures, such as the suspension of grants, loans and aid (Kreutz 2004). The EU measures, most of which are diplomatic sanctions, ceased to be valid in October 1990 (Wacker 2004), while the arms embargo remained in place. The fact that the arms embargo was never formalised in a CFSP instrument has significant implications. Firstly, the measures were adopted on an indefinite basis, unlike most CFSP regimes currently in force, which contain an expiry date, or 'exit-clause'. Secondly, no common list of goods covered by the embargo was agreed, as is routine practice with current CFSP arms embargoes; thus, individual member states remain responsible for interpreting the embargo. Given that the embargo was interpreted as excluding the supply of equipment under agreements that were already concluded, European arms sales under those contracts continued. Some items with military applications, such as early warning systems, were also supplied. However, a US study published in 1998 estimated that European arms sales to China were not substantial, making up only 2.7 per cent of China's imports of military equipment (cited in Wacker 2004:2). In 2003, EU member states refused applications for 44 export licences for military equipment to China, and granted 159. However, the volume of sales remains 'relatively small' according to experts' estimates (Austin 2005:9).

The continuing arms embargo regained attention after some EU leaders, notably France and Germany, publicised their intention to review it in the autumn of 2003. China has lobbied for the lifting of the embargo since 1997 (Kreutz 2004), and the initiative that finally brought about the EU's reconsideration of the embargo seems to have been instigated by the Chinese mission to the EU in Brussels (interview 2007). The Chinese argument in favour of lifting the embargo is that China has become an important partner to the EU, and that as such it should not be subjected to the embarrassment of being a target of its sanctions (Kreutz 2004). The then-Commissioner for External Relations Patten reports that Chinese representatives claimed that China wanted the embargo relaxed not in order to make huge new arms purchases, but so as 'to end a humiliating situation in which it was placed on the same category as Burma and Sudan' (Patten 2005:280). Secondly, China announced that it was not planning to increase massively its arms imports from Europe, and that it was prepared to respect the EU's Code of Conduct on Arms Exports (Wacker 2004).

The European Council's announcement in December 2003 that it was prepared to reconsider the arms embargo was followed by a heated debate involving disagreements at the EU intra- and inter-institutional level that lasted for several months. The backdrop to the planned lifting of the embargo was the substantial upgrade in bilateral EU–China relations that took place in the second half of the 1990s. China had become the EU's third biggest trading partner by 2002, and EU exports to China rose by 40 per cent the following year. The robust health of bilateral links is best illustrated by China's participation in the Galileo satellite navigation system, to which it contributed 300 million euros. The Council's argument went along these lines. In its discussion of April 2004, it noted that the embargo had been 'imposed as a response to specific events in 1989 and that a solution for the matter had to be found which was in line with the current situation in China, the increasingly close bilateral relations and the EU's intention to develop a strategic partnership with China' (quoted in Austin 2005:1). As regards the human rights situation, the Council assessed China's progress in the field of human rights as follows:

> The Council … acknowledges that China has made considerable progress over the last decade in its social-economic development and economic freedom for ordinary citizens. It welcomes steps towards strengthening the rule of law …. It also welcomes moves to enhance cooperation with UN human rights mechanisms and China's work thus far towards the ratification of the International Covenant on Civil and Political Rights …. On balance … and from a long term perspective, a positive trend can be seen, with improvements in the rule of law and respect for economic rights and decline in the influence of the state on citizens' daily life.
>
> (Council of the European Union 2004f)

The EU's stated intention to lift the embargo was not only opposed by the European Parliament and civil society organisations dismayed at China's human rights record, it also met with fierce resistance from the US and some of China's neighbours, principally Taiwan. The adoption by the National People's Congress in March 2005 of an anti-secession law contemplating the use of force in the event of Taiwan's secession reinforced fears that tensions could escalate in the Taiwan Strait, even though the language employed in the law did not depart from previous Chinese rhetoric (Austin 2005:16). The Council's willingness to lift the embargo transformed the EU into the target of a coercive attempt by the US Congress, which passed a bill restricting military exports and technology sharing with those European countries selling arms to China. The EU's failure to lift the embargo can primarily be attributed to US pressure (interview 2007). Patten documents that dropping the embargo 'was likely to lead to a sharp deterioration in Europe's relationship with America' (Patten 2005:281).

IMPACT AND EFFICACY

In economic terms, the 1989 measures did not create any major annoyance for China. The 'very limited', 'low key' programmes that were suspended in the

1980s were resumed in the period 1991–94 (Bridges 1999:100). Broader trade relations were not damaged, as European businessmen returned to the Chinese market 'within months or even weeks' (Bridges 1999:106). The suspension of talks on WTO membership, which were only resumed in 1992, probably represents the most serious inconvenience posed to China – although the question of Chinese WTO membership was also compounded by the 1990 bid by Taiwan.

Despite the continuation of European arms sales, the embargo led to a general restraint among EU member states on the signature of new contracts with China (Osteneck 2004:11). In the field of human rights, scholars agree that little headway has been made (Wulteputte 2004). The most significant step taken by the leadership so far has been to amend the constitution to include formal guarantees of human rights. The fact that the EU never transformed the original document imposing the sanctions into a CFSP position meant that the conditions for lifting them were never specified. The Council's behaviour is illustrative of the leeway it wished to maintain over the decision to lift sanctions by leaving the evaluation of progress to the member states. Improvements in the human rights situation in China had been meagre; however, it was still prepared to lift the embargo on the basis of the 'long-term positive trend' observed. In 2004, the EU came so close to lifting the embargo that it is possible to argue that it would have done so were it not for the US pressure to maintain it, particularly in view of its persistent argument that, thanks to the Code of Conduct, the policy of arms sales to China would not have been affected. In spite of this often-voiced argument, there are indications that the European defence industry, which suffers from the embargo due to its dependence on exports for the bulk of its revenues, expected to benefit from trading with China, whose growing military expenditures are among the world's largest: according to Klenner, lifting the ban 'would amount to a political rehabilitation of China in return for which Beijing could reward Europe by buying more planes from Airbus, satellites from Astrium, telecommunication systems from Nokia, or even nuclear power plants and high-speed rail systems' (Klenner 2005:345).

In turn, the fact that the arms embargo was not lifted also proves the close link between EU and US sanctions. This circumstance also illustrates an equally interesting point, namely the role that the interests of the European arms industry played in the calculations of EU leaders. The China arms embargo emerges as one of the rare EU sanctions cases where the promise of commercial benefits linked with the lifting was offset by the commercial loss that would have been entailed, especially in view of the dependence of European arms production on the US: 'Europe is especially dependent on the import of high-tech components whose flow to us would be threatened if the US believed that they would make their way to China' (Patten 2005: 281)

In contrast to the other CFSP sanctions cases, EU officials have an answer ready when asked about the impact of the China arms embargo. They claim that the measure has been effective in 'preventing China from using European items for internal repression' and 'maintaining some degree of irritant in bilateral relations', motivated by China's poor human rights record. The evidence that China proactively promoted the idea of lifting the embargo on the basis of its embarrassment at being the target of EU sanctions – 'an affront on China's dignity' as presented to Patten (2005:280) – lends credibility to the idea that the discomfort caused had some impact. This can be explained in terms of the country's ambition to establish its international prestige. China is certainly interested in being regarded globally as a 'responsible power' (interview 2007).

The Chinese case constitutes a magnificent example of the degree of cooperation that can exist between the EU and one of its targets. Trade figures and, centrally, participation in Galileo testify to the shape of relations that, in the succinct assessment of one EU official, are 'going very well' (interview 2007).

CODING SUMMARY

Only very minor concessions were achieved from the target. Yet, the goals of the sanctions were not achieved; therefore, the EU cannot be credited for any contribution (contr 0). The measure did not affect the economy as a whole (eco 0), although it did have some impact, reflected in the Chinese uneasiness with the embargo. The measures did not endanger the position of the leadership (grip 0). The measure was not managed coherently (coh 0). The sanctions enjoyed scarce international support (int 0).

Diplomatic sanctions: Cuba

The EU is Cuba's main trading partner, its largest source of foreign investment and tourism, and its principal donor. Yet Cuba remains the only country in the Caribbean not to have signed a cooperation agreement with the EU. As part of Cuba's move towards participation in regional structures, shown by its membership of CARIFORUM and the signing of a free-trade agreement with CARICOM, Cuba acceded to the ACP group in 2000, and was granted informal observer status for the Economic Partnership Agreement negotiations. It applied for accession to the ACP–EU Partnership Agreement on two occasions, in early 2000 and in January 2003, both times unsuccessfully.

EU policies towards Cuba have been described as a 'mixture of engagement and light coercive measures' (Smith 2006:156). In spite of the significance the EU bears for Cuba, improvements in relations since the end of the Cold War have been only slight, and characterised by a series of setbacks. The basis for the EU's policy towards Cuba is a Common Position first adopted in 1996 and periodically renewed (Council of the European Union 1996d), which sets out a series of measures geared towards facilitating peaceful change, particularly through the promotion of human rights. It foresees a gradual, reciprocal strategy for support to Cuba: 'As the Cuban authorities make progress towards democracy, the European Union will lend its support to that process and examine the appropriate use of the means at its disposal for that purpose', including the intensification of dialogue and cooperation, which may open up the possibility of negotiating a Partnership and Cooperation Agreement. The objective of the Common Position is both political and socio-economic, as it claims to 'encourage a process of transition to pluralist democracy and respect for human rights and fundamental freedoms, as well as a sustainable recovery and improvement in the living standards of the Cuban people'. The EU explicitly rules out the use of economic coercion in order to achieve this objective: 'It is not European Union policy to try to bring about change by coercive measures with the effect of increasing the economic hardship of the Cuban people'.

After Cuba was granted observer status during the Cotonou negotiation process, the possibility of accession appeared to be in sight. Following Cuba's application to accede to the Cotonou Treaty, which found support in the ACP group, an exploratory EU Presidency Troika visit was scheduled for April 2000. However, in response to EU support for a resolution against Cuba passed by the UN Commission on Human Rights, Cuba cancelled this visit and withdrew its application. A mission sent later by the ACP group reported that the Cuban authorities had withdrawn because they believed that they 'had been subjected to discriminatory treatment which had never before been applied to other candidate countries … The EU Troika had stated that its visit to Cuba was a fact-finding mission, after which the EU would make a decision regarding Cuba's entry into the ACP–EU partnership. According to Cuban authorities, such a procedure had never been applied before to any other country' (quoted in Arts 2005:168). Thanks to the ACP group, which took the unprecedented step of admitting the country as a new member by amending its constituent document, the Georgetown Agreement, Cuba formally became an ACP country in December 2000. In early 2003, a Commission Delegation opened in Havana.

It was against the background of Cuba's renewed application for accession to the ACP-EU Partnership Agreement that the so-called 'cocktail crisis' took place in January 2003. This journalistically originated term denotes the diplomatic sanctions imposed on Cuba following the imprisonment of seventy-five political opponents in April 2003. The Council froze Cuba's application to accede to the Cotonou Treaty (Smith 2006:160) and adopted a series of diplomatic measures, namely:

- to limit the bilateral high-level governmental visits
- to reduce the profile of member states' participation in cultural events
- to invite Cuban dissidents to national day celebrations
- to re-evaluate the EU Common Position.

The idea of inviting dissidents to national day celebrations at the embassies of the member states is innovative – it was the first time that this sanction was wielded at all. It also appears to be the sanction that the Cuban authorities resented most. They dramatically denounced the measures as an unjustified retorsion, freezing diplomatic relations and imposing restrictions on cultural exchanges. Contacts with diplomats from EU member states took place rarely, and whenever Cuban authorities agreed to meetings, these involved only low-ranking officials. Official Cuban representatives did not attend national festivities to which dissidents were invited.

Following the conditional release of a number of the detainees in June and November 2004, the Council decided in early 2005 to suspend all measures. However, it protested the fact that the release of the prisoners was conditional, and announced that it would intensify contacts with the peaceful political opposition and civil society in Cuba (Council of the European Union 2005a). It also reiterated its demand that all political prisoners be released, as only about one-fourth of the detainees had been freed. Interestingly, the suspension of the measures was followed by the release of more political prisoners.

The decision by the Council triggered EU internal dissent. Following the conclusion of the meeting where the decision was taken, the Czech representative announced that his country would not respect the decision to suspend the measures. As a result, the practice of inviting political dissidents to receptions in Havana continues to be pursued by certain member states, with which the Cuban authorities have not resumed contact. The Council remained unable to reconcile the positions of member states advocating intensified cooperation and those in favour of further isolation in the face of Cuban insistence that the 2003 measures be fully lifted to allow an improvement in relations (Reuters 2007a). The eventual full lifting in June 2009, which took place after power had been handed over to Raul Castro, who subsequently introduced several reforms, was motivated by a desire to support the democratic transition of the country rather than by compliance.

IMPACT AND EFFICACY

The impact of these apparently low-key sanctions was very visible. The Cuban authorities felt that the measures, particularly the invitation of dissidents to national festivities, questioned their legitimacy, and were reportedly unsatisfied with the fact that the measures were only suspended, rather than withdrawn. They made the normalisation of relations with the EU conditional on the lifting of the measures, the repeal of the Common Position, and the termination of the practice of adopting resolutions condemning Cuba in the framework of the UN Human Rights Committee (interview 2007). Significantly, Cuba has consistently referred to the measures as 'sanctions', a term contested by the EU side.

The 2003 crackdown on the opposition met with widespread international condemnation, including that of its Latin American neighbours. It has not been possible to ascertain how the liberation of about fifteen dissidents in two waves during 2004 was connected with EU actions and international condemnation. Nevertheless, the fact that the resumption of contacts with most

EU states following the suspension of measures was accompanied by the release of further dissidents suggests that the Cuban authorities were sensitive to the sanctions, and that freeing further prisoners was intended to send a goodwill signal. Two years on, the Cuban authorities released another seven political detainees ahead of high-level meetings with EU member state Spain (Usborne 2007).

In this sense, the sanctions were partially effective. Before the suspension of the measures, about one-fourth of the detainees had been freed. The fact that shortly after the suspension a new wave of liberations took place reveals an interesting insight: it seems that the Cuban authorities felt compelled to reciprocate the EU's positive move. This situation contrasts with other cases where leaderships have become less forthcoming after the lifting of measures, as with the Central African Republic (interview 2007). Cuban leaders remained uncomfortable with the fact that the EU has not lifted the sanctions completely. Thus, the post-suspension liberations may have been inspired by Cuba's desire for a formal and complete lifting. However, the Council's capacity to reciprocate Cuba's move is limited by the US-inspired stance of Eastern European newcomers.

In view of the uncertainty surrounding Cuba's motivations, it is difficult to find an explanation for its amenability to EU influence in this seemingly minor episode. However, the international standing of the target appears to be relevant. Cuba's international position is heavily influenced by the comprehensive US embargo to which it has been subject for decades. Although presence of the embargo initially favoured the adoption of a policy of isolation and autocracy, over the past decade Cuba has shown a desire for international recognition, compelling its accession to the UN and other international organisations. This policy has been reasonably effective. Diplomatically, Cuba is increasingly integrated into the international system. Against this background, the EU bears importance for Cuba. Complicating factors account for the various setbacks witnessed in the short history of tentative rapprochement between the two; in particular the EU's political proximity to the US. Despite these drawbacks, Cuba has continued to demonstrate an interest in rapprochement with the EU, reflected in its renewed application to the EU–ACP partnership, as well as its participation in successive EU–Latin American Summits. Cuban elites bear in mind that despite their criticism, Europe still constitutes a major source of revenue. As put by an adviser to National Assembly president Miguel Alvarez in the midst of the crisis: 'To invite dissidents to their national parties was a real provocative action. … But at the same time, we have excellent trade with European businessmen, and a lot of Europeans are coming to Cuba as tourists' (Cuba News 2004).

The Cuban 'cocktail sanctions' episode is instructive in several respects. Firstly, it illustrates how the imposition of sanctions, as light as these may be, can create a 'trap situation' for both sender and target. According to an official, both Cuba and the EU miscalculated. Cuba staged the crackdown at a time when international attention was focused on Iraq, in the hope that it would escape notice. For its part, the EU did not count on the harsh reaction of the Cuban authorities to its diplomatic measures. The EU 'came to realize that without entertaining any contacts with the Cuban authorities, it could neither advance its interests, nor help Cuban dissidents – everybody was in a trap situation' (interview 2007).

Secondly, it demonstrates how leaderships care about the symbolic aspect of sanctions, even where the target country has faced deprivation for decades. Trade relations and the provision of aid remained untouched, and the diplomatic measures taken did not cause any disruption to the Cuban authorities beyond the perceived questioning of their legitimacy.

Thirdly, the lack of a pre-established framework reduced the room for manoeuvre of the EU, whose internal composition had been altered by the Eastern enlargement that took place in 2004. While CFSP Common Positions may be renewed on an annual basis, measures adopted in the form of Presidency declarations do not foresee any timetable for renewal. Thus, sanctions embedded in Common Positions will automatically expire unless renewed, while measures adopted through Presidency Declarations will continue indefinitely unless the Council deliberately interrupts them, or member states cease to apply them. In the case of the Cuban sanctions, Spain made some early efforts to lobby for the suspension of the sanctions following its own change of government, but encountered resistance from the Eastern European newcomers, who subscribed to a harder position, due to both their socialist legacies and US influence.

CODING SUMMARY

The goals of the sanctions were partially achieved, for which the EU alone can be credited (cont 1). The measures had some economic character, albeit the diplomatic crisis they triggered indicates that they had a considerable impact (eco 1). The sanctions did not directly threaten the continuance of the regime (grip 0). The management of the measures constitutes a prime example of inconsistency (coh 0). The EU's stance found considerable international support (int 1).

Redirection of aid: Russia

The first time that the EU agreed a measure as a result of Russian human rights violations was during the first Chechen crisis of 1995. This consisted in postponing the signature of the interim agreement that was to precede the implementation of the Partnership and Cooperation Agreement (PCA) signed the previous year.

By the time the EU came to consider sanctions against Russia in response to human rights violations perpetrated in the second Chechen war, post-Soviet Russia–EU relations were already well developed. The EU already had three legal instruments in place which included references to the protection of human rights: the PCA, the TACIS Regulation and the CFSP Common Strategy towards Russia. With the exception of the Common Strategy, which is not contractual in nature, these instruments include human rights conditionality, i.e. references to human rights as essential elements accompanied by a suspension clause.

The measures taken by the EU in response to the human rights violations resulting from what the Council called 'Russia's disproportionate use of force' in Chechnya in late 1999 have been described as 'pseudo-sanctions' (Stangos 2000). The European Council denounced Russian human rights violations in Chechnya as 'totally unacceptable' and mandated the following measures:

- a review of the Common Strategy towards Russia, which had been adopted six months earlier
- the suspension of some provisions of the PCA, and the strict application of trade provisions
- the transfer of some of the funds granted under TACIS towards humanitarian assistance, and
- the limitation of TACIS funds for the year 2000 to a number of priority areas, which included human rights, rule of law, support for civil society and nuclear safety (Council of the European Union 1999d).

The European Council's statement came close, but ultimately failed, to activating the human rights clause. It also failed to specify how and to what extent the Common Strategy on Russia was to be revised. Ample room for manoeuvre was left in these instructions, to be hashed out at a later date by the Council. Drawing a parallel to the Lomé agreement, Fierro suggests that 'the political signal was given, so that the Commission or one Member State could have had the initiative of calling … consultations' (Fierro 2003:346). The activation of the human rights clause was indeed considered, along with other measures such as the suspension of the Most-Favoured Nation (MFN) status that Russia enjoys under the PCA, or the suspension of GSP privileges, which affected 10 per cent of Russian exports to the EU. The Council finally decided on milder measures (Council of the European Union 2000a):

- the revision of the Presidency's work plan for the implementation of the Common Strategy towards Russia
- the suspension of the signature of the Scientific and Technological Agreement
- the Commission's decision not to carry over 30 million euros of unspent funds of food aid from the 1999 to the 2000 budget
- the prohibition on extending GSP privileges to products not yet covered
- the redirection of TACIS funds towards programmes in support of humanitarian assistance, democracy and civil society.

As a result, a total of 90 million euros of aid was frozen, and credits for food and trade preferences were blocked (Heller 2008:188). TACIS aid was reduced from 140 million euros in 1998 to 92 million euros, and a new financial heading in support of democratic values and civil society was created and endowed with 34 million euros (Heller 2008:179). On the diplomatic front, the EU encouraged the OSCE and the Council of Europe to 'review' their relations with Russia, and tabled a resolution condemning developments in Chechnya at the UN Commission for human rights.

Russian officials rejected EU criticism as an 'interference in internal affairs' (Heller 2008:188). Six months later, the Council relaunched its cooperation with Russia, notably through the reactivation of the TACIS programme, inviting the Commission to prepare a proposal for an action plan for the year 2000 (Council of the European Union 2000c).

IMPACT AND EFFICACY

These measures had no impact on the behaviour of the Russian leadership. The EU's timid reaction to Russian human rights violations in Chechnya shows how the availability of the legal framework matters, but does not determine the scope of the EU's reactions. The Council had several instruments at its disposal which it failed to use, and the half-heartedness of the measures taken may have encouraged Russia to disregard them. Even the 'minimal sanctions' that were imposed were lifted in the same year in the absence of any step taken by the Russian side to warrant such a change of strategy. The formulation used by the European Council allowed for sufficient room to limit the scope of the measures to be decided by the Council. The overall weakness of the EU's reaction has been denounced as a 'subtile manière de donner l'impression de "faire quelque chose" sans rien compromettre d'essentiel' (de Wilde d'Estmael 2000b:179). Indeed, the measures had no impact on economic, energy or security cooperation between the EU and Russia (Heller 2008:188).

Criticism also subsided at the level of declarations. After the tenth EU–Russia summit in November 2002 Chechnya was left off the official agenda. This reconsideration was part of a general trend: 'the loudly voiced demands of late 1999 and early 2000 about Chechnya, and how Russia should seek a political solution ... and that failure to do so would have far reaching consequences, had ... disappeared by 2002' (Smith 2005:120–21).

Yet the Commission had never advocated sanctions, backing instead the continued nurturing of the partnership emerging between the two actors. In the midst of the crisis, Commissioner Patten claimed in an address to the European Parliament that 'it is only by trying to maintain that partnership that we have any chance of getting the Russians to heed our message' (Patten 1999a). In response to calls to cut off financial assistance, he questioned the usefulness of such a move:

> There would be no direct impact on Russia's public finances because the money is all channelled through contractors mainly in the EU. But it

> would undermine the pace of economic and social modernisation that we have been pressing for so hard.
>
> (Patten 1999a)

Finally, commenting on withholding IMF and European Bank for Reconstruction and Development lending, he questioned whether it would be in the EU's interest to 'provoke a political backlash against the international community in the run-up to the Duma elections in December' (Patten 1999a). In sum, the option of imposing more serious measures was dismissed not only on the grounds of an expected lack of success in terms of improving the situation in Chechnya, but also due to fears of obstructing Russia's democratic course.

CODING SUMMARY

The goals of the sanctions were not achieved, and the EU's contribution was nil (contr 0). The measure was economic in character but remained without impact (eco 1). It hardly posed a threat to the leader's permanence in power (grip 0). The measure was managed incoherently (coh 0). EU measures found only limited international support (int 0).

Redirection of aid: the Palestinian Authority

The suspension of aid to the Palestinian Authority (PA) is a case of informal sanctions which has attracted high levels of public attention in recent years. It is in fact an instance of the redirection of aid rather than a freeze. The suspension was agreed following the Palestinian elections of March 2006, in which Hamas obtained an overwhelming majority of the votes. The EU justified the measure on the grounds of Hamas's lack of respect for the principles for continued engagement with the Palestinian Authority, set out by the Council jointly with the Quartet in the framework of mediation efforts in the Middle East conflict. Pointing out that Hamas is an organisation included in the EU's terrorist list, Commissioner Ferrero singled out its refusal 'to renounce violence, recognize the right of Israel to exist or accept existing agreements' as the reasons for the EU's decision to 'temporarily put on hold assistance to, or through, the Palestinian government and its ministries' (Ferrero-Waldner 2006c). The EU declared that it wished to 'see an evolution of the positions taken by the Palestinian Authority government, not its failure', thus signalling the EU's readiness to resume aid as soon as Hamas accepted the principles formulated by the Quartet.

Paradoxically, the suspension was coupled with an increase in EU aid to Palestinians in response to the deterioration of the social, economic and humanitarian crisis in the Palestinian territories. As stated by Ferrero 'we have suspended payments going to the Palestinian government, but we have not suspended aid to the Palestinian people'. In June 2007, the Commission claimed to have committed 320 million euros in Community funds in the first half of 2007 alone (Ferrero-Waldner 2007).

The suspension concerned not only EU funds – assistance from the West ceased entirely. An EU-inspired special arrangement was put in place shortly after the freeze, in order to allow for the resumption of international assistance circumventing the Hamas-led PA government. From June 2006, aid was channelled through a Temporary International Mechanism (TIM), bypassing the PA, with the exception of its Presidency. As EU total aid to the occupied territories rose to 700 million euros in early 2007, UN envoy Alvaro de Soto commented: 'Europeans have spent more money in boycotting the PA than what they had previously spent in supporting it' (quoted in Tocci, 2007a).

Following some indications from the EU in the first half of 2007 that it was ready to cooperate with some 'reliable' ministers of the Unity government, the EU 'aid embargo', as it was referred to in the media, was relaxed in July 2007 (Goldirova 2007). The European Commission signed an agreement allocating 4 million euros for technical assistance and the training of officials in the Palestinian finance ministry, led by an independent politician, Mr Salam Fayyad.

IMPACT AND ASSESSMENT

The Western suspension of aid is reported to have hit PA employees, the vast majority of whom are Fatah supporters, the most harshly. There is no evidence supporting the claim that Western policies weakened the movements backing Hamas. The effects of sanctions are considered to have been counterproductive, having a negative impact on the evolution of democracy and governance. Due to Western coercive policies, Palestinians have by and large not held Hamas responsible for non-delivery of its programme, nor for the worsening security situation on the ground (Tocci 2007a). In addition, the TIM reversed the limited progress made in PA governance reform in previous years, since the bypassing of official institutions led to the re-centralisation of powers in the (non-Hamas) Presidency. In addition, the focus on humanitarian rather than development assistance generated a dangerous culture of dependence amongst beneficiaries.

From a broader perspective, the imposition of sanctions on a democratically elected government has discredited the legitimacy of Western policies and enhanced Hamas's image of resistance in the eyes of the Palestinian population. According to Tocci, these policies have 'most likely raised support' for Hamas (Tocci 2007a:3).

CODING SUMMARY

The goals of the sanctions were not achieved, thus, the EU cannot be credited for any contribution (cont 0). The measure was economic in character but its impact was minor, due to the parallel system put in place (eco 1). It did not directly threaten Hamas's permanence in power (grip 0). The measure was managed incoherently (coh 0). The EU's stance found limited international support (int 0).

Deferral of signing agreements: Pakistan

The EU reacted to the consecutive nuclear tests conducted by India and Pakistan in May 1998 with political declarations condemning the tests and invitations for both countries to join the Non-Proliferation Treaty (NPT) and the Comprehensive Test Ban Treaty as non-nuclear-weapon states. The Council adopted some measures in its conclusions. In its Declaration of 25 May 1998, which followed the Indian tests, it instructed the Commission to reconsider India's eligibility for the Generalised System of Preferences (GSP). Following the tests conducted by Pakistan shortly afterwards, the Council released a new declaration issuing similar instructions to the Commission, and temporarily postponed the conclusion of an impending Partnership and Cooperation Agreement with Islamabad.

In the CFSP Common Position issued the following October, no reference to these measures was made (Council of the European Union 1998d). This document contained a general pledge to support the 'efforts of the international community to achieve enhanced confidence-building measures among India and Pakistan and in the region in general'. An attempt was made to put together a package of positive measures and incentives to support non-proliferation, featuring the organisation of seminars and the establishment of links with European think-tanks. The Common Position also foresaw the provision of technical assistance in the implementation of export controls.

The late release of the Common Position reveals the lack of general consensus on proliferation that existed at the time. Reactions were not homogeneous among EU member states. While Denmark, Germany and Sweden froze development aid, other countries, such as France and Spain, were against any measures beyond condemnation, arguing that as non-signatories of the NPT, these countries were under no obligation to refrain from acquiring and testing nuclear weapons (Portela 2003). Secondly, the absence of references to the measures agreed at the time of the tests may indicate a change of priorities at Council level. Having realised that its primary objective should consist in ensuring the implementation of effective export controls on nuclear-sensitive technology, the Council may have dropped the threat of countermeasures in order to obtain the target countries' agreement to the provision of assistance to those ends.

So far, the consideration of countermeasures here remains the only example in which a measure from the EU in reaction to a nuclear proliferation case has not simply accompanied UNSC sanctions. The US adopted legislation interrupting cooperation with these countries following the tests; however, the half-heartedness of these measures became evident, as they were repealed shortly after (Meier 1999). Thanks to the flexibility provided by the informality of the decision, the EU was able to retreat from its condemnatory position, to refrain from fulfilling its threat to suspend GSP preferences, and to provide for the implementation of export controls in these countries. Finally, the threat of revising the GSP helped to make up for the asymmetry between the reactions to the two cases. Since there was no impending agreement with India, there was no equivalent tool available which would have permitted a symmetrical response to two cases where the 'wrongdoing' was identical.

CODING SUMMARY

The goals of the sanctions were achieved; only partially (cont 0). The measure was economic in character but its impact was nil (eco 0). It did not pose any threat to the leader's permanence in power (grip 0). The measure was managed incoherently (coh 0). The EU's stance found considerable international support (int 0).

Freezing of aid: Peru

The temporary freezing of Community aid to Peru is a unique 'informal sanction' case in the sense that the measure was not decided by the Council, but by the Commission. No document on the adoption of measures in response to the Peruvian crisis exists. From this perspective, the freezing is more 'informal' than the other episodes grouped under this heading.

In view of the irregularities observed in the first round of the 2000 presidential elections in Peru by both local and international independent observers, President Fujimori's main rival, Mr Toledo, decided to withdraw his candidacy. As a result, Fujimori won the second round of the election in May 2000 and started his third mandate as President amidst widespread international criticism, including that expressed by the European Union. In response, the Commission froze all new cooperation programmes with the country. As with ACP suspensions, ongoing programmes were left in place. Technically, this measure was accomplished through the Commission's refusal to sign the financial agreements required for the implementation of previously agreed programmes because of a Peruvian refusal to abide by the established terms, e.g. the reduction of the Peruvian share in the financing of the projects.

A political crisis provoked by a corruption scandal involving a member of the Presidential cabinet compelled Fujimori to step down in September 2000 and to announce general elections for April 2001. Cooperation was resumed once the flawless transition phase had been completed by President Paniagua. In addition to the unfreezing of 61 million euros, the EU signalled its support to the new government by organising a donors' conference in October 2001, whose objective was, according to an internal Commission note, 'the political support to the new Peruvian government of President Toledo through support to its programme' against unemployment (Commission of the European Communities 2001a). Equally, the report of a mission conducted in December 2001 with a view to the agreement of a country strategy paper underlines: 'Le Pérou est en pleine transition démocratique … L'appui politique au Président Toledo est crucial actuellement. A ce sujet, le déboursement imminent de 8 Million d'Euros constituera un signal politique très important' (Commission of the European Communities 2001c).

IMPACT AND EFFICACY

There is no doubt that the Commission's decision to freeze aid was not in itself a determining factor in the resignation of President Fujimori, which in turn allowed the organisation of new elections. It was the internal political crisis that ultimately brought about the President's decision to allow a democratic transition. However, the Peruvian authorities that came to power after the democratic transition had repeatedly underlined the contribution that the Commission's measures made to international pressure on President Fujimori.

This episode came about in a highly atypical way. In the absence of a mandate by the Council of Ministers, the legal basis of the measure remained very shaky. At the same time, the episode displays a striking similarity with ACP suspension cases, where flawed elections repeatedly led to the opening of consultations with the governments responsible. The Commission showed a substantial degree of initiative by using its capacity to defer the signature of financial protocols in order to contribute to political pressure on Fujimori. This is especially the case because it based its actions on difficulties of a technical-legal nature rather than a political one. In the present case, the entrepreneurship of the Commission complemented the condemnation of the Council at the time of the flawed elections.

CODING SUMMARY

The goals of the sanctions were achieved, and the EU can be credited for its contribution (cont 1). The measure had economic character and would have had some impact (eco 1). It posed a threat to the leader's permanence in power (grip 1). The measure was managed coherently (coh 1), and the EU's stance found some international support (int 1).

Freezing of aid: Guatemala

The Guatemala episode was successful, but extremely brief. The EU suspended new project aid to Guatemala immediately after the 'self-coup' of President Serrano in May 1993, where sections of the constitution were revoked, and the Congress was dissolved. The EU's was not the most forceful measure imposed in response to the coup, given that the US agreed a full suspension of aid in the same month. The coup proved short lived, given that within a month a return to democratic rule was accomplished.

IMPACT AND EFFICACY

Assessments of the importance of international pressure in bringing about the reversal of Serrano's self-coup vary widely. While some analysts claim that Serrano's resignation only a week later was due to a combination of domestic and external pressure, other experts believe that intense internal pressure alone accounts for the return to democracy (interviews 2007). Be that as it may, the EU's reaction is unlikely to have played a central role, given that the US, more influential in Central America, suspended all government aid at the same time as the EU.

CODING SUMMARY

The goals of the sanctions were achieved, but the EU can only be credited for a modest contribution to the international condemnation of the coup (contr 0). The measure was economic in character and would have had some impact (eco 1). It posed a threat to the leader's permanence in power (grip 1). The measure was managed coherently (coh 1). The EU's stance found some international support (int 1).

Suspension of agreement: Serbia

The background to this Serbian sanctions episode can be found in a CFSP Common Position adopted by the EU concerning the extradition of indictees of the International Criminal Tribunal for the Former Yugoslavia (ICTY). While the Common Position refers to the imposition of sanctions, they are not addressed as such in the present investigation because they affect individuals who are not connected to governments. In 2004, the EU released a Common Position freezing the assets of indictees of the ICTY who had not yet been extradited, which affected Bosnia Herzegovina, Croatia and Serbia and Montenegro (Council of the European Union 2004g).

The origins of the Serbian episode lie in the establishment of a conditionality link between the cooperation of local authorities in extraditing ICTY indictees – in particular four generals indicted in late 2003 – and progress in negotiations for a Stabilisation and Association Agreement (SAA) with the EU. Similar to the *Europe Agreements* concluded with the Eastern European states, the SAA is meant to provide a legal framework for relations between the EU and Serbia for the entire period prior to a possible future accession. The government's lack of cooperation with the ICTY in the extradition of indictees was the subject of severe criticism from the US and the EU. In January 2005, the EU enlargement Commissioner announced that ICTY compliance was a precondition for the positive assessment of Serbia's readiness for the SAA. The Serbian government then gave assurances that it would fulfil its obligations to the tribunal, followed by a wave of voluntary surrenders which reached a total of sixteen new extraditions, including high-profile indictees (Rajkovic 2007). As a result, the Commission confirmed that sufficient progress had been made and opened negotiations on the SSA, stating that further negotiations were conditional upon Serbia's continued cooperation with the ICTY.

The crisis that triggered the freezing of negotiations arose when it became clear that the government under Prime Minister Kostunica was not ready to arrest and forcibly extradite the indicted General Mladic, whose whereabouts were apparently known. The government's refusal to cooperate was partly due to domestic considerations, as one of the main parties in parliament had threatened to withdraw its support for the government, were Mladic to be arrested (Rajkovic 2007). In May 2006, the EU called off negotiations with Serbia on the SAA, announcing that they would remain so until Mladic was delivered to The Hague.

In the days that followed the suspension, the Kostunica government indicated that it was prepared to take a tougher stand on Mladic, and in July of the same year it presented the EU Council of Ministers with an action plan for cooperation with the ICTY which included the arrest and extradition of Mladic. The Council's reaction to the document was reported to be so positive that it considered the resumption of negotiations. However, this did not take place, as it would have been contrary to the previously stated condition that talks would only resume once Mladic had been extradited (Rajkovic 2007). Similarly, the pledge for full cooperation with the tribunal formulated by the new Kostunica government formed in May 2007 during a visit by the EU Enlargement Commissioner Rehn again failed to bring about the resumption of talks.

While SAA talks remained frozen, cooperation continued. Negotiations for visa facilitation and readmission with Serbia began in November 2006, and the EU has recently allocated 600 million euros to the institutional and economic development of Serbia (Bilandzic 2007). Commissioner Rehn decided to resume talks in 2007, in the midst of calls by the ICTY prosecutor Mr Brammertz that improved Serbian cooperation was needed, notably by arresting the remaining fugitive war crimes suspects (EU Observer 2008a). While negotiations for the agreement continued and were eventually finalised, the signing of the agreement was made conditional on full cooperation with the ICTY. In a speech in front of the European Parliament, Commissioner Rehn announced that the Commission had finalised technical work on the text of the draft SAA:

> We are, as the EU, technically ready to sign the Agreement soon, provided that the political conditions are in place, namely full co-operation with the ICTY leading to the arrest of the remaining indictees.... Signature will depend on full co-operation with ICTY. This requires Serbia to do everything in its powers to locate the fugitives and provide the ICTY with all necessary information leading to their arrest and transfer to The Hague.
> (Rehn 2007)

Yet, the agreement was signed in April 2008, although one element of conditionality was still kept: the Presidency of the Council, held by the Slovenian Foreign Minister Rupel, announced that the agreement would only come into force after Serbia had fully cooperated with The Hague (Frankfurter Allgemeine Zeitung 2008). In its conclusions, the Council confirmed that the Community had 'decided to implement the interim agreement as soon as the

Council decided that Serbia fully co-operates with the ICTY', and announced that the Council and Commission would 'regularly monitor that Serbia continues to fully co-operate with the ICTY' (Council of the European Union 2008b). In spite of these conditions, the Bosniak chairperson of Bosnia and Herzegovina's tripartite state presidency complained about the signing of a pre-accession deal with Serbia while Bosnia had not been offered a similar agreement, accusing the EU of double standards: 'this act shows that Serbia enjoys some benefits like no other country' (EU Observer 2008b).

IMPACT AND EFFICACY

The EU's behaviour in the Serbian case can be best described as taking a step back from a sanctions measure to conditionality. The EU took a risk by freezing talks with Serbia from which it decided to backtrack. The Serbian episode provides an example of contradictory EU aims in a target country in which the organisation is highly involved. On the one hand, EU conditionality proved reasonably effective in bringing about compliance with ICTY demands in the ex-Yugoslav republics, including, at first, Serbia. The underlying reasoning is visible in the statement by Serbian President Tadic in December 2004: 'without co-operation there is … no entry into the EU, no increase in the standard of living. Our poverty rate will rise, we will have no political stability, so long as we are excluded from the international community' (quoted in Rajkovic 2007)

On the other hand, the EU also has a stake in the country's development into a stable democracy, as well as in its cooperation on the question of the final status of Kosovo. These two interests collided in this crisis, given the negative impact that a possible extradition could have had on Serbian domestic politics. This is especially so in view of the fragile situation of the Kostunica governments. The forcible extradition of Mladic risked endangering Kostunica's rather fragile power base and increasing the chances of a nationalist backlash. Indeed, the division between these sets of interests seems to coincide with the Commission–Council cleavage. While the freezing of talks was a Commission initiative, some resentment emerged in the Council about the loss of the EU's main source of influence at a time when Serbian cooperation was needed for the resolution of the status of Kosovo (interview 2007). These considerations did eventually override the EU's original stance. The suspension turned into conditionality in the face of the question of recognition of Kosovar independence, and conditionality was redefined on the eve of the Serbian parliamentary elections in May 2008, in an attempt to strengthen the increasingly precarious position of Serbian pro-EU parties.

CODING SUMMARY

So far the outcome has been nil, and the contribution of EU sanctions cannot be but zero (contr 0). The EU's approach has been characterised by a high degree of inconsistency (coh 0). The measure is economic in nature, with noticeable impact (eco 1). It hardly endangers the leadership's permanence in power (grip 0). It enjoyed some international support, or at least it encountered little international opposition (int 1).

Freezing of aid: Turkey

The suspension of aid to Turkey dates back to the early 1980s and follows a highly atypical pattern. Following a coup d'état in Turkey in 1980, and the reluctance of the generals who staged the coup to commit to a timetable for a return to parliamentary democracy, Germany decided to withhold an aid package to Turkey. This was followed by a European Council decision in late 1981 not to approve an EC aid package, while the following year the European Parliament dissolved the Joint Parliamentary Assembly with Turkey until such time as the Turkish Parliament had been elected by direct universal suffrage. Following the positive outcome of a referendum on a new Constitution, coupled with assurances that steps towards the restoration of democracy were forthcoming, Germany resumed aid (Hufbauer et al. 1985). However, EU aid remained blocked until the Council agreed on the resumption of financial cooperation and the European Parliament gave its approval to the creation of a customs union in 1995 (Crawford 1997:50). Only then could the Financial Protocol to the Association Agreement enter into force, permitting the disbursement of EC aid. However, the Greek–Turkish crisis that erupted in January 1996 over the Aegean island of Kardak/Imia delayed the disbursement of aid once more, as a result of Greece's veto in the Council, supported by the European Parliament. Aid to Turkey was effectively resumed following its nomination as a candidate for EU accession in December 1999. Since then, Turkey has received aid in order to prepare for EU membership.

The Turkish episode is atypical in the sense that two short-lived, formally decided sanctions regimes coexisted with the repeated postponement of the signature of a Financial Protocol. According to one expert, one could speak of two distinct EU sanctions episodes corresponding to the periods 1981–85 and 1996–97 (interview 2007). Yet the lack of a formal legal basis for imposing sanctions and the fact that the aid package originally agreed in 1981 was never effectively disbursed warrant Turkey's characterisation as a single informal sanctions episode.

IMPACT AND EFFICACY

The evaluation of the Turkish case is not straightforward. On the one hand, the influence of EU sanctions has undeniably been effective in bringing about democratic reforms in Turkey. The military junta which seized power in 1980 only agreed to new elections on the condition that former political leaders be banned from standing, and after the adoption of a constitution foreseeing that the head of the junta remain President of the Republic for seven years.

After a civilian government came to power in 1983, remarkable headway was made in the fields of democratisation and human rights, lifting political restrictions and taking steps to eradicate the influence of the military in politics. There is no doubt as to the importance of the EU in prompting this evolution, as steps were explicitly taken with reference to EU demands and the aim of normalising relations. In addition, the EU was the only donor to block aid. As one analyst puts it, progress in democratisation and human rights took place 'because Turkish policy-makers realised that Turkey needed the help of Europe not only for economic reasons to release the blocked aid and to increase textile and agricultural exports, but also for political reasons to increase the level of co-operation' (Arikan 2003:118).

At the same time, the reforms were also part of Turkey's preparations to apply for EU membership, an intention that was publicly announced in early 1986. In the words of the then Prime Minister Ozal, the motive behind the economic and political reforms of the 1980s was to facilitate Turkey's integration into the EU as a full member. Ozal even turned Turkish compliance into a pro-accession strategy by suggesting that 'if the EU wanted Turkey to have a viable and durable democracy, the best way of doing this was political integration of Turkey into the EU' (Ozal quoted in Arikan 2003:119). Thus, the EU's influence over the Turkish leadership can almost be viewed through the same prism of accession conditionality that characterised relations with Eastern European countries in the late 1990s. Crawford confirms this assessment: 'As a lower middle-income state, Turkey is not aid dependent, and aid sanctions will have limited economic impact. Nevertheless, given the strong desire of … recent Turkish governments to join the EU, aid sanctions confer a powerful symbolic message with the potential to leverage improvement in the human rights situation' (Crawford 1997:51).

The peculiarity of this case is that the EU's strategy in Turkey changed once the leadership announced its intention to apply for membership in 1986: 'Turkey became more vulnerable to pressure from the EU … Turkey's wish to apply for membership increased European public interest in … the domestic politics of Turkey, which led to continuing public scrutiny of Turkey's human rights record' (Arikan 2003:120). The number of European Parliament (EP) Resolutions regarding the situation of human rights in Turkey in the 1980s and 1990s is telling in this respect (Soler 2005). The EP's increased emphasis on human rights contrasts with the fact that tensions in bilateral relations between the member states and Turkey had eased remarkably by the mid-1980s – Germany had resumed aid after Foreign Minister Genscher reported the junta's commitment to return to democracy in late 1982. According to Crawford, a majority of member states in the Council was prevented from enforcing the protocol, due to a blockade by Greece and the EP: '11 out of 12 member states in the European Council have wanted to normalise relations since 1986. Only the lack of unanimity prevented such a decision' (Crawford 1997:50).

The Turkish episode is especially illuminating from the point of view of institutional dynamics. What started as a German aid blockade developed into a suspension maintained by one member state's veto and by the EP's power to refuse its assent to international agreements. This may explain some member states' general reluctance to initiate EU sanctions regimes, given the difficulties that may arise in lifting them. At the same time, this case shows the EP as a successful policy entrepreneur, given its key role in framing the EU's approach to Turkish membership aspirations and its willingness to withdraw its assent to several agreements with Turkey (Zanon 2005). The Commission, originally reluctant to interrupt association relations with Turkey (and to some extent also the Council), moved to increase human rights conditionality after Turkey announced its ambition of full membership.

CODING SUMMARY

The coercive effort was fruitful, and the EU sanctions can be exclusively credited for success (contr 1). It is a measure of economic nature, with some impact (eco 1). It hardly endangered the leadership's permanence in power (grip 0). It enjoyed some international support, or at least it encountered little international opposition (int 1). The measure was managed with little consistency (coh 0).

Evaluating informal sanctions

The parallels between CFSP measures and informal sanctions are evident. The distinction between them is purely legal, and only came about with the creation of the CFSP and the definition of its legal instruments in the treaty of Maastricht. While the first instances of CFSP sanctions appeared to be 'all-encompassing', including measures ranging from the interruption of high-level meetings to arms embargoes, the allocation of measures to different legal instruments can be observed over time. CFSP sanctions regularly feature measures from a seemingly fixed catalogue comprising visa bans, arms embargoes and the freezing of assets. In contrast, diplomatic sanctions, the deferral of the signature of treaties and the redirection of aid have been reserved for less formal frameworks. The almost arbitrary nature of the distinction between formal and informal sanctions was nicely illustrated in the context of the Chechen wars, when some European leaders considered freezing certain provisions of the agreement with Russia. Having questioned how such measures should be presented to the press, Commissioner Patten was told by the President of the European Council that that was 'a matter of bureaucratic detail' (Patten 2005:206).

There is no apparent logic behind the allocation of these particular sets of measures to each of these frameworks. The division does not correspond to the identity of the implementing agency. Member states are responsible for the implementation of CFSP arms embargoes and informally adopted diplomatic sanctions alike. The Community is in charge of carrying out the redirection of aid or postponing the signature of agreements. The choice of legal basis emerges as a clear indication of the degree to which the Council wishes to be bound by the sanctions. In the cases of Pakistan and Russia, the flexibility provided by the use of European Council Conclusions/Presidency statements, combined with deliberately vague formulations, allowed the Council to refrain from fully substantiating the announcement of upcoming sanctions. Another illustration is the Council statement imposing a series of measures against China following the events of Tiananmen Square. Except for the rather exceptional survival of the long-lasting arms embargo, the diplomatic sanctions died a 'natural death', in the words of one EU official (interview 2007). That is to say that member states simply ceased to apply them, in the absence of a formal Council act or notification of member states. Given that no official justification accompanied these decisions, there is no reason to believe – and no way of ascertaining – that the unofficial lifting of the measures was meant to reciprocate any concession made by the target. Tellingly, Presidency statements, Council Conclusions and, since their creation, statements by the High Representative for the CFSP, are the communicative tools chosen for the issuing of threats of sanctions. The threat to adopt measures against Uzbekistan if the authorities failed to consent to an international independent inquiry into the Andijan events serves as an example (Council of the European Union 2005c).

Interestingly, informal measures have sometimes been adopted in parallel with CFSP Common Positions outlining the EU's stance on the specific event that triggered their adoption. However, no reference was made in these documents to the measures adopted, despite the fact that they were agreed jointly by all member states. This is the case with Cuba. An EU Common Position on this country is renewed annually, yet measures in place against Cuba in reaction to the imprisonment of dissidents are not reflected in it. The reasons for choosing the informal framework can be explained by the lower profile and visibility of the decision vis-à-vis the European public and the third country in question. However, the consideration that it is easier to distance oneself – if need be – from a commitment reflected in Council Conclusions rather than in a CFSP act remains decisive.

6 The efficacy of development aid suspensions in the context of the Partnership Agreement between the EU and the African-Caribbean-Pacific Group

Since 1995, the European Union has suspended development cooperation with a number of ACP countries. These suspensions have taken place within a specific legal-institutional regime, namely that of the Partnership Agreement between the EU and ACP countries contained in the Cotonou Convention, which in 2000 succeeded a series of Lomé Conventions detailing a privileged trade relationship between the EU and some former colonies of its member states. Art. 96 of the Cotonou Convention provides for a consultation procedure which can be invoked in cases of serious breaches of human rights and democratic principles, and empowers the Council of the EU to suspend development aid.

At first, an exploration of the efficacy of development aid cut-offs may appear a departure from the theme of sanctions. The suspension of development aid is generally discussed in the context of relations between the EU and the developing world, and left out of the mainstream sanctions debate. The EU does not label these measures 'sanctions', and keeps them legally separate from CFSP measures. There is a considerable distance between classical embargoes and EU suspensions, as these are designed in such a way as to spare the population of the country concerned from any suffering. Yet the suspension of aid under Art. 96 remains an attempt to influence in which benefits – aid and trade preferences – are withdrawn that would otherwise be available, and whose restoration is dependent on the fulfilment of a series of conditions defined by the EU. Comparing the efficacy of development aid suspensions with targeted sanctions directed exclusively at leaders will enable us to ascertain how economic pressure fares in the overall sanctions toolbox. Are targeted sanctions delivering better results in terms of target compliance than traditional economic tools?

The present chapter looks at the efficacy of development aid cut-offs in the framework of the Cotonou Convention as a coercive instrument of EU foreign policy. It does so by reviewing the cases in which this instrument has been wielded. While the dataset features cases prior to the signing of the Cotonou Convention, this chapter focuses on cases since 2000, given that these are better documented. Table 6.1 features major cases of suspensions of development cooperation under Art. 96 of the Cotonou Convention, and indicates the nature of the 'appropriate measures' taken. A brief overview of each case follows the table, and these serve as a basis for the concluding analysis.

Table 6.1 Suspensions of Cotonou Convention under Article 96

	Measure	*Time Period*	*Main goal*	*Outcome*
Central African Republic	Partial suspension	2003–2005	Free election and reforms	compliance
Ivory Coast (I)	Partial suspension	2000–2001	Free elections and reforms	compliance
Ivory Coast (II)	Partial suspension	2001–2002	Free elections and reform	compliance
Fiji	Partial suspension	2001–2003	Free elections and reforms	compliance
Haiti	(Almost) total suspension	2001	Free elections and reform	compliance
Guinea–Conakry	Partial suspension	2003–ongoing	Free elections	limited concession
Liberia	Partial suspension	2001	HR violations in Sierra Leone	no compliance
Togo (I)	(Almost) total suspension	1993–94	Redress of illegal constitutional change; new elections	no compliance
Togo (II)	(Almost) total suspension	1998 –2006	Redress of illegal constitutional change; new elections	compliance
Zimbabwe	Partial suspension	2002 – ongoing	New elections	no compliance

Article 96 suspensions: what kind of sanction?

The Lomé Conventions, a series of treaties embodying the privileged relationship between the EU and some of its member states' former colonies located in the African, Pacific and Caribbean regions, constituted the legal basis for the granting of development aid and trade preferences to these countries from 1975 to 2000. Originally, the Conventions contained references only to human rights in their preamble, and there was no legal provision for the interruption of cooperation in the form of a conditionality clause. Before 1995, the granting of EU development aid to ACP countries took the shape of an entitlement: 'the EU was obliged to support an ACP country even if it was implementing policies that were contrary to development, human rights, rule of law, etc.' (Babarinde and Faber 2004:37).

In the 1990s, development aid to various ACP countries was suspended on several occasions. However, no formal procedure existed, and no agreement seems to have existed at the time on the actions that would warrant the freezing of aid, or even on whether the Council or the Commission were the competent institutions to decide on such measures (Schmalz 1997). Early suspensions were thus handled in informal ways (Hazelzet 2005:4). This situation of uncertainty is reflected in the cases of Equatorial Guinea and Nigeria. While the decision to freeze aid to Equatorial Guinea in 1992 was taken by Commissioner Marin, the Council mandated the interruption of cooperation with Nigeria in 1995 through a CFSP Common Position (Council of the European Union 1995).

The 1995 mid-term review of Lomé IV first saw the introduction of conditionality. It identified respect for human rights and democratic principles as 'essential elements' of the treaty (Art. 5), thereby reflecting the increased interest in the promotion of human rights that followed the end of the Cold War. This provision was accompanied by a conditionality clause empowering any of the parties to call for a consultation procedure where a breach of any of the essential elements of the treaty by another party had been observed (Art. 336a). The consultation procedure consists of a period of intensive contacts whereby the country in question is requested to present a programme for the re-establishment of the 'essential elements': human rights and democratic principles. The conditionality clause also provides for the adoption of so-called 'appropriate measures', depending on the outcome of the consultations. These might entail, amongst others, the suspension of development cooperation with the country in question. The actual procedure for the application of Art. 336b was only agreed in 1999, based on a Commission proposal presented in 1996. It established that the initiative for calling consultations could come from the Commission or from a member state, and it fixed the decision-making procedures for suspensions. The signature of a new ACP–EU Partnership Agreement in Cotonou (Benin) in June 2000, replacing the Lomé Convention series, saw two important novelties. The 'rule of law' was added to the 'essential' elements of the treaty, while 'good governance' became a 'fundamental' element. The introduction of good governance was accompanied by a new conditionality clause enabling the parties to call for consultations in serious cases of corruption (Art. 97). The mid-term review of the Cotonou Agreement in 2005 also incorporated important changes. A new provision on an 'intensified political dialogue' provided a middle ground between regular political dialogues and Art. 96 consultations, and the time period for the opening and closure of consultations was doubled. The legal framework for suspension is relevant insofar as the establishment of clear rules facilitated its employment as a political tool. Indeed, the precision of the consultation procedure under what is now Art. 96 in three consecutive revisions since 1995 (Lomé VI *bis*, Cotonou 2000, Cotonou 2005) has been accompanied by its incremental use to tackle violations of human rights and democratic rule.

The consultation procedure

According to Art. 96, 'if a party considers that the other party has failed to fulfil an obligation stemming from respect for human rights, democratic principles and the rule of law', it shall supply the other party and the Council of Ministers with the relevant information 'with a view to seeking a solution acceptable to the Parties. To this end, it shall invite the other Party to hold consultations that focus on the measures … to be taken by the party concerned to remedy the situation.' Art. 96 also foresees deadlines. Consultations shall begin no later than 30 days after invitation and shall not last longer than 120 days. The adoption of appropriate measures is foreseen in cases in which

1. Consultations do not lead to a solution acceptable to both parties;
2. Consultations are refused; or
3. There is 'special urgency', defined as 'exceptional cases of particularly serious and flagrant violation of one of the essential elements … that require an immediate reaction'.

Treaty provisions leave considerable leeway to the Council, as they merely stipulate that appropriate measures will be taken in accordance with international law, and should be proportional to the violation. When selecting the measures, 'priority must be given to those which least disrupt the application of this agreement'. Finally, suspension is referred to as 'a measure of last resort'.

The procedure for consultations is highly institutionalised. Once a serious breach of human rights or democratic principles is observed, the Council of the EU invites the ACP country in question to participate in consultations under Art. 96. The decision to invoke Art. 96 is preceded by a discussion in the relevant geographical Council working party under the CFSP and the ACP working party. The decision to start consultations is taken by the Council on the basis of a proposal tabled by the Commission.

Consultations start with a meeting in Brussels between the EU troika and the ACP country considered in breach, accompanied by a number of ACP countries of its choice, and representatives from regional organisations such as the African Union and the ACP Secretariat. The objective of the consultations is to agree on measures to rectify the breach. The EU and the responsible government adopt a list of commitments to be fulfilled within a timetable. When consultations are closed, the EU evaluates the progress made by the government in fulfilling the commitments undertaken and may then decide to take 'appropriate measures'. In the early days of the application of the non-execution clause, when debating the opportunity of opening consultations with Guinea-Bissau, the Council concluded that consultations should be seen as a positive measure, implying a dialogue in which the parties would strive to find a solution to the breaches, and that the suspension of cooperation would not be automatic (Fierro 2003:332). Albeit they may entail the suspension of development cooperation, appropriate measures can also consist of positive measures, such as the release of new funds or the redirection of aid. Suspension can be total – for which unanimity in the Council is required – or partial – for which a qualified majority suffices. In practice, proposals are adopted unanimously (Hazelzet 2005:6). Subsequently, the EU conducts regular monitoring, including missions to the country to assess progress in implementation.

The behaviour of the sender towards the ACP countries displays some trends that are visible in the contractual basis of the partnership. In the light of the innovations brought in by the Cotonou Treaty, some authors have identified a number of forces 'altering the nature of the relationship in a fundamental way' (Babarinde and Faber 2004:28). The evolution observed consists in a progressive shift towards increasing conditionality in the provision of aid, which started with the introduction of the non-execution clause and culminated in the establishment of a performance-based partnership which follows the principle of differentiation. At the same time, it has been noted by a number of authors that the ACP countries have been downgraded in the EU's 'pyramid of preferences' (Smith 2003, Petiteville 2003).

One of the factors accounting for these trends is the perception of the EU's relative failure in terms of promoting the development of the ACP countries, in spite of the considerable resources it has devoted to this aim over several decades. While few countries profited in terms of development, most ACP economies struggled and even regressed during the Lomé era. The resulting donor fatigue may explain the trend towards an increasingly performance-based relationship. Yet, if aid is unable to advance social and economic development in these countries, it can at least be useful in promoting democratic and accountable governance and human rights. A linkage is believed to exist: a lack of respect for these principles hinders development; therefore, their promotion could be conducive to development.

Measures applied under Art. 96 often entail the redirection of aid, rather than its suspension. This frequent tactic consists in the redirection of funds towards aims other than those they had been originally allocated to. The EU has also taken this approach, e.g. with Zimbabwe, where funds foreseen for budget support were redirected towards humanitarian aid and projects in direct support of the population. The most common strategy followed by the EU in the context of consultations consists of:

1. The redirection of aid to measures designed to fulfil the authorities' commitments to redress breaches, most notably actions supporting the preparation of elections; and
2. The incremental resumption of development cooperation on a conditional basis. This is referred to as the 'gradual and conditional approach'.

As in all aspects of its coercive policies, the EU attempts to ensure that the population is spared from deprivation. Not even in cases of total suspension is the entire flow of aid interrupted. Suspensions only affect one strand of development funds administered directly by the state, namely budget support, which affect mostly infrastructure projects. The suspension often takes the form of non-notification of the upcoming European Development Fund (EDF) programme.

Despite a suspension, substantial portions of development aid may remain in place. The suspension is only enforced for projects that are not yet in place, leaving ongoing programmes unaffected. Humanitarian aid, which is funded through a different budget, is expressly exempted from suspension. Cross-border regional projects involving several countries are not interrupted as a result of the suspension of development aid against one of the participants. Aid in direct support of the population is channelled through NGOs; therefore, it is often left in place. This may include health, education and food security programmes, programmes in support of civil society, human rights and democracy, and rural development projects. Fisheries agreements typically concluded between the EU and ACP coastal states, offering financial compensation and development measures in exchange for access to resources in territorial waters, also remain unaffected by Art. 96 suspensions. So-called 'third generation' fisheries agreements constitute a major source of income for ACP countries, often providing coastline countries, such as Mauritania, with more generous funds than those granted to them as development aid. Finally, development aid provided by EU member states is also unaffected by Art. 96 suspensions, as it is up to the individual member states to decide on the discontinuation of their bilateral aid programmes. The continued provision of aid by member states to beneficiaries under an Art. 96 suspension has sometimes created internal, and especially inter-institutional, friction in the EU.

ACP sanctions practice

Given the large number of ACP suspension cases, this chapter excludes some early episodes, either because information was unavailable or because they repeat the characteristics of other episodes described at length.

A suspension of development aid in the pre-Lomé IV **bis** *era: Rwanda*

The EU halted benefits to the Rwandan government in reaction to the genocide in 1994. In the post-genocide period, the EU contributed a reconstruction aid package worth 22 million ECU, conditional on the new government's respect for human rights. A framework for the conditional resumption of aid was stipulated in the Common Position 94/697/CFSP (see Council of the European Union 1994b). According to this document, 'aid should be disbursed progressively depending on the observed performance' in a number of areas, particularly concerning the return of refugees and the 'creation of essential conditions for their return'. Under this framework, the EU suspended payment of the package, appealing to the Rwandan government to investigate the massacre and to arrest the perpetrators as a precondition of payment. As the authorities initially refused to impose sanctions on members of the army, aid was withheld until the following year, when the government agreed to prosecute those responsible (Hafner-Burton 2005).

A suspension under Lomé IV **bis***: Comoros*

The first instance of application of Art. 336a under Lomé IV *bis*, once the procedure had been finalised, was in the Comoros Islands. The motive was a military coup in May 1999, which overthrew the legitimate government and dissolved the Constitution and legal institutions. Consultations took place in July 1999, in which the Commission threatened that if democracy was not rapidly restored, appropriate measures, including the partial or total suspension of the convention, would be taken. During the consultations, which the Commission described as 'constructive' (Fierro 2003:328), the Comoros delegation committed to preparing a new constitution and organising elections. The measures taken by the EU reflected a gradual, conditional resumption of cooperation, combined with positive measures, which included a support package for the electoral process, humanitarian aid and decentralised cooperation for the transitional period. Further assistance to local communities was foreseen for the post-election phase, but full cooperation would only be resumed after elections. A fact-finding mission sent by the Commission in 2000 concluded that elections had been satisfactory and cooperation was fully resumed.

Article 96 suspensions under Cotonou

Central African Republic

The Central African Republic has not been favoured by the donor community, despite its heavy dependence on foreign aid. The EU has a prominent role among donors, especially since the IMF cut budgetary support in 2001 (Mbangu 2005:8, Laakso et al. 2006:75). Art. 96 was invoked following a coup d'état by General Bozizé in 2003, which overthrew President Patassé. Consultations, starting in June 2003, were not limited to the discussion of democracy and human rights, but also addressed economic governance and corruption, and respect for the Kimberly process concerning the export of diamonds. As analysts have observed, this reflected 'the fact that the political crisis was linked to public finance mismanagement and corruption' (Laakso et al. 2006:75). Acute problems of financial governance could be observed before the coup, and are believed to have been at the root of the increasing unpopularity of Patassé's regime. Following the conclusion of consultations, the Council opted for a partial suspension. Reportedly, the Council refrained from a total suspension, due to the 'catastrophic' situation of the economy. Instead, a more creative solution was found: first, it left in place selected fields of aid: 'Existing cooperation will remain centred on the social fields, in particular health, and on direct support for the population. Ad hoc support for measures will be taken by the authorities to fulfil their commitments, in particular regarding preparation of the elections, good governance, institutional support and technical assistance for the adoption of an action plan to improve public finance.' The resumption of suspended cooperation was linked to the following:

> The resumption of macroeconomic support alongside a programme with the IMF, once an electoral plan has been adopted laying down the steps and procedures for the organisation of the various elections and provided respect for human rights is ensured. … The full and complete resumption of cooperation when democracy and the rule of law have been re-established following the elections, which should take place by early 2005 at the latest.
>
> (Council of the European Union 2003d)

In particular, the originality of the Council's approach is reflected in the announcement that 'in the event of non-fulfilment of the commitments made by the Central African authorities, the European Community reserves the right to reduce the ninth EDF allocation to the Central African Republic by 20 per cent a year as of the end of the consultations' (Council of the European Union 2003d:4).

A monitoring mission of October 2003 concluded that while dialogue on reconciliation had been successful, progress made regarding the freedom of the opposition, the timetable for elections and the reform of the military was unsatisfactory. Therefore, the Council decided to partially suspend development cooperation on some road projects, macro-economic support, and a progressive reduction of the ninth EDF funds by 20 per cent per year. Cooperation was resumed following presidential and legislative elections in 2005, which were considered to have met the appropriate standards.

Haiti

As the poorest country in the Western hemisphere, Haiti is heavily dependent on foreign aid. However, the EU's importance as a trading partner for this country is low, due to the overwhelming commercial weight of the US. Article 96 was invoked as a consequence of the electoral fraud observed in the May 2000 legislative elections. The EU is reported to have been encouraged to make use of this instrument by the contact group of donors in Haiti, composed, among others, of the international financial institutions, the Organisation of American States and the UN (Laakso et al. 2006:88). As a result of the consultations held in September 2000, the Haitian government promised to arrange new elections for senators. Following the failure to abide by its commitment, the EU decided to suspend budget aid and food security as well as the second instalment of the eighth EDF. The remaining funds were redirected to projects in direct support of the population, civil society and the private sector. The Council agreed the non-notification of the ninth EDF. These amounted to severe sanctions; only humanitarian aid was left in place. In the following years, the EU modified its measures several times as a result of its participation in the Consultative Group of Haiti, whose members encouraged the EU to lift the suspension. Development aid was resumed in October 2005 as a result of a commitment to hold elections, which eventually took place in February 2006.

'Chronic' cases: Togo, Ivory Coast and Fiji

Togo (I)

Despite being the ACP state whose capital gave the name to EU–ACP Partnership Agreements since 1975, Togo is one of the most endemic cases of development suspension. Cooperation with Togo was first suspended in 1992, at a time when no procedure was yet in place, as a consequence of the breakdown of the democratisation process and of an illegal change to the constitution made by

President Eyadema. Both Germany and France cut off bilateral assistance programmes. Presidential elections took place in June 1993, but Eyadema's victory was widely regarded as fraudulent (Crawford 1997: Annex). After the constitution was restored in 1994, a partial resumption of aid was announced in March 1995.

Togo (II)

Art. 336a was first invoked against Togo before the procedure had even been finalised, as a result of the flawed presidential elections of 1998. At the request of the Togolese government, the EU financially supported the establishment of an independent national electoral commission for the presidential election. However, the electoral commission was dissolved by President Eyadema and elections were again reported to be flawed. Consultations were held in 1998, following the Togolese government's failure to provide proof of concrete measures taken to remedy the irregularities of the presidential elections. As a result, the Council decided to end consultations with Togo and to suspend cooperation with the country, all the while declaring that it would support any initiative intended to allow Togo to comply with the essential elements of the Convention.

Togo (III)

As a result of a succession of interruptions in the democratic process (see above), Togo did not receive any EU funds under the eighth and ninth EDF; assistance from the EU was obtained only in the form of humanitarian aid. The consultations that took place in 2004 are atypical in that they were called at the request of the Togolese government, encouraged by other ACP countries (Mbangu 2005:12). Togolese activism even took the form of a visit to Brussels by Prime Minister Mr Sama in October 2003 to address the Development Committee of the European Parliament (Laakso et al. 2006:85). Consultations started in March 2004 and closed in November with an agreement by the Togolese authorities to implement a list of commitments, mainly related to the re-establishment of democratic rule. The EU offered institutional aid for the implementation of measures to carry out the undertakings made during the consultations. The resumption of full cooperation was made conditional on the holding of free elections. The gradual approach taken in the case of Côte d'Ivoire was repeated in the list of appropriate measures, which the Council Decision stipulates as follows:

> The ninth EDF allocation will be notified once electoral arrangements that will ensure transparent and democratic elections acceptable to all parties are established and a date for the holding of parliamentary elections is set ....

1. once the ninth EDF allocation is notified, aid for preparing the elections may be given as long as the conditions stipulated in the above electoral arrangements are adhered to;

2. once free and fair parliamentary elections have been held, cooperation with the European Union will resume in full, with implementation of the ninth EDF.
(Council of the European Union 2004h:3)

A number of problems arose at the implementation phase, mainly due to diverging interpretation of commitments and lack of administrative capacities (Mbangu 2005:13), and the monitoring mission reported that no conclusive evaluation was possible, despite the goodwill shown by the government. However, the EU decided to release funds to support the preparation of elections, human rights programmes and justice reforms. Following the signing of the Global Political Agreement by government and opposition, elections were announced for the following year. However, President Eyadema's sudden death in 2005 set back the initial timetable. The presidential elections were preceded and accompanied by violence, which compelled the European Parliament to contest the validity of the results, in open contradiction to the Commission assessment. Thus, highlighting that the 'several important measures concerning essential elements of the Cotonou Agreement' had yet to be implemented (Council of the European Union 2006c), the EU extended the application of the appropriate measures before fully resuming aid.

Ivory Coast (I)

The military coup in Ivory Coast of December 1999 provoked widespread international condemnation, from African, European and North American countries alike. It was in this context that the EU decided for the first time to adopt restrictive measures prior to the opening of consultations. These measures consisted of refraining from any new financial commitments in Ivory Coast, apart from possible humanitarian projects or projects of direct benefit to the poorest sections of the population. In the consultations held in February 2000, the authorities committed to a timetable for elections and the adoption of a constitution, and to guarantee the separation of powers, a free press and transparency. Consultations were concluded in May 2000. Satisfied with these commitments, the EU agreed a package of measures to support the transition to democracy (Fierro 2003:335). Existing cooperation was not altered, but it was decided that for the programmes for which financial agreements had not yet been signed 'a gradual and conditional approach would be undertaken'. Thus, this episode corresponds more to a pseudo-sanctions than to a sanctions scenario, given that aid was not suspended. However, consultations reopened just one year later, due to the Ivorian authorities' failure to honour a number of these commitments.

Ivory Coast (II)

The EU called for consultations following the flawed presidential and legislative elections of 2000, pointing to unfulfilled commitments that had been agreed in the previous rounds of consultations under Art. 366a of the Lomé

Convention (see above). The EU did not regard the presidential and legislative elections organised in October and December 2000 as sufficiently open, due to violence and restrictions preventing the opposition from participating freely (Laakso et al. 2006). In addition, grave human rights violations against the civilian population were reported. In the consultations which were launched in February 2001, the Ivorian party promised to conduct a transparent investigation into the atrocities perpetrated during the military regime, and to open up the political system. However, in order to ensure that the authorities would this time follow up on their commitments, the EU engaged in an intensive round of dialogue on the various controversial points. Following the closure of consultations in July 2001, the EU decided to take a gradual and conditional approach towards the implementation of new projects in support of the restoration of democracy, rule of law and good governance. This decision was motivated by the mixed record of the Ivorian authorities. Despite satisfactory local elections, the political system had not yet been fully opened up, nor had a judicial investigation into the atrocities been launched. The EU's 'gradual and conditional approach' is visible in the letter addressed to the Ivorian President following the conclusion of consultations. Noting that significant measures had already been taken, although some were still to be implemented, the Council outlined the following process for resumption:

> i. The initial disbursements will focus on social themes, institutional support and the private sector. …
> ii. The situation will be reviewed in September 2001. Once new and substantial progress has been made towards fulfilling undertakings, over and above that already achieved, aid will be rolled out progressively and new measures may be adopted ….
> iii. Following a further review of the situation in January 2002, establishing that the undertakings have been fulfilled, full cooperation will be resumed.
>
> (Council of the European Union 2001a)

Cooperation was fully resumed in January 2002, in view of satisfactory progress by the Ivorian government. Consultations were again proposed by the Commission in 2004, in view of the human rights breaches that followed the intensification of fighting in the north of the country that had begun in 2002. However, the Council rejected the proposal, arguing that the threat of civil war would render Art. 96 consultations ineffective (Laakso et al. 2006:85). What followed was the imposition of mandatory sanctions by the UNSC Res.1572 (2004) and 1643 (2005), which featured a comprehensive regime comprising an arms embargo, a visa ban and freezing of assets, as well as an import ban on diamonds.

Fiji (I)

Fiji is one of the ACP countries least dependent on European aid; indeed, it is barely eligible for aid at all. However, the main economic link with the EU is sugar export, for which Fiji enjoys special access. A coup was perpetrated by a military unit and was motivated by the perceived political dominance of Indo-Fijians. Consultations under Art. 96 were initiated in October 2000, following a coup d'état in May of that year. During the consultations, power shifted from the original perpetrators of the putsch to the military, and eventually to a nominated President. In view of the commitments made by the Fijian authorities in the course of the consultations, and the encouraging development of the country since the opening of consultations, the Council decided on relatively mild measures.

The EU made the notification of ninth EDF allocation and the financing of new programmes under the previous EDF (sixth to eighth) conditional on the holding of elections and the appointment of a legitimate government. Regional projects, humanitarian aid and trade-related preferences were left in place. Once the conditions were fulfilled, the EU decided on a gradual resumption of cooperation in November 2001, consisting of projects in support of the rural population and on human rights and democracy. However, an irregularity observed in the allocation of seats in the parliament – a number of elected Indo-Fijian MPs from the Labour Party had been excluded – left the EU unsatisfied. Full cooperation was only resumed in November 2003 after the nomination of Labour cabinet ministers.

Fiji (II)

The coup d'état staged in Fiji in December 2006 surprised many observers. The 2006 election had brought about the first-ever multi-party government and introduced policies focusing on inequality which departed from the ethnic dissensions witnessed hitherto. This had created the impression that Fiji might be heading 'into a new political era with more stable constitutional development, a more stable environment for economic development, an increase in trade, and the reduction of poverty' (Laakso et al. 2007:65). Upon seizing power, commander Bainimarama announced a state of emergency and dissolved the parliament, action which met with immediate universal condemnation. The EU opened consultations with Fiji in January 2007, demanding, among other things, a plan for elections by May 2009. Despite calls by the European Parliament to cease all non-humanitarian aid, the Commission suggested that activities supporting the sugar reform be continued in view of 'the importance of the sugar industry for Fiji's economy, employment and poverty situation' (Commission of the European Communities 2007b:5). The Council followed its time-honoured approach of selective suspension: while leaving the sugar reform assistance in place, the EU suspended the allocations for sugar from 2007 onwards. As a result of the leadership's failure to abide by the core demand of holding elections by May 2009, the suspension of the sugar allocation, which totalled 24 million euros in 2009, remains in place. It is noteworthy that the EU has not exploited Fiji's main vulnerability, by leaving tariff preference in place. As explained by Chand, ending the sugar preferences would impose significant adjustment costs on the domestic economy, likely 'including a severe economic contraction, loss of government revenues, dislocation of households from rural to urban areas, and a worsening in the balance of payments position with consequences for the sustainability of the fixed exchange rate regime' (Chand 2006:196).

CODING SUMMARY

In most cases the goals of the sanctions were largely achieved, and the EU can be largely credited for success in most cases (cont 1). The measures had an unequivocally economic character and were bound to have an impact on the target (eco 1). The suspensions endangered the leader's permanence in power (grip 1). The measures were managed coherently in all cases (coh 1). The EU's stance found considerable international support (int 1).

Yet, in a few cases the record is less positive. In Fiji II, e.g., only some of the secondary goals of sanctions were achieved, such as the lifting of the state of emergency, for which the EU can be largely credited (cont 0). The measures had economic character and were bound to have an impact on the target (eco 1). The suspensions endangered the leader's permanence in power (grip 1). The measures were managed coherently in all cases (coh 1). The EU's stance found universal international support (int 1).

The interface between CFSP and Article 96 sanctions

Zimbabwe

Given that there have been certain cases of overlap between development aid cut-offs and CFSP sanctions, the relationship between Art. 96 suspensions and CFSP measures must be explored. At first, the fact that both types of measures are imposed on identical targets seems straightforward, as both serve the purpose of pressuring the target into making concessions. Yet, the relative frequency of cases of aid cut-offs lies in contrast with the rarity of CFSP episodes in the ACP region. A cursory examination of the only targets subjected to both Art. 96 suspensions and CFSP sanctions reveals that this coincidence is related more to the EU's legal constellation at the time when measures were imposed than to any teleological distinction between them.

The case of Zimbabwe is exceptional in a number of respects. Along with Guinea-Conakry, it is the only example in which a suspension of aid under Art. 96 has been complemented by CFSP sanctions. Zimbabwe has also been described as a deviant case in studies of governance, human rights and democracy in ACP countries, where it has been singled out as the only case in which, according to relevant indicators, freedom of participation had improved in the year previous to consultations under Art. 96 (Laakso et al. 2006). The Zimbabwean crisis has its origins in the agrarian reform begun by President Mugabe in 2000/1, which entailed the expropriation of land from white farmers, and which was accompanied by a wave of political violence and the intimidation of the opposition (Kreutz 2006). The expropriation campaign was initiated against the background of declining support for President Mugabe's party (ZANU-PF), which embarked on this policy in an attempt to expand its power base with a view to the forthcoming parliamentary elections. Consultations were launched in January 2002. Yet, despite unsatisfactory progress, aid was suspended only after the Zimbabwean authorities refused entry to a team of EU electoral observers on the eve of the 2002 elections, and their harassment of the opposition. The EU moved very quickly from political dialogue under Art. 8 of the Cotonou Agreement to Art. 96 consultations, which were apparently exceptionally short (interview 2007). Immediately after the suspension, the EU imposed an arms embargo along with a visa ban and a freezing of assets against individuals included in one of the longest blacklists the EU had ever produced.

In parallel to the political crisis, an economic crisis of catastrophic dimensions unfolded, due to corruption and mismanagement of the economy: Zimbabwe became the world's fastest shrinking economy with the world's highest annual inflation rate, featuring unemployment figures of 70 per cent and above (Weiland 2004:129, International Crisis Group 2009:8). Exacerbated by drought, the continued deterioration of the economy compelled the EU to increase humanitarian aid.

Support offered to the Mugabe regime by neighbouring countries has been central to Zimbabwe's resistance to EU pressure. Zimbabwe's neighbours continue to back Mugabe not only politically, but also through the supply of energy. The EU's attempts to garner support for its sanctions on Zimbabwe from the Southern African Development Community (SADC) remained unfruitful. African powers such as Nigeria and South Africa criticised the imposition of EU sanctions. Tellingly, the African group, headed by Nigeria, led opposition to EU-sponsored resolutions condemning Zimbabwe in two consecutive sessions of the UN Commission on Human Rights (Smith 2006:167). Few CFSP sanctions regimes have exposed so publicly EU internal disagreements. Mugabe's attendance at the French–African Summit of February 2003 spurred considerable irritation (Weiland 2004:139). The EU's ban on Mugabe's participation in summit meetings provoked the cancellation of a Europe–African summit planned for 2003. When the summit finally took place in 2007, British Prime Minister Brown refrained from attending, in protest at Mugabe's presence (Castle 2007).

SADC has played a central role in pressuring Zimbabwe to comply with the organisation's newly agreed electoral standards in the 2005 parliamentary elections, thus acknowledging the existence of democratic deficiencies in the country. Following the electoral victory of the opposition in the presidential and parliamentary elections of April 2008 – a development ascribed to the miserable state of the economy, coupled with divisions in the ruling party – SADC managed to broker an agreement among the opposition and the Mugabe regime (Mair 2008:2).

EFFICACY

The Zimbabwean aid sanctions constitute the only Art. 96 suspension case triggered by a government refusal's to accredit election monitors, a move precipitated by the fact that an ultimatum had been issued to that effect in the context of consultations held in 2002. Some analysts credit EU and US sanctions in bringing about the fragmentation of the ruling party: 'Targeted EU and US sanctions on senior regime figures are working. ZANU-PF leaders cite their personal financial situations as motivation for wanting Mugabe out' (International Crisis Group 2007:13). One of the ZANU-PF leaders who is also a businessman, Solomon Mujuru, is reported to have 6 million dollars of his funds frozen in European banks (International Crisis Group 2009:6). A senior member of the politburo, supportive of the faction demanding Mugabe's retirement, was quoted as saying: 'We need to look at … what measures … should ensure … that ZANU-PF remains in power. One of those measures is clearly to have a new leader and to begin to make moves to engage with the international community' (International Crisis Group 2007:6). According to another senior member, ZANU-PF's overall objective during the negotiations to bring the opposition party into a coalition government was to help stabilise the economy and obtain removal of Western sanctions targeted on the ruling party's leadership (International Crisis Group 2009:4)

CODING SUMMARY

The goals of the sanctions were not fully achieved; however, they can be credited for compelling the ruling party to accept the opposition as a coalition partner (cont 1). The measures were predominantly non-economic in character (eco 1). They had some noticeable impact. They endangered the leader's permanence in power (grip 1). The measures were not managed entirely coherently (coh 0), except for the aid suspension (coh 1). The EU's stance found endorsement from the US, but not from Zimbabwe's neighbours (int 0).

Guinea-Conakry (I and II)

A second case of overlap between ACP suspension and CFSP came about in 2009, when the government of Guinea-Conakry, a country already under Art. 96 suspension, staged a crackdown on demonstrators, which triggered CFSP sanctions by the Council. The democratic standards and rule of law in the Republic of Guinea had been deteriorating for some time before the flawed presidential elections of December 2003 gave rise to consultations with the EU. At the conclusion of these lengthy consultations in April 2005, which concentrated on improvements in the electoral process, such as freedom of the press and the opposition, the EU decided to redirect the unexpended balances of previous EDF towards decentralisation, liberalisation of the press and economic governance, while ninth EDF funds continued for programmes in direct support of the population. Slight progress by the Guinean authorities, for example with respect to the operation of independent radio broadcasters, was reciprocated with a partial lifting of measures. However, delays in the key commitment, namely the organisation of elections, led to the extension of the implementation phase to April 2009.

Before the implementation phase came to an end, a coup d'état was perpetrated, following which the constitution and political and trade unions were suspended and a provisional government was installed. Nigeria and the US joined the EU in condemning the seizure of power, and Guinea was suspended from the African Union, Economic Community of West African States, and the Organisation Internationale de la Francophonie. Consultations thus reopened in April 2009, leading to the leadership's commitment to hold parliamentary elections in October and presidential elections in December. Following the already well-established 'gradual and conditional approach', the EU tied the resumption of aid to steps to be taken by the Guinean authorities in accordance with the roadmap. It was against this background that the crackdown on the demonstration of September 2009 took place: the government's action constituted a set-back in terms of the roadmap implementation, and the violent repression of a pro-democracy demonstration, with 150 casualties, according to UN estimates, perfectly fits the classical CFSP sanctions pattern. The Council imposed an arms embargo and a visa ban on the military junta (Council of the European Union 2009b).

CODING SUMMARY

For the purpose of coding, only the suspension initiated in 2004 is taken into account. Coherence was not perfect, as the resumption of aid hardly appeared to reciprocate concessions by the target (coh 1). The goals of the sanctions were not achieved (cont 0). The measures had economic character and an impact on the target (eco 1). External support was considerable (int 1).

Evaluating Article 96 suspensions

When does the EU invoke Article 96?

Most consultation cases are officially justified as reactions to both human rights violations and the interruption of democratic processes. However, there is a clear predominance of the democracy element. Article 96 was invoked whenever democratic governance was obstructed – such as in cases of flawed elections – even if no human rights breaches took place. In contrast, human rights violations were never the only motive for holding consultations. A glance at the instances of Art. 96 consultations reveals that the majority of cases are triggered by coups d'état (Bradley 2005).

The most frequent criticism of EU development aid suspensions is their alleged lack of coherence. Decisions to begin consultations are significantly associated with deteriorations in human rights, governance and democracy in a given country, rather than with their absolute levels (Laakso et al. 2006:12). In addition, breaches of human rights to which the EU reacts concern civil and political rights closely associated with democracy, such as the freedom of speech and association and the right to peaceful demonstration. Some breaches – such as harassment of the press or the opposition – are defined in terms of their capacity to disrupt the organisation of free and fair elections. Interestingly, the commitments to which ACP leaderships are encouraged to subscribe under Art. 96 consultations often encompass governance issues such as anti-corruption measures, theoretically covered by a different provision of the Cotonou Agreement, Art. 97.

A possible explanation for the predominance of coups d'état as triggers of consultations is that clear-cut coups d'état seem to garner more support among EU member states than other democratic flaws. Portugal's resistance to the opening of consultations with Guinea-Bissau serves as an illustration. The call for consultations following fraudulent elections by rulers already in power tends to encounter more resistance from the ACP group. However, a further explanation is the fact that the perpetrators of coups are often more amenable to EU influence than are democratically legitimised rulers who breach the constitutional order. Coups d'état often unseat leaders with flawed democratic records whose reluctance to abide by democratic standards is driven by their desire to retain power at all costs. In contrast, transitional authorities often perceive considerable benefits in maintaining dialogue with an interlocutor like the EU. The successful conclusion of consultations guarantees the continued flow of development aid. Being accepted as an interlocutor by the EU confers legitimacy upon them. New elections will not always unseat those who carried out the coup. Albeit the EU often requires that the coup perpetrators do not stand for office, the case of the Central African Republic shows that democratic elections can in fact legitimise their power.

As in all strands of EU autonomous sanctions practice (Brummer 2009), the EU has been accused of inconsistency in the selection of its targets (Crawford 1997). France has sometimes been accused of displaying a stronger tendency to protect its former colonies from aid cut-offs than the UK, albeit research exploring the link between the use of the consultation tool and the identity of the former colonial ruler of the target does not fully confirm this (Hazelzet 2001). The view that former colonial powers France and the UK display different orientations on the use of sanctions in general also overlooks the fact that they do not necessarily treat all of their former colonies in the same way. The threshold that must be crossed in an ACP country for the opening of consultations may diverge even among the former colonies of the same metropolis. Illustratively, France entertains a different link with the Central African Republic than with its neighbour, the Ivory Coast. Finally, the attitude of the former colonial powers in the Council is not the sole determinant. While Portugal is virtually the only stakeholder in Guinea-Bissau, several member states have trade interests in the former British colony Nigeria. The fact that the government in question maintains effective control over most of the territory of the country also seems to be a precondition for the opening of consultations. The involvement of other organisations, notably the UN, in many of the countries engaged in conflicts renders Art. 96 consultations redundant. The EU has become involved in these countries by participating in broader political processes, such as in the DRC (García-Pérez 2007:4). This official justification given by the Council when it rejected the Commission's proposal to open consultations with Ivory Coast in 2004 confirms this criterion. In addition to multilateral efforts, the EU has typically imposed arms embargoes and interrupted military cooperation with African countries engaged in conflicts, such as Zaire/DRC in 1990, Sudan in 1994 and Ethiopia/Eritrea in 1999.

In sum, the EU invokes Art. 96 whenever it believes that it stands a reasonable chance of influencing the leaderships concerned. In the immediate aftermath of a coup d'état, the EU's call for consultations is certain to be supported by both ACP group members and the donor community, while the new leadership is likely to be interested in the political and financial benefits it can derive from collaboration with the EU. When a country is involved in large-scale violent conflict which prevents its leadership from exercising control over its territory, the EU prefers to address the situation within the framework of broader multilateral efforts rather than through the mechanism of consultations. The inadequacy of this mechanism in conflict situations finds some support in the academic literature: 'The standard strategies for promoting democracy, including governance conditionality, tend to become ineffectual in crisis situations and can sometimes compound the problems that prompted the crisis in the first place' (Santiso 2003:152).

Development aid cut-offs: how successful?

The high rate of success of development aid cut-offs stands in sharp contrast with the record of CFSP sanctions, which are mostly unsuccessful. Here, in contrast, few episodes were total failures. The population of unsuccessful cases seems to be restricted to those targets simultaneously subject to CFSP sanctions or to chronic cases where coups d'état are recurrent. Tellingly, Guinea-Conakry and Togo are located in West Africa, the region characterised by the highest rate of military coups of sub-Saharan Africa (McGowan 2003). Consultations tend to (eventually) deliver the expected results, and whenever they fail, the suspension of development cooperation has often proved effective as a coercive tool. In virtually all cases, the EU is both an important trading partner and a major donor of the country in question. However, a central factor contributing to the success of consultations is backing for the EU's actions from the target's neighbours.

However, this positive record must be qualified with some considerations. First, the EU tends to call consultations with countries over which it expects to gain some influence. Art. 96 is not invoked in *every* case of the violation of human rights and democracy. This selective approach partly accounts for the high success rate. Secondly, an eventually positive outcome fails to reflect the fact that success in some cases was more complicated and tortuous than in others. The uncooperative Haitian authorities, as opposed to the more forthcoming coup leaders of the Central African Republic, are a case in point. Failed consultations under Lomé IV show that the amenability of ACP countries to EU influence cannot be taken for granted: Ivory Coast and Togo had taken part in consultations prior to 2000, with poor results. Thirdly, the fact that conditions were met to the extent considered sufficient by the EU for the full resumption of cooperation in 2002 did not prevent a recurrence of violence and grave human rights breaches in Ivory Coast. Moreover, EU officials resent the fact that leaderships that have behaved cooperatively during consultations are far more reluctant to implement reforms after their closure (interview 2007). The concentration on fair and free elections diverts attention from the fact that the establishment of stable democracies requires further conditions that may remain absent: 'the holding of elections has tended to be the main focus of international pressure, overlooking wider dimensions of the electoral system and the democratisation process' (Santiso 2003:153). The 'chronic' cases of Fiji, Côte d'Ivoire and Guinea-Conakry, where democracy does not take root despite repeated consultation efforts, reveal the limitations of this mechanism; however suitable it is in tackling crises, it remains inadequate to enable the consolidation of democratic rule. This is, however, a different issue: Art. 96 was designed as an emergency tool to redress violations of the 'essential elements' of the treaty, a purpose they accomplish to a mostly satisfactory degree.

When and why do aid suspensions work?

The central determinant for the success of EU development aid cut-offs remains the cooperative attitude of the leadership targeted. In a number of cases, coups d'état were conducted to unseat leaders with poor democratic records, and with the ultimate goal of restoring civilian democratic rule. These circumstances provided a 'favourable terrain' for consultations. In these cases, the EU found itself in the role of 'accompanying' a democratic transition alongside coup leaders willing to cooperate from the start. This was the case for the Central African Republic, and also for Mauritania and Guinea-Bissau, whose forthcoming attitudes prevented the EU from interrupting aid. One of the central benefits that the leadership obtains from participating in consultations is some degree of legitimacy. The EU's holding of consultations with the authorities constitutes a *de facto*, albeit not *de jure*, recognition of that body as the country's representative (Laakso et al. 2007:66). The fact that the EU treats them as interlocutors provides them with some legitimacy in a climate of volatility. This is especially the case when the commitments entered into by the leaders during the consultations are made public. The public nature of the consultations process has the effect of making the transitional authorities accountable not only internationally, but also domestically.

Legitimacy is not all, though. The disutility that the EU expects to inflict on the target via the suspension of aid arises from a series of interlinked considerations, which have a 'snowball effect' (Stokke 1995:43–45). The absence of donor support and of private foreign investment visibly weakens economic performance. The lack of new infrastructure projects creates a negative business environment in the country, which will then fail to attract foreign investment. Moreover, the donor community often coordinates its policies. The EU's withdrawal is often followed, if not preceded, by that of other donors such as the international financial institutions. Donor coordination is most evident in the fact that, to determine whether structural adjustment programmes can receive funding, the EU has accepted the criteria of the principal multilateral donors such as the IMF and the World Bank (Holland 2004:121). As a result, the government becomes unpopular with the general public and business elites. The multiple effects of aid suspension provide the concerned government with a strong incentive to avoid it.

The forthcoming attitude of certain coup leaders should not, however, obscure the fact that the ACP group is generally resentful of the EU's practice of freezing development aid. During consultations with Niger, the ACP group requested that the EU refrain from suspending aid, alleging that such a measure would punish the population and obstruct a return to democracy. In the aftermath of the failed 1998 consultations with Togo, the ACP group claimed that options for political dialogue had not been exhausted when consultations closed. Similarly, the ACP group regretted that the 2000 consultations with Haiti consisted in only one meeting, and appealed to the European side to 'engage in true consultations' with Haiti (ACP Press Release 5 February 2001).

Finally, the low proportion of non-African cases in the sample may obscure the role of the geographic location of the target. As a Caribbean state, Haiti belongs to the sphere of influence of the US, which contrasts with the prevalence of the EU in the sub-Saharan region. While the result of the consultations was eventually positive, the Haitian leadership proved less forthcoming than in other cases. The heavy involvement of the Organisation of American States in the resolution of the Haitian crisis seems to have strongly influenced the behaviour of the EU – the decision to resume aid has been described as being driven by the desire to appear as a 'credible partner' in the Consultative Group on Haiti (Laakso et al. 2006:37). Involvement with other interlocutors seems to have reduced the EU's room for manoeuvre.

Some authors, and especially EU officials, credit the highly institutionalised framework in which consultations take place for their success. 'Appropriate measures' have to be preceded by consultations invoked under Art. 96. These consultations provide a venue where the country in question has the opportunity to present a plan for remedying the breach of democracy and human rights by making specific commitments and drafting a timetable jointly with the EU. The suspension of development cooperation is a last-resort measure. The EU considers it only if consultations fail to produce satisfactory results. Transitional authorities have come to realise the benefits they can obtain from

Art. 96 consultations, in both political and financial terms. Finally, consultations also offer a venue to address politically sensitive issues, such as the question of slavery in Mauritania (García-Pérez 2007:8).

At first sight, the observer may be tempted to dismiss the argument that the institutional framework matters in favour of the more commonly accepted idea that the inherent inequality between the EU and developing countries explains their amenability, or simply that 'money talks'. However, this idea is contradicted by the manner in which the procedure for interrupting development aid has been progressively institutionalised. Most suspensions agreed in the early 1990s, when the non-execution clause did not yet exist, were unsuccessful. The establishment and perfection of a mechanism of consultation foreseeing intensive discussions at a high political level within a limited time frame in the direct aftermath of a crisis has been accompanied by an increase in satisfactory outcomes. Finally, the proliferation since 2000 of successful cases of Art. 96 consultations in which aid was not interrupted – for example Niger and Mauritania – seems to indicate that the existence of the consultation procedure not only facilitates the transitional period and the resumption of cooperation, but may even render the use of coercive instruments unnecessary. Only Guinea-Bissau provides a regrettable example of a target being shielded by its former ruler, where two consecutive rounds of consultations without suspension were unable to compel the country to implement institutional reforms. In addition, the existence of an institutionalised procedure has allowed the inventiveness of EU institutions to unfold. Not only have practices been perfected, but several innovations have been tried out. Notably, the approach of the 'gradual and conditional' resumption of aid piloted in Ivory Coast has become common practice.

7 Withdrawal of trade privileges under the Generalized System of Preferences

The granting of trade preferences to third countries by the EU in the form of the Generalized System of Preferences (GSP) constitutes a unilaterally granted benefit. Trade preferences granted to developing countries represent an exception of the WTO's Most-Favoured Nations (MFN) principle, which stipulates that members are not allowed to discriminate between trading partners. An exceptional clause allows for a more favourable treatment for imports stemming from developing countries. Tariff preferences additional to the WTO's MFN are granted by a number of industrialised countries. However, only the EU and the US link their GSP programmes to conditions (Bartels 2005:68). While the suspension of trade preferences is not considered a sanction by the EU, its study as a form of sanction has become established practice in political science scholarship (Hufbauer and Oegg 2003, Orbie and Tortell 2009). Table 7.1 displays the only two cases of GSP suspension so far.

The nature and legal framework of GSP withdrawal

The granting of GSP benefits by the EU

The granting of trade privileges to third countries by the EU under the General System of Preferences takes the form of a unilateral regulation. These preferences belong to the field of development cooperation, since they are designed to further the economic development of the third country to which they are applied. Unlike the human rights conditionality clauses embedded in bilateral agreements, unilateral regulations are not subject to negotiation with

Table 7.1 GSP withdrawal cases

	Measure	*Time Period*	*Goal*	Outcome
Burma	Suspension of GSP	2003- ongoing	Abolition of forced labour	No compliance
Belarus	Suspension of GSP	2007- ongoing	Improvement in freedom of trade unions	No compliance

the third country. While in the framework of bilateral agreements the third country concerned commits to the respect of human rights and democratic principles, this commitment is absent in the case of unilateral regulations such as the GSP.

The GSP scheme constitutes a perfect example of the thin line that separates 'positive' and 'negative' incentives. From a legal point of view, the suspension of trade privileges is not technically a sanction. However, several considerations warrant its inclusion in the present investigation. Firstly, the EU regards the use of trade preferences as a coercive instrument. Commissioner for External Relations Patten stated:

> In all our programmes, there is a clear conditionality linked to our assistance .... The Union has also developed quite an arsenal of sanctions and restrictive measures. These range from restrictions on visits and diplomatic contacts through the *suspension of aid or trade privileges* to fully fledged sanctions or embargoes, stopping trade, blocking transport and freezing financial assets and transactions.
>
> (Patten 1999b; my emphasis)

The juxtaposition of the terms 'sanctions' and 'restrictive measures' seems to suggest that each refers to a different set of measures. What is noteworthy is that the suspension of aid and trade privileges is classed among measures which are unambiguously considered sanctions, such as diplomatic sanctions, embargoes and financial sanctions. While the formulation is ambiguous, since in EU parlance they are used synonymously – 'restrictive measures' is the term generally used to refer to CFSP sanctions – it leaves no doubt about the fact that suspensions of aid or trade privileges are used to coerce. Secondly, the removal of a privilege is considered by targets as a sanction – certainly so by the targets of the two GSP suspensions studied here, Burma and Belarus. Finally, given that countries subject to GSP withdrawal are simultaneously the objects of CFSP sanctions, it is worth exploring the interrelations between the two sets of measures.

The legal-institutional framework: evolution and instruments

The aim of tariff preferences is to allow developing countries to increase their import revenues. Their emergence was the result of a decision of the United Nations Committee for Trade and Development of 1968 recommending the creation of a Generalized System of Tariff Preferences under which industrialised countries would grant trade preferences to all developing countries on a non-reciprocal and non-discriminatory basis, and authorising them to establish individual GSP schemes. The EC was the first to implement a GSP scheme in 1971. The EU's GSP grants products imported from GSP beneficiary countries either duty-free access to the Community market or a tariff reduction, depending on which of the GSP arrangements applies. The GSP is implemented by means of Council regulations in ten-year cycles. This unilateral regulation has from the outset contained a conditionality clause, called the 'social clause', in light of the social rights it intends to protect. The selection of the rights protected corresponds to an emerging consensus on the existence of certain 'core labour standards' recognised by virtually all states. According to the International Labour Organisation (ILO), the rights enshrined in Conventions Nr 87 and 98 on 'Freedom of Association and Collective Bargaining'; Nr 138 on 'Elimination of Exploitative Forms of Child Labour'; Nr 29 and 105 on the 'Prohibition of Forced Labour' and Nr 100 and 111 on 'Non-Discrimination in Employment' constitute the core labour standards. This list was confirmed by the 1995 Copenhagen World Social Summit.

The GSP social clauses represent a fine example of the combination of positive and negative conditionality. In the original scheme, beneficiary countries may request additional preferences if they had adopted and actually applied domestic legal provisions 'incorporating the substance' of the standards laid down in the relevant ILO Conventions (Art. 7 of the EC 3281/94 and EC 1256/96). In order to benefit from the scheme, the beneficiary's authorities must not only incorporate the substance of the ILO regulations, they must also provide proof of the measures taken in order to apply and monitor legislation effectively. In contrast, the non-execution clause is foreseen for cases where the beneficiary country practises any form of forced labour or exports goods made by prison inmates. The rationale for this distinction, granting a special status to the prohibition of forced labour, can be found in the fact that the Convention prohibiting it (Nr 29) is the ILO instrument ratified by the most states. In addition, the prohibition of forced labour enjoys the status of *ius cogens* – obligatory law of a superior status – and is covered by customary international law, which makes the prohibition valid and enforceable even in the absence of a contractual instrument. Subsequent GSP regulations have maintained this distinction.

There is an overlap between the rights covered by the regular human rights conditionality clause routinely employed by the EU, and the social clause, as some of the rights covered also fit into the category of civil and political rights. At the same time, this clause does not cover the entire range of social rights (Fierro 2003:366). The definition of a specific clause covering labour-related rights in the GSP Regulation may be the result of the idea that compliance is easier to achieve when protected rights are few in number, concrete, and identifiable. In any case, some streamlining took place in the subsequent GSP regulation by the dropping of this distinction. The special incentive arrangement includes the same rights as the temporary withdrawal clause. This approach has been criticised because it decreases the incentives for adherence to all standards. To trigger the incentives clause, all standards must be implemented, while if just one of them is breached the non-execution clause may be activated.

EC regulation provisions

So far, only two beneficiary countries have been suspended from the scheme, namely Burma in 1997 and Belarus in 2007. During the first suspension

(Burma), the scheme presented a fragmented legal basis, consisting of two Council regulations adopted in 1994 and 1996, granting preferences for various industrial and agricultural products respectively (EC 3281/94 and EC 1256/96). These were subsequently substituted by a single legal text to which are annexed the lists of products covered and eligible countries. The GSP regulation of 2005 provides for three different schemes. Beneficiary countries may enjoy preferences under:

1. The general arrangement.
2. The GSP+, a 'special incentive arrangement for sustainable development and good governance' stipulating even more favourable terms. Eligibility for this scheme is restricted to countries classified as 'vulnerable' (i.e. whose five largest sections of its GSP-covered imports to the Community represent more than 75 per cent in value of its total GSP-covered imports, and whose GSP-covered imports to the Community represent less than the 1 per cent in value of total GSP-covered imports to the Community). The scheme is granted to those countries which have ratified and 'effectively implemented' sixteen UN/ILO conventions on core human and labour rights, and at least seven of eleven conventions related to the environment and governance principles.
3. The special arrangement for the least developed countries (LDCs), also known as the *Everything but Arms* (EBA) initiative, provides for the most favourable treatment of all.

Subsequent reforms of the GSP regulation have allocated increasing weight to ILO assessments. While the initial regulations only required beneficiaries to implement the substance of some conventions, the ratification and effective implementation of the eight fundamental ILO Conventions became a necessary condition in the regulation of 2005 (Orbie and Tortell 2009:671).

Procedure leading to GSP withdrawal

The possibility of temporary withdrawal of preferential arrangements was introduced in 1995. At that stage, withdrawal could take place only on grounds of 'forced labour' or 'export of goods made by prison labour', which were extended in 2001 to '*serious and systematic violation of any standards referred to in the ILO Declaration on Fundamental Principles and Rights at Work*' (Orbie and Tortell 2009:668). Currently, withdrawal is foreseen for any of the following reasons:

1. Serious and systematic violations of principles laid down in the core human rights and labour conventions on the basis of the conclusions of the relevant monitoring bodies;
2. Export of goods made by prison labour;
3. Serious shortcomings in customs controls related to drug-trafficking, or failure to comply with international conventions on money laundering;

4. Serious and systematic unfair trading practices;
5. Serious and systematic infringements of the objectives of regional fishery organisations;
6. Reversal of the adoption of relevant legislation, or failure to implement the same: it is explicitly mentioned that withdrawal will result 'if the national legislation no longer incorporates those conventions referred to in Annex III which have been ratified in fulfilment of the requirements of Art. 9, or if that legislation is not effectively implemented'.

The Commission and the member states are entitled to request consultations with the Committee if they receive information that might justify the temporary withdrawal of preferences. The launch of an investigation leading to the withdrawal of the GSP can only be triggered by a duly substantiated complaint from a natural or legal person, or an association not endowed with a legal personality, which can demonstrate it has an interest in the temporary withdrawal. The Commission does not have the power to open the investigation on its own initiative. This complaint must be accompanied by all the documentary evidence required by the Commission in order to examine its admissibility and determine the relevance of the allegations made. The decision to open an investigation is subsequently taken by the Commission after consulting the member states in the Committee for the Management of Generalized Preferences, where it considers sufficient evidence exists. Following the consultations, the Commission has one month to decide to initiate an investigation. If it decides to do so, it is obliged to publish a notice in the Official Journal of the European Union calling for interested parties to communicate their views in writing. The Commission then completes what is a remarkably exhaustive inquiry. Apart from the general call issued in the Official Journal, the regulation mentions the assessments and recommendations of international organisations such as the ILO as the point of departure of the investigation. The regulation provides for the extensive participation of the beneficiary country at fault, which shall be provided 'with every opportunity to cooperate in the investigation'. The Commission can terminate the investigation if it considers that the findings do not justify withdrawal. Otherwise, it announces to the beneficiary country that it intends to submit a proposal to the Council for withdrawal, unless the country concerned commits to remedy the breach. The Commission monitors and evaluates the situation for a period of six months. In the absence of progress during this period, it submits a proposal to the Council, which decides by qualified majority to withdraw the GSP or not. In the event of a decision to withdraw, it is stipulated that the decision shall enter into force six months later.

The highly institutionalised nature of the procedure for GSP withdrawal recalls ACP Art. 96 consultations, as it provides for direct contacts with the authorities at fault and for the regular monitoring of the situation, including the dispatch of fact-finding missions to the country. The prominence of the Commission's role in the process, especially in its initiation, is another point the two procedures hold in common. Yet another similarity between ACP Art.

96 consultations and GSP suspensions is the presence of a series of 'antechambers', allowing multiple opportunities for formal exchanges between the EU and the third country. Opportunities for contacts with non-state actors, including economic operators, local opposition and civil society, and international NGOs during the investigation are ample. However, a fundamental difference is the length of the process, whose deadlines allow a 'creeping process' of almost two years. Nevertheless, the rationale for this prolonged period appears justified. Firstly, it ensures that every withdrawal is based on solid evidence; secondly, it provides the authorities of the beneficiary country with generous opportunities for dialogue and for correcting its misbehaviour.

The conditionality embedded in the GSP scheme has been criticised for setting a high threshold for benefiting from the privileges, in particular for GSP+. This, it is argued, may detract from the attractiveness of the scheme (Orbie et al. 2005:166–67; Orbie 2010). It is also striking that the causes for suspension extend to very heterogeneous fields – from unfair trading practices to the failure to comply with norms on money laundering. This situation belittles the moral authority of the provision on prison labour, which is further weakened by its formulation. It is not prison labour that triggers the suspension, but the 'export of goods made by prison labour'. Furthermore, the regulation envisages withdrawal on the abovementioned grounds not merely as a measure to promote the objectives of those conventions, but also 'to ensure that no beneficiary receives unfair advantage through continuous violation of those conventions' (point 18 of preamble, p.2).

Withdrawal of the GSP: what kind of sanction?

To the extent that GSP withdrawal can be considered a sanction, it is a mild one, as it implies no more than the re-establishment of normal trade flows. However, its impact is highly dependent on the level of development of the suspended beneficiary. While it has major consequences for LDCs or 'vulnerable' countries, its impact on developed countries – such as Belarus – is minor. Fundamental differences from other frameworks for human rights conditionality lie not only in the delimitation of the rights covered, but especially in the specification of the conditions for readmittance to the scheme. The regulation suspending Burma's access to the GSP stipulates:

> The Council … shall bring the application of this regulation to an end in the light of a Commission report on forced labour in Myanmar, showing that the practices mentioned in Art. 9(1) … of regulations 1256 which have caused the withdrawal of access to the generalized preferences from Myanmar no longer exist.
>
> (Council of the European Union 1996a)

The specificity of this provision contrasts with the pattern found in CFSP Common Positions, where the practice of including the conditions for lifting in CFSP instruments started almost a decade after the first GSP withdrawal. The 'social clause' also presents an advantage, compared with the human rights clauses embedded in bilateral treaties. Given that the GSP is a unilateral instrument, it provides the EU with a legal basis to pursue human rights objectives in the form of conditionality in countries not bound by a bilateral agreement with the Community. This is the case for both of the suspended beneficiaries.

GSP withdrawal practice

Burma

Burma was the first country to have its GSP preferences withdrawn by the EU, and indeed remained the only case for almost a decade. The Burmese case set a precedent in procedural terms, as the procedure for withdrawal in later EC GSP regulations was modelled on the steps followed here. The suspension procedure was triggered by a joint complaint to the Commission issued by the European Trade Union Confederation (ETUC) and the International Confederation of Free Trade Unions (ICFTU) in June 1995. The Commission opened a consultation in the GSP Committee, which released an opinion favourable to the opening of an investigation. The Commission did not obtain permission from the Burmese authorities to dispatch a fact-finding mission to the country, and the investigation that followed, which included hearings with NGOs and experts, pointed to the existence of forced labour. The Burmese authorities contested the Commission's charges on legal grounds, arguing that the practice was covered by an exception in ILO Convention Nr 29 allowing the population to carry out work as part of community service (Art. 2(2)), an interpretation which was challenged by the ILO. The Commission also consulted representatives of the democratically elected government of Burma, which was favourable to the GSP withdrawal. The decision on withdrawal was eventually taken by the Council in March 1997 (Council of the European Union 1997a). Equally, and despite its recognised status as one of the least developed countries in the world, the EU excluded Burma from the *Everything but Arms* scheme for states classified by the UN as Least Developed Countries (LDCs) initiated in 2001, which entitles this group of countries to more favourable terms of trade than those of the GSP.

IMPACT AND EFFICACY

More than ten years after the withdrawal of EU trade preferences from Burma, no progress towards the abolition of forced labour has been recorded. Only the trade sanctions imposed by the US, which were initiated with the withdrawal of GSP in 1989, are known to have displayed a noticeable economic impact on the population, as they are reported to have forced the closure of a number of garment factories, leaving their workers unemployed (Steinberg

2003). By contrast, the suspension of GSP by the EU is reported to have had a minor impact on the Burmese economy (Lerch 2004:259).

However, the non-granting of trade preferences under the GSP and *Everything but Arms* schemes has been singled out as one of the measures affecting the economy generally, and by implication penalising the general population. Pointing to Burma's status as a labour-intensive agricultural country whose GDP is mostly generated in the private sector, Tonkin argues that 'any assault on the formal economy is ... bound to have its effect on the ordinary people, who at the very least will continue to suffer stagnation in their living standards and more probably a deterioration' (Tonkin 2006:3). Indeed, the case of GSP suspension in Burma underlines an inherent contradiction in the idea of withdrawing trade preferences from countries where undesirable labour practices exist. By reverting to less favourable terms of trade, the general economic situation of the country worsens, which is in turn likely to translate into an increase in child and forced labour.

CODING SUMMARY

The outcome of the coercive effort was nil; thus, the EU sanctions contribution is accordingly nil (contr 0). The EU is Burma's fifth trade partner according to EU 2007 statistics. The withdrawal is a measure of economic nature, which in a context of poor economic performance causes some noticeable impact (eco 1), and hardly endangers the leadership's permanence in power (grip 0). It does enjoy some international support, but only from Western countries, notably the US and Canada, who levied comparable measures (int 0). The measure was managed consistently (coh 1).

Belarus

The process of suspension of GSP privileges to Belarus was triggered by a joint request to the Commission by three international trade unions, the International Confederation of Free Trade Unions (ICFTU), the European Trade Union Confederation (ETUC) and the World Confederation of Labour (WCL), in January 2003 on the basis of alleged violations of the ILO Conventions Nos 87 and 98, which concern freedom of association and the right to collective bargaining. In December of the same year, the Commission initiated an investigation which corroborated the existence of serious and systematic violations of these rights. In parallel with, but independently from, the Commission's process, the ILO had appointed a Commission of Inquiry to investigate trade union freedom in Belarus, which issued twelve recommendations in July 2004, urging Belarus to implement them within a one-year time frame. In view of the lack of implementation, the Commission initiated the six-month period of monitoring and evaluation of the labour rights situation in June 2005, and announced that it intended to submit a proposal for withdrawal to the Council unless Belarus 'made a commitment to take the measures necessary to conform with the principles referred to in the 1998 ILO Declaration on Fundamental Principles and Rights at Work' (Council of the European Union 2006e:37).

While the Belarusian authorities failed to make the required commitments, they endeavoured to give the impression of compliance. First, they presented a report on the situation of freedom of association rights in Belarus in March 2006. After analysing the report, the Commission concluded that it did not contain sufficient evidence of commitment. Indeed, an ILO follow-up report adopted in the same month pointed to an actual worsening in the situation of trade union rights in Belarus. Two months later, Belarus issued a communication on the situation of freedom of association rights, which was again judged insufficient by the Commission. This opinion was confirmed by the ILO. A new letter sent by Belarus in October 2006 was assessed again by the Commission as lacking any 'indication of effective implementation of ILO Conventions Nr 87 and No 98' (Council of the European Union 2006e:39).

In accordance with the procedure stipulated for GSP schemes in 2006, the Regulation is meant to enter into force only six months after its adoption 'unless the reason justifying it no longer prevails' (Council of the European Union 2006e:39). As in the Burma Regulation, the conditions for reversing the withdrawal of the scheme are spelled out in Art. 2 in the following terms: 'The Council ... shall re-establish the preferential arrangement for products originating in Belarus, if the violations of the freedom of association and of the right to collective bargaining in Belarus no longer exist' (Council of the European Union 2006e:40). In a December 2006 speech, trade Commissioner Peter Mandelson declared: 'Almost four years after the start of the withdrawal process ... Belarus has not taken any real, tangible measure to remedy the situation' (Mandelson 2006). In the absence of progress by Belarusian authorities in the six months that followed, the Regulation entered into force in June 2007.

IMPACT AND EFFICACY

The withdrawal was not expected to cause any substantial harm to the Belarusian economy, as only 12 per cent of Belarusian exports to the EU were covered by the GSP. Belarus had not even taken full advantage of the preferences before their withdrawal (Kryvoi 2007). Only 57 per cent of the potential benefits were exploited. Although it is difficult to evaluate the actual impact of the withdrawal, since the regulation entered into force as recently as mid-2007, the economic harm caused by the GSP withdrawal is generally considered to be marginal (Bosse and Korosteleva-Polglase 2009). In the view of one official, 'the political aspect of the withdrawal is more important; it is rather a political sign' (interview 2007). It is evident that the procedure created some discomfort for the Belarusian authorities, given that they engaged in several last-minute efforts to avert the decision on withdrawal. This is especially remarkable, given that these reports were not accompanied by any sincere endeavour to remedy the situation; on the contrary, the ILO detected a deterioration in the situation of trade unions in Belarus. Yet the leadership seemed to prefer to create at least the impression that the withdrawal of trade preferences was due more to a difference of opinion with the Commission than to its own failure to take corrective action.

CODING SUMMARY

So far, the withdrawal has been futile, thus, the EU sanctions contribution is zero (contr 0). The sanctions have been managed consistently, given that there were no developments to reciprocated (coh 1). It is a measure of economic nature with noticeable impact (eco 1), given the high level of trade between Belarus and bordering EU members Poland and Lithuania. The EU is Belarus's second trading partner, according to 2006 European Commission statistics. The measure hardly endangers the leadership's permanence in power (grip 0). The withdrawal enjoys some international support, but only from Western countries, notably the US and Canada, which suspended their trade preferences some ten years before the EU did (int 0).

Evaluating GSP withdrawal

The interface between GSP withdrawal and CFSP sanctions: Burma and Belarus

GSP withdrawals are endowed with a number of 'antechambers' which provide the concerned leadership with numerous opportunities to avoid an eventual withdrawal. If the authorities submit sufficient evidence to the Commission proving that they are taking steps to remedy the breach to the ILO Conventions, the Commission can terminate the investigation. Fierro documented how, by showing a cooperative attitude, Pakistan managed not only to prevent the withdrawal, but to even bring about the disbursement of additional aid to help it address the breach (Fierro 2003:375). In addition to the opportunities that the leadership is granted during the process, following the conclusion of the investigation the procedure foresees two six-month periods during which the authorities are able to take corrective measures, both in the run-up to and in the aftermath of the Council decision. Finally, the conditions for reversing the withdrawal are clearly spelled out, and the Council's decision to grant access to the GSP scheme is taken by qualified majority. This situation contrasts with CFSP sanctions, where the decision as to whether compliance is sufficient to lift the sanctions is left to the discretion of the Council, which decides by unanimity. This overall state of affairs would suggest that regaining access to the GSP scheme would be easier than securing the lifting of CFSP sanctions. Yet neither of the suspended beneficiaries has seriously attempted to redress the GSP withdrawal. However, it may well be the status of the suspended beneficiaries as targets of CFSP sanctions that prevents them from taking any steps toward regaining GSP access. The interrelation between CFSP sanctions and GSP withdrawal reveals itself in the 2005 regulation, which reads: 'Due to the *political situation* in Myanmar, temporary withdrawal of all tariff preferences in respect of imports of products originating in Myanmar should remain in force' (Council of the European Union 1997:2; my emphasis).

This provision is contrary to the 1997 regulation withdrawing access to the GSP, which stipulated that the regulation would cease to apply when the practices of forced labour disappeared, rather than when the 'political situation' changed. This reformulation of the conditions for lifting indicates that access to GSP preferences will not be granted to Burma unless the objectives of the CFSP Common Position are fulfilled, giving the impression that the withdrawal of the GSP, rather than being a separate measure, has been subsumed into the CFSP sanctions regime. While there is no evidence that this interpretation corresponds to the calculations of the target, this circumstance would render superfluous the benefits arising from the specificity of the conditions for lifting.

In conclusion, the overlap between GSP withdrawals and CFSP sanctions can be held to obstruct the efficacy of the first of these measures. While GSP withdrawals present characteristics that appear to facilitate their lifting, the presence of CFSP sanctions may prevent targets from benefiting from these advantageous features. This is especially the case since, as in the non-case of Pakistan, the Commission is ready to settle for suboptimal outcomes – i.e. the persistence of child labour – as long as the responsible authorities demonstrate that they are addressing the problem.

When does the EU withdraw GSP privileges?

Belarus and Burma constitute an odd pair in the EU's record of GSP withdrawals. The selection of targets, and in particular the dismissal of the Pakistani case, has left analysts puzzled by the criteria the EU follows when withdrawing preferences. Observers pointed to the imbalance between the breaches committed by each of these governments, noting that 'the magnitude of violations of core labour standards is very different'. While in Burma thousands of civilians were forcibly recruited and put to work, in Belarus the reported violations 'did not amount to torture, physical injuries or systematic use of force' (Kryvoi 2007:38–39). The fact that both kinds of breaches are penalised with identical measures appears disproportionate, adding a new peculiarity to the GSP suspension regime. It has been posited that the degree of government involvement in labour rights violations is central to triggering penalties. Labour rights violations in Burma and Belarus were perpetrated by the authorities themselves, while in Pakistan they took place in the private sector. Thus, while the Belarusian and Burmese governments are directly responsible for the violations, the Pakistani government can be blamed only for its failure to enforce labour rights (Kryvoi 2007).[1] However, the reason why these particular countries were suspended seems to lie with the ILO assessment. Orbie and Tortell detected a clear consistency between the application of GSP sanctions by the

EU and the hierarchy of ILO condemnation: since 1995, the ILO has only established a Commission of Inquiry, which is the highest instance in terms of condemnation, with regard to Burma and Belarus. Thus, the EU appears to have set a high threshold for suspension: it withdraws trade preferences only in cases in which the ILO has unambiguously held that the breach of labour standards has been persistent and serious (Orbie and Tortell 2009:675–76).

A conspicuous feature of the countries under GSP suspension, Burma and Belarus, is that both are simultaneously subject to CFSP sanctions. This overlap is all the more surprising since, in principle, the two types of sanctions are unrelated. The withdrawal of the GSP and CFSP sanctions appear to be unconnected measures, given that they are taken on different grounds (labour standards as opposed to the more general CFSP objectives), rest on different legal bases (unilateral regulations as opposed to CFSP instruments) and are subject to different levels of involvement of EU institutions (the predominance of the Commission as opposed to intergovernmental cooperation in the Council). The similarities between the cases of Belarus and Burma are therefore evident. In both cases, the imposition of CFSP sanctions predates the withdrawal of the GSP. Despite their differences, both are under authoritarian rule and have been the object of ever-tightening CFSP sanctions regimes. The fact that the situation of trade unions is often precarious in countries under non-democratic regimes could justify the link between CFSP sanctions and GSP suspension.

Still, the relation between the types of sanctions thus appears to lie elsewhere. Targets of CFSP sanctions are more likely to be suspended from the GSP scheme than others, given that, in the absence of a contractual relationship and high-level contacts, there is no other framework available in which breaches of the ILO Conventions can be addressed. It is revealing that CFSP sanctions predated GSP investigations in both cases. Secondly, some degree of CFSP contamination is visible in the reference to the Burmese 'political situation' in the latest GSP regulation. Finally, a certain inconsistency in the selection of targets also emanates from the Commission's and the Committee's discretion to open and close investigations. This arises partly from the bizarre legal situation that entitles affected third parties, but not the Parliament or the Commission itself, to initiate investigations into breaches of the social clause standards.

In this light, the small number of cases of GSP withdrawal is hardly surprising. The social clause embedded in these unilateral regulations functions as a 'default' instrument. Given the overlap between the rights covered in the social and human rights clauses, the EU will first open political dialogue with the beneficiary country in question to address the issues that may lead to withdrawal. In the case of non-compliance, it would then consider activating the human rights clause included in the bilateral agreements before opening an investigation. In the case of ACP countries, the subject would be discussed in the course of Art. 96 consultations. From this vantage point, it comes as no surprise that the two existing cases of suspensions were already, as Fierro has put it, 'on the blacklist of the international community' (Fierro 2003:371). No contractual relation with the EU existed at the time of withdrawal with either Burma or

Belarus, and high-level dialogue had been suspended for several years by the time investigations were initiated. Indeed, the freezing of negotiations on a PCA was one of the first measures taken by the EU in response to the constitutional crisis in Belarus, while the limitation of contacts was one of the measures included in the first round of sanctions in both cases.

Nevertheless, the contrast between the grounds on which Burma and Belarus were suspended remains stark. While in the Burmese case the withdrawal was based on documented evidence of forced and prison labour in the country, Belarus's suspension was motivated by the Commission's finding that 'Belarus is impeding the right to establish trade union organisations freely, the right to organize, the right to choose among trade union organisations, and the right of such organisations to legal recognition and to external funding' (Commission of the European Communities 2006b: point 5). The EU decision to suspend Belarus was opposed by some neighbouring countries, given that the withdrawal of GSP preferences would be bound to have adverse effects on cross-border enterprises with Lithuanian and Polish involvement. Finally, the list of GSP withdrawals is unlikely to display any consistency, due to the fact that Community institutions such as the Parliament, or indeed the Commission itself, are not entitled to instigate the investigation procedure. An official from one of the international trade unions involved in the initiation of the Burma complaint recognises that the international standing of the beneficiary plays a role in the decision to submit a complaint, claiming that a complaint against an important power in the world economy was unlikely to succeed. Yet, he also acknowledges the gravity of the breaches: 'The degree of human rights violations does have an impact. Burma is considered one of the worse in the world' (interview 2005). In any case, the fact that Burma was joined in the list of suspended beneficiaries by a country with lesser violations of core standards can be easily explained by the progressive broadening of grounds susceptible to warrant the withdrawal. The originally rather narrow 'practice of forced labour' and 'export of goods made by prison labour' has been widened, thereby enlarging the potential population of targets as compared to the mid-1990s.

GSP withdrawal: how (un)successful, and why?

GSP withdrawals have the worst record of success of all EU sanctions. As one analyst has observed, 'the situation with freedom of association in Belarus and with forced labour in Myanmar has not improved despite the sanctions introduced by the EU' (Kryvoi 2007:46). The low N does not allow any meaningful exploration of the reasons behind this failure. However, it is plausible to venture the conclusion that the presence of CFSP sanctions was an obstructive factor. Targets perceived the withdrawal of GSP as 'yet another sanctions regime' through which the West attempted to undermine them. This impression may have been reinforced by the Council Regulation's reference to the political situation in Burma as the reason for the withdrawal. This spill-over from CFSP sanctions may have reinforced the leadership's impression that the suspension of the GSP would not be reversed until the demands of the CFSP sanctions are met, i.e. when the transition to a civilian government is completed. In the Burmese case, the effects on the economy were more noticeable than in Belarus, where the leadership's attempt to avert the measure was due to prestige considerations rather than a desire to avoid economic harm.

The apparently 'compartmental nature' of GSP withdrawals suggests that compliance should be more forthcoming than with CFSP sanctions, given that the conditions for renewed access to the scheme are restricted to a single, specific and verifiable objective. This could make suspended beneficiaries more likely to comply than with CFSP aims such as democratic transition, which equates to the replacement of the current rulers by a democratically elected leadership. However, the 'basic labour standards' that the EU intends to promote through the GSP scheme do have a certain – if remote – bearing on the leadership's grip on power. This is most evident in the case of Belarus, where the granting of freedom of speech and association is directly linked to the strengthening of civil society and political opposition. Thus, respect for these rights is perceived as endangering the leaderships' power base. For the impoverished Burma, the existence of forced and prison labour is not directly linked to the emergence of a challenge to the junta's rule. However, the leadership presents forced labour as a 'community service', i.e. as a resource that alleviates the state's inability to provide services to the population. In this sense, both motives for withdrawal are directly or indirectly linked to the political situation in the affected countries.

8 Sanctions theory and the efficacy of EU sanctions

Some fresh air coming into the sanctions debate

The findings stemming from the examination of the efficacy of EU sanctions practice have significant implications for the understanding of the operation of targeted sanctions and for the international role of the European Union. The most original finding of the investigation consists in the connexion between the legal framework under which the sanctions are wielded and their efficacy. This unexpected outcome points to a pattern whereby ACP Art. 96 suspensions prove most successful, CFSP sanctions achieve their objectives only sometimes, and informal sanctions are often abandoned in the absence of any progress. The residual category of GSP withdrawal encompasses only two episodes, both unsuccessful, which can hardly bear any lesson in view of their concurrent status as CFSP sanctions targets. The coincidence between the legal framework chosen for the imposition of sanctions and the outcome of the coercive attempt warrants closer exploration.

Art. 96 suspensions constitute one of the most homogeneous groups in the EU sanctions universe, and thus lend themselves to generalisations. The abundant successes in this group contrast sharply with the predominance of failures in the rest of the universe. The most straightforward explanation is the presence of a selection bias. There is support for this idea in each of the groups: Art. 96 can only be invoked with ACP countries which reduce *a priori* the population of potential targets. However, sanctions are not applied to *every* ACP country through Art. 96 exclusively. Consultations susceptible of leading to suspension are called only in cases of coups d'état and in the absence of hostilities. ACP countries endowed with strategic importance become the object of CFSP sanctions. Never summoned for consultations, oil-rich Nigeria and Sudan became CFSP sanctions targets. In view of the acute crises of Zimbabwe and Guinea-Conakry, the EU wielded both Art. 96 *and* CFSP measures. While in Sudan some fighting with rebel groups made the situation less amenable to consultations than cases free of armed conflict, the type of situation addressed in Nigeria, Guinea-Conakry and Zimbabwe largely corresponds to the democratic crises that characterise the rest of the Art. 96 suspensions universe.

The selection bias becomes most visible in the case of the CFSP and informal sanctions. The choice between enshrining the sanctions in a CFSP instrument versus adopting them informally is unconnected to any geographical criteria or prior contractual relationship between the EU and the target. Such decisions remain political in nature and are left almost entirely to the Council's discretion. The legal definition of the frameworks requires breaches in democratic rule, good governance or human rights to invoke Art. 96. Violations of the ILO Conventions are required to activate the GSP suspension mechanism. However, the EU has flexibility in determining the goals of CFSP and informal measures, as they do not feature as a response to violations in pre-existing unilateral or contractual frameworks. CFSP sanctions must merely be linked to the pursuance of the objectives of the CFSP stipulated in Title V of the TEU. In reality, these are defined so broadly that they can accommodate a large variety of demands, featuring the preservation of peace 'in conformity with the principles of the UN Charter', the strengthening of the security of the Union 'in all ways', the development of 'democracy and the rule of law' and 'respect for human rights and fundamental freedoms' (TEU, p.14). The informal arms embargo on China corresponds to a type of sanction which is recurrent in CFSP practice. Many measures, however, are *sui generis* and imposed on a one-off basis, such as the cocktail sanctions against Cuba or the pseudo-sanctions against Russia. The reluctance to act under the legal framework of the CFSP can be ascribed to a weak determination to pursue the sanctions or a fragile consensus among member states vis-à-vis a controversial target, which prevents the Council from legally committing to the measures. Similarly, the EU has chosen to withdraw GSP only from those countries that have been found by the ILO Commission of Inquiry to persist in systematic violations of core labour standards. Taken together, the different groups form a 'hierarchy of tractability': Art. 96 suspensions are employed whenever there is a reasonable expectation of success, while CFSP sanctions are reserved for more intractable cases. The apex is represented by the informal sanctions, which are wielded in cases where not only is the expectation of efficacy low, but the internal cohesion in the EU is fragile. While the selection bias explains Council behaviour in the choice of framework and instruments, it is unable to fully account for the core concern of the present investigation: the efficacy of sanctions in bringing about their intended aims. The positive record of Art. 96 suspensions is particularly puzzling, given that it contradicts the hypothesis that sanctions are less likely to be effective when they threaten the leadership's permanence of power. This is certainly true in a group composed almost exclusively of sanctions geared towards the restoration of democratic rule following a military coup. Several interconnected explanations can be advanced.

It is tempting to conclude that ACP suspensions are effective because they deprive the target of substantial economic benefits in terms of tariff preferences and aid; in ACP countries material and non-material aspects can hardly be wholly dissociated from each other. Given that the conditionality criteria for the allocation of aid from the international financial institutions and the EU are comparable, EU suspensions are typically accompanied – if not preceded – by identical measures by other donors. Another aspect is what could be labelled 'transitory legitimacy'. Being a recipient of development aid and an interlocutor of the EU is a source of prestige for leaders vis-à-vis other ACP countries, the domestic political elite, and the general public. This is especially valued by transitional authorities with fragile legitimacy. The impact of EU cut-offs is magnified by their secondary – or 'snowball' – effects. Private economic operators are likely to move their businesses to neighbouring countries offering more favourable economic environments. Foreign businesses prefer to invest in countries which are recipients of aid, as this indicates that the country is stable, and because they can only obtain export credits for operations conducted in such third-states. The economic aspect is closely linked to the question of international support. EU objectives frequently find support among the neighbours of the target country, and some ACP members of the target's choice are allowed to participate in the consultation process which precedes suspension. Thus, the economic and symbolic harm inflicted on the target and the international cooperation variables combine to maximise the impact of the sanctions in this group. In this sense, the centrality of the economic element to the Art. 96 tool refers us back to classical sanctions theory. While Art. 96 suspensions fall short of blanket trade embargoes, this measure can induce compliance by fear of destabilisation in the sense suggested by Galtung. Withdrawing trade preferences from states whose economies depend on exports to the EU can provoke social unrest, or even an upheaval which could unseat those in power.

While in most cases the objective of the sanctions was the organisation of free elections that could easily unseat rulers, perpetrators are often prepared to restore democratic rule after staging a coup d'état with the aim of dislodging authoritarian rulers. This circumstance makes the influence attempt less challenging. Perpetrators sometimes undergo a genuine 'learning process' as members of the military profession who discover, once in power, that the withdrawal of aid by external donors threatens to bring about the collapse of the country's economy. This underscores that a key dimension to the EU–ACP relationship is the economic incentive, a reflection of how ACP dependence on aid and tariff preferences facilitates EU influence over these countries. This situation involves a stark inherent inequality between both groups which is absent in other frameworks. Art. 96 suspensions are likely to inflict considerable economic damage on the targets, countries dependent on trade links with the EU and deprived of regional protectors. This group includes countries of doubtful viability in the absence of external aid. Several ACP countries belong to the group classified as Least Developed Countries (LDC).

As repeatedly highlighted by scholars, the relationship between the EU and the ACP states is unique, 'unparalleled for its time' (Holland 2004:125). But which aspects of this partnership, beyond the link of economic dependence, account for the successful resolution of challenges to democratic rules endemic to the ACP group? The partnership is based on a contractual agreement which enshrines respect for certain principles – 'essential' elements – whose violation gives rise to the suspension of the treaty. In other words, a contractual agreement stipulates that these principles need to be respected, and that failure to do so can provoke the suspension of development aid. This creates a situation of legal certainty, especially given that the treaty currently provides clear definitions of the 'essential' elements. In particular, the consultation procedure offers a relatively amicable venue for conciliation, constituting an 'antechamber' to suspension which can render the adoption of sanctions unnecessary. In its current configuration, the consultation procedure offers the party in breach the possibility of averting sanctions by redressing the violation. Indeed, sanctions are only imposed where the ACP state affected refuses to make commitments or consistently fails to abide by them. The EU may release additional funds to support the government's compliance. The highly structured nature of the consultations procedure can partly be credited with the successes observed in this group. A glimpse at the cut-offs performed before the introduction of the suspension mechanism under Lomé VI *bis* in 1995, which displays a higher number of failures, suggests that the availability of the institutionalised procedure of consultations, coupled with the legal certainty in which that process is embedded, played a role in the efficacy of these measures. In addition to this 'antechamber', the ACP–EU framework relies on a long-standing and mature comprehensive political dialogue. It is virtually all-encompassing: 'any subject could be addressed' (Arts 2005:161). It acts as a 'pre-antechamber' in which the EU can discuss its expectations well before the situation degenerates to the point that the EU contemplates sanctions. The legal and procedural arrangements for conducting political dialogue have gradually increased in sophistication: ACP countries have a 'uniquely long history of political dialogue' with the EU. Scholars continuously emphasise the unique nature of the EU–ACP contract. Despite some shortcomings, Arts describes the headway made in ACP–EU political dialogue as 'unique, certainly when compared to other fora, on all accounts' (Arts 2005:158). Holland celebrates that the EU–ACP Partnership links 'politics, trade and aid in an as yet untested way' (Holland 2004:125). The efficacy of ACP sanctions can be regarded as a reflection of the synergy produced by such linking.

Thus, with the notable exception of the predicted failure of pro-democracy sanctions, the findings from the examination of ACP suspensions underscore the validity of the selected variables. Through the consultation procedure, targets are offered ample institutional 'antechambers' prior to suspension. With a single actor – the Commission – bearing responsibility for conducting the consultations, benchmarking commitments and monitoring their implementation, the sanctions strategy is consistently managed. The sanctions strategies were reasonably coherent, in the sense that progress by the leadership in the implementation of commitments was rewarded with the resumption of aid. The introduction of the 'gradual and conditional' approach to aid resumption constituted a major step in facilitating responsiveness to partial implementation of EU demands.

Those factors which, beyond the economic element, facilitate the success of sanctions seem to corroborate Drezner's proposition that sanctions are more effective when imposed against friends than when wielded against enemies. At the same time, the observer's attention is drawn to the contrast between the presence of sophisticated procedures involved in the suspension, monitoring of implementation and resumption of aid and the absence thereof in the CFSP framework. The emphasis on dialogue and the legal necessity of calling consultations with the ACP country at the highest level prior to deciding on suspension appears to offer a useful venue for negotiation in which the EU, represented solely by the Commission, speaks with 'one voice'. Of central importance is that once both parties have agreed on a timetable in the consultation phase, the Commission conducts its own regular monitoring of progress by the target in accordance with pre-established benchmarks. This situation considerably reduces the difficulties posed by a composite actor like the Council, where each member state relies on its own assessment, often following diverging criteria. The use of qualified majority voting for partial suspension eliminates the possibility of veto by one single member state, thus facilitating both the imposition and the termination of the measures. While Art. 96 procedures have been criticised for their rigidity and slowness (Laakso et al. 2007), the highly structured nature of the suspension and resumption procedure, coupled with the Commission's role in negotiating with the target and monitoring its progress, can be held to be favourable to sanctions efficacy.

The suggestion that the likelihood of success increases when the Commission is in charge is at first sight disconfirmed by the sad failure of the GSP withdrawals. However, a record of only two episodes makes this group hardly representative – if not negligible – while the fact that the delinquent beneficiaries are simultaneously CFSP sanctions targets does not allow an assessment of the efficacy of this tool in isolation. Finally, a closer look at the procedure leading to withdrawal reveals that, while highly structured and endowed with plenty of antechambers, it is not as genuinely led by the Commission as are Art. 96 consultations. It is not in the power of the Commission to initiate the procedure. Largely due to the lack of in-house expertise in DG Trade, increasing weight has been placed on ILO evaluations, to the extent that the EU has so far withdrawn preferences only from those countries with grave breaches in the eyes of the ILO Commission of Inquiry. As a result of its reluctance to make use of the withdrawal option, the EU has suspended only the most intractable delinquents of labour standards. By contrast, the positive impact of the Commission-led, structured nature of Art. 96 procedure is underscored by the failure of the early ACP suspensions. Cases of suspension in the pre-Lomé IV *bis* era almost invariably remained ineffective. After the introduction of the suspension clause, the failure of Art. 96 is more often the exception than the rule. Trends are conspicuous: as the legal tools were perfected, both the frequency of suspensions and their success rate increased. In the Cotonou era, some consultations managed to bring about a return to democratic rule in the absence of suspension, an encouraging development. Most ACP sanctions failures are to be found in episodes from the early 1990s, where the procedure was still at an embryonic stage – albeit some of the targets of that period might represent the most intractable cases in the entire ACP experience. Failure remains pervasive in a number of countries where coups are chronic: Guinea-Conakry, Côte d'Ivoire or Fiji. The persistence of instability in these countries, however, cannot be ascribed to Art. 96 sanctions. Devised as an emergency remedy geared towards the restoration of essential elements, aid suspensions are ill equipped to address problems of long-term instability.

The patterns of efficacy in CFSP sanctions differ greatly from the ACP context. The CFSP universe is a highly heterogeneous group which features a high failure rate and little variation. The selection bias identified at the beginning of these paragraphs finds its most evident expression in the CFSP universe: targets are characterised by the support of neighbouring powers which act as 'protectors', weakening the international pressure to which the target is subject. Burma, Zimbabwe and Transnistria are examples of targets politically and economically backed by neighbouring powers. A distinguishing feature of this group is that sanctions have often been in place for long periods of time, mostly without any progress. The frequent failure of CFSP sanctions appears to corroborate the validity of most of the factors put forward by the present study. Often no other tool can be used to exert leverage on these countries with which bilateral agreements were never signed. The CFSP sanctions toolbox is composed of measures unable to deprive targets of anything valuable, and therefore ill suited to disrupting the activities of the leaders. The measures wielded produce limited harm, and in particular their economic impact remains marginal. Informal sanctions largely share these features. Yet, the few cases in which CFSP sanctions proved at least partially effective are rich in insights illuminating the operation of targeted sanctions, and particularly revealing of how the EU has availed itself of this instrument to achieve its political goals. What distinguishes these episodes from the bulk of CFSP cases?

A factor central to success is proactivism on one of the sides of the dispute. In order to set in motion the easing process, one of the parties approached the other with the intention of promoting the lifting of measures. The easing of the measures against Uzbekistan emerges as an excellent example of 'negotiated' lifting: in the aftermath of the imposition of sanctions, some EU actors conducted a sustained effort to persuade the Uzbek authorities to make concessions that would allow the measures to be diluted. Togo represents another perfect illustration, where the 'negotiated' lifting was initiated by the target. The planned, if ultimately aborted, lifting of the arms embargo against China largely resulted from intense lobbying by the Chinese mission in Brussels. The Commission published a non-paper detailing what it could offer to Belarus, and dispatched a visit to the country to present it. Even when diplomatic campaigns fall short of bringing an end to sanctions, attempts at approximation are fruitful in other respects. The idea that sanctions are but one element of a broader negotiating process is well known. However, the traditional image of a defeated, 'repenting' target conforming to the sender's demands in search of accommodation is replaced in EU practice by a sender often as interested in restoring cooperation as is the target. The EU proved highly responsive to limited compliance, reciprocating even modest concessions. The EU's remarkable responsiveness becomes especially – albeit not only – evident in those areas where lack of cooperation affects its own economic interests. The rapidity with which the Commission established a 'quasi-dialogue' on energy with Belarus after Russia withdrew its support indicates that the lack of cooperation in this area was resented on the EU side. The very first step in the easing of sanctions against Uzbekistan consisted in reactivating the technical subcommittees under the PCA. The desire for cooperation is not always frustrated by the presence of sanctions. The persistence of the arms ban has not prevented China from becoming the EU's second trading partner, nor from participating in its Galileo satellite project.

A set of innovative findings highlighted by the investigation relate to the motivations that led targets to make progress towards compliance. The EU has embraced the notion of targeted sanctions, distancing itself from the employment of economic embargoes in CFSP practice. This circumstance might create the impression that economic considerations have no role to play in the calculations of the sender – certainly not among CFSP sanctions targets, middle-income countries which are not dependent on aid. However, albeit non-economic in nature, CFSP sanctions operate against the background of the EU as an economic power and as a source of assistance. One of the most powerful forces compelling targets to seek accommodation with the EU is the 'promise of wealth' stemming from cooperation and trade. A case in point is Belarus: the underlying reasons motivating the Belarusian leadership to comply with EU requirements arose from the economic difficulties that followed the energy crisis. While sanctions were not at the root of the deterioration of the economy, the prospect of decline prompted the leadership to work towards their lifting. The leadership perceived the imminent decline in the country's living standard as a danger to its permanence in power. In this sense, the scarcity of foreign investment from EU countries proved a more effective 'sanction' than CFSP blacklists. Statements by affected leaders corroborate this point. Belarusian President Lukaschenko was quoted as saying 'if we have a free trade zone with Europe, we will be twice as rich', while Serbian President Tadic declared 'without co-operation there is … no entry into the EU, no increase in the standard of living'.[1]The primarily economic rationale underlying Belarusian accommodation with the EU evidences an irony in the notion of targeted sanctions: despite the efforts devoted to crafting sanctions to target elites without damaging the population, they only prove effective when leaders perceive economic decline as jeopardising regime stability. The promise of enhanced access to foreign investment, trade and additional assistance constitutes a powerful incentive operating 'in the background'.

Nevertheless, the presence of a compelling economic component in EU sanctions does not assimilate its operation to that of traditional trade embargoes. It departs from the operation of trade embargoes in two fundamental ways. Firstly, it abandons the 'all or nothing' approach of trade embargoes, consisting in depriving the target of all imaginable benefits of cooperation until compliance has occurred. The use of the economic element by the EU, as most evident with the ACP but increasingly visible in the easing of CFSP sanctions, is modulated in a gradualist fashion that rewards concessions by the target with the progressive resumption of cooperation. The easing of CFSP sanctions against Uzbekistan reflects this approach. The inclusion of Belarus in the multilateral track of the Eastern Partnership, with the option of participation in the bilateral track in the event of further progress towards EU demands, illustrates the fluid passage from an adversarial relationship to a first stage of cooperation. Thus, the target is granted access to selected benefits, whereby the EU hopes to encourage further steps towards compliance. This strategy comes close to blurring the distinction between the notion of sanctions and that of conditionality, locating EU coercive instruments in a 'grey zone'. Secondly, the EU's employment of sanctions departs from that of trade embargoes, in that sanctions are often initiated with the idea that the most powerful tools should not be activated from the onset. Illustratively, the Commission proposed that the suspension against Fiji should not entail the freezing of financial support for the restructuring of the sugar sector, in view of the 'importance of the sugar industry for Fiji's economy, employment and poverty situation' (Commission of the European Communities 2007b:5). This policy is in full consonance with the notion of targeted sanctions, and particularly with the objective of avoiding the suffering of the population. However, the renunciation of the freezing of support for sugar sector reform appears to follow considerations of pure humanitarianism. From the point of view of sanctions efficacy, the threat of freezing the sugar reform support would have made Art. 96 suspension more potent. One could speculate whether the fact that ACP suspensions are managed by the Directorate-General concerned with development might have a 'contamination' effect in the design of ACP sanctions.

The 'promise of wealth' associated with cooperation with the EU does not solely account for success. The stigma that sanctions carry enhances their efficacy. Evidence suggesting that blacklisted individuals are dismayed at EU bans in their private capacity seldom goes beyond the anecdotal. With the exception of a prominent Zimbabwean official reportedly unable to access a considerable sum held in a British bank, due to the assets freeze, CFSP measures seem to have caused little material disutility to blacklisted individuals. They have had no impact on efficacy, as the malaise provoked did not compel leaders to accommodate. Thus, the stigmatisation of individuals in a private capacity does not appear to have inconvenienced them to the extent of affecting their behaviour. However, rulers are often concerned that sanctions do impinge upon their international prestige in their official capacities, or leadership roles. Certain leaders aspire for their countries to achieve widespread recognition as regional or even global powers. Therefore, they resent the stigma of being blacklisted, to the extent that they seek an accommodation. The desire for international prestige proved central in Uzbekistan's progress towards meeting EU demands. As highlighted by experts, Uzbekistan does not want to be a 'pariah'. Although the arms embargo also represented an inconvenience in other respects, Chinese officials were very vocal about their uneasiness at being put on a par with countries such as Burma or Sudan. The need to be externally recognised as a 'responsible' power translates into leaders' readiness to enter into a bargaining process with the sender. By contrast, the leadership of states which do not regard themselves as regional powers, and do not have any aspiration to become such, are less concerned with their external image. Thus, for countries such as Transnistria and Burma the survival of the state or regime takes precedence over prestige considerations. The desire for international prestige brings us back to the centrality of international support, one of the keys to sanctions success. The positive developments in relations with Uzbekistan can be ascribed partly to the absence of support from neighbouring powers. This is underscored by Belarus' rapprochement with the EU following the rise of tensions with Russia. The only episodes featuring positive outcomes correspond to target countries which are aspiring or actual regional powers, such as Uzbekistan, Indonesia or Nigeria, while remaining unprotected by any patron state in the way that China and Thailand shield Burma, Russia shields Belarus and Transnistria, or South Africa supports Zimbabwe.

Little insight can be gained from the universe of informal sanctions, which contrasts with the other groups in that its outcomes do not display any clear pattern. They are highly heterogeneous in terms of the tools they wield and the goals they pursue, ranging from the restoration of democratic rule and the respect for human rights to unique instances such as state recognition, cooperation in the extradition of indicted war criminals, or accession to the NPT. A defining feature of this group is that the management of sanctions is characterised by a high degree of inconsistency. Regimes were often modified for reasons exogenous to the behaviour of the targets, lifted in the absence of progress towards compliance, or left in place despite considerable progress. The lack of compliance by most targets might have been due to the target's realisation of the sender's lack of determination. In any event, measures were soon revoked anyway, so that lack of compliance only interrupted aid or normal relations for a few months. In those episodes where progress was observed, the EU played a limited role: Peru's and Guatemala's speedy returns to democracy following coups d'état warranted the lifting of measures; however, these outcomes can be credited mostly to domestic pro-democracy forces. In Turkey and Serbia, included in the dataset because the object of the dispute was unconnected to reforms formally stipulated in the accession process, eventual compliance can largely be explained by their desire to join the EU.

From embargoes to targeted sanctions

While confirming the continued validity of a number of determinants of success established in classical sanctions theory, the findings point to the relevance of aspects so far neglected by scholarship. Firstly, the study appears to corroborate the assumption that economic measures are more likely to succeed in inducing policy changes than are non-economic measures. Most EU sanctions, especially CFSP sanctions, tend to cause little material disutility. By contrast, Art. 96 suspensions, which are likely to produce economic harm, are mostly successful. Whenever CFSP sanctions have been accompanied by economic measures, sanctions tended to fare somewhat better. Some progress has been witnessed in Zimbabwe and Belarus – albeit not in Burma – and the oil embargo and freezing of state assets against the FRY yielded promising results before the EU sanctions exercise was cut short by NATO's operation in Kosovo. Wherever non-economic CFSP sanctions have contributed to positive outcomes, they have done so largely by depriving the target of international prestige. However, this restricts the potential for efficacy of sanctions to targets aspiring to international prestige: to the extent that the target cared about its reputation, the EU is capable of exerting some influence. While the discomfort that sanctions cause among elites often compels those targeted to manifest their desire for the removal of measures, it does not induce them to implement the reforms demanded by the EU. This finding does not, per se, represent a 'thumbs-down' on targeted sanctions. However, it sheds new light on the employment of stigmatisation as a coercive tool in international relations.

One of the most innovative contributions to the understanding of the operation of sanctions is the relevance of the management of sanctions. The consistent management of sanctions, coupled with the availability of an institutionalised framework which reassures the target of the EU's commitment to mutual agreements, can be considered a major conditioning factor. The example *par excellence* in this study of such a scenario lies in the procedures for consultation embedded in the EU–ACP framework. Sanctions scholars have devoted little attention to issues of sanctions management so far, especially in the case of EU sanctions. De Wilde d'Estmael claims that the requirement for unanimity in CFSP decision making does not allow the Council to manage the tool flexibly, thus hampering its efficacy (de Wilde d'Estmael 1998, 2000, Watson Institute 2007). There seems to be some truth in this assertion. Regardless of the nature of the sanctions imposed, the sender should retain the capacity to respond to both progress and setbacks in the target's conduct. The rigidity of the processes for the adoption and modification of CFSP sanctions has sometimes hindered a more flexible management of the measures. Aware of this difficulty, the Council addressed its lack of flexibility from the late 1990s by introducing some changes to its legal acts. CFSP Common Positions now clearly spell out their demands and provide an 'expiry date' which makes renewal rather than termination subject to unanimity. As a result, the removal of sanctions has – procedurally – become easier. Still, easing or lifting sanctions regimes remains far more difficult than adopting them, and the unanimity requirement continues to limit their bargaining power vis-à-vis the targets. In order to bring about the easing of sanctions against Uzbekistan in 2006, certain member states had to be persuaded to relax their resistance. Most CFSP episodes display a reasonably high level of coherence in the handling of the sanctions tools. Where regimes were adjusted, it was more often in the negative sense of tightening than in the positive sense of easing sanctions. The Council encountered little difficulty in escalating existing sanctions regimes in reaction to such setbacks, as illustrated by the gradualist strategies applied in Zimbabwe and Burma. However, reciprocating progress, or even lifting the measures, remains complicated in the EU framework. This is mainly due to the unanimity requirement in the Council, which gives a veto to individual member states. Germany inspired an EU aid blockade against Turkey, which the European Parliament and Greece managed to keep in place for more than fifteen years after Germany lifted its own sanctions. Spain instigated the imposition of diplomatic sanctions against Cuba, but only three years later was unable to bring about their removal, due to the hard line followed by the new Eastern European member states. Other factors can also make it difficult for EU member states to relinquish sanctions regimes they no longer fully subscribe to. Plans to lift the arms embargo against China in 2003 had to be abandoned, largely due to opposition from the US, although actors such as the EP and human rights organisations also played a role. Conversely, certain modifications in the sanctions regimes appear unrelated to the behaviour of the leaderships concerned. While Belarus, Burma, the FRY and Zimbabwe are examples of responsive incrementalism, the lifting of measures against Pakistan and Russia are unconnected with developments in the leaderships' conduct.

A highly counterintuitive finding consists in the invalidation of the assumption that sanctions goals jeopardising the leadership's grip on power are less likely to succeed. The positive record observed in Art. 96 suspensions is almost invariably connected to the restoration of democratic rule. However, the study's original assumption about the leadership's grip on power holds in the CFSP cases. Episodes where EU demands were unrelated to the re-establishment of democratic rule proved successful, such as the Drozny crisis in Belarus and the Andijan inquiry in Uzbekistan. Interestingly, the goal of the Uzbekistan sanctions merely referred to the dispatch of an 'international inquiry', leaving the leadership's permanence in office unaffected from the start. In Belarus, where EU demands aimed at the re-establishment of democratic rule, the leadership managed to manoeuvre itself into a situation whereby it satisfied most EU demands, while failing to fully meet the core demand of reforming the electoral code and holding free elections. Also 'technical' improvements such as the increasing specificity of goals in Common Positions may have facilitated efficacy. In the case of Uzbekistan, the EU requested the conduct of an inquiry into the Andijan events, while no specific demand was formulated when the arms embargo on Sudan was agreed. However, EU practice has also evolved in the opposite direction. Incremental strategies have not only upgraded sanctions, but have also progressively added new conditions for their lifting. EU sanctions predominantly aim at correcting flaws in democratic rule often intertwined with human rights issues. All goals have in common some international legitimacy emanating from international legal instruments (such as Covenants on Civil and Political Rights, the Non-Proliferation Treaty, the Geneva Conventions), which emphasises the normative intent of the measures. Also, some demands echo demands of other international entities, such as the Assembly of the Council of Europe (Pouridges Report about Belarus) or the International Criminal Tribunal for the Former Yugoslavia (ICTY). Results remain mixed. Perhaps more atypical goals have lower chances of success, but this is probably more closely related to the lack of domestic pressure in the target countries than to the perceived legitimacy of democratic and human rights objectives. No domestic forces pushed for the sanctions' agenda of nuclear disarmament in Pakistan or for cooperation with ICTY in Serbia in a way comparable to democratic forces pushing for elections against authoritarian rulers. Under this scenario, sanctions are unable to contribute to pressure exerted in the domestic arena.

Despite the fact that the present investigation reveals the importance of factors that have not so far been contemplated in mainstream sanctions research, the presence of international support, particularly from major powers geographically close to the target, remains a key determinant of success. After more than thirty years of research into sanctions efficacy, it retains full validity. Targets across all EU sanctions groups are more likely to respond positively when the EU's position is shared by other states, and particularly if they are not shielded by states in their vicinity.

The investigation has not only illuminated the actual operation of targeted sanctions. It has revealed that the efficacy of EU sanctions is directly connected to (unwritten) criteria guiding the choice of which measures to impose in each particular case. The implicit categorisation of targets corresponds to different expectations of success. Those targets most likely to be receptive to EU demands are ACP countries that are tackled in the framework of Art. 96 consultations. CFSP sanctions are wielded against countries it can afford to antagonise, given that their cooperation is not vital. While the targets of CFSP sanctions are protected by major powers and thus in a good position to resist EU pressure, the EU's main trading partners have never been targeted within this group. The EU chose to protest Russian and Chinese misconduct through 'informal' sanctions that allowed more flexibility, and which did not require official Council decisions to be revoked. The withdrawal of GSP preferences has been employed only against long-term CFSP targets. Finally, informal sanctions are levied with little hope not only that the target will yield, but also that the members of the Council will uphold them for long.

More revealing of the EU's distinctive character than the criteria followed in the imposition of sanctions is perhaps the pattern observed in their easing. The activism preceding the lifting of sanctions reveals that the EU often has as strong an interest in the removal of the measures as has the target. Uneasy with the presence of obstacles, the EU often exploits available possibilities of cooperation with targets in priority areas. This trend is particularly evident in prolonged sanctions episodes which remain unfruitful. The prospect of enhancing relations, and the hope of encouraging further compliance, compels the EU to ease sanctions in face of suboptimal concessions. While accommodating a target attracts criticism from those who accuse the EU of half-heartedness or even double standards, the selective resumption of cooperation allows the EU to reap some benefits while at a stage when it is uncertain whether full compliance will eventually occur. Thus, the EU's pragmatic calculus responds to a preference for limited compliance over indefinite political deadlock.

Annex I

Overview of Variables (dataset)

Episode	*Legal tool*	*Economic nature (eco)*	*Grip on power (grip)*	*Coherence in strategy (coh)*	*International support (int)*	*EU sanctions contribution (contr)*
Belarus I	inf	1	1	1	0	1
Belarus II	CFSP	0	0	1	0	1
Belarus IIIa	CFSP	0	1	1	0	1
Belarus IIIb	CFSP	1	1	1	0	1
Belarus IV	GSP	1	0	1	0	0
Burma Ia	inf	1	1	1	0	0
Burma Ib	CFSP	0	1	1	0	0
Burma Ic	CFSP	1	1	1	0	0
Burma Id	CFSP	1	1	1	0	0
Burma II	GSP	1	0	1	0	0
Burma Ie	CFSP	1	1	1	0	0
Burundi	inf	1	1	1	1	1
Cambodia	inf	1	1	1	1	0
Central African Republic	96	1	1	1	1	1
China	inf	0	0	0	0	0
Comoros	96	1	1	1	1	1
Congo/Zaire Ia	inf	1	1	1	1	0
Congo/Zaire Ib	CFSP	0	1	1	1	0
Côte d'Ivoire	96	1	1	1	1	1
Cuba I	inf	1	0	1	1	0
Cuba II	inf	0	0	0	1	1
Djibouti	inf	1	0	1	1	1
Equitorial Guinea	inf	1	1	0	1	0
Ethiopia–Eritrea	CFSP	0	1	1	1	1
Federal Republic of Yugoslavia Ib	CFSP	0	1	1	1	0
Federal Republic of Yugoslavia Ic	CFSP	0	1	1	1	0
Federal Republic of Yugoslavia Id	CFSP	1	1	1	1	0

(*Continued on next page*)

Episode	*Legal tool*	*Economic nature (eco)*	*Grip on power (grip)*	*Coherence in strategy (coh)*	*International support (int)*	*EU sanctions contribution (contr)*
Federal Republic of Yugoslavia Ie	CFSP	1	1	1	1	0
Federal Republic of Yugoslavia If	CFSP	1	1	1	1	0
Federal Republic of Yugoslavia Ig	CFSP	1	1	1	1	0
Federal Republic of Yugoslavia Ih	CFSP	1	1	1	1	0
Fiji I	96	1	1	1	1	1
Fiji II	96	1	1	1	1	0
Gambia	inf	1	1	1	1	1
Guatemala	inf	1	1	1	1	0
Guinea-Conakry[a]	96	1	1	0	1	0
Haiti	96	1	1	1	1	1
Indonesia	CFSP	0	0	1	1	1
Kenya	inf	1	1	1	1	1
Liberia	96	1	1	1	1	0
Malawi	inf	1	1	1	1	1
Moldova I	CFSP	0	0	1	0	0
Moldova II	CFSP	0	0	1	0	1
Nigeria	CFSP	1	0	1	1	1
Pakistan	inf	1	0	0	1	0
Palestine Authority	inf	1	0	0	0	0
Peru	inf	1	1	1	1	1
Russia I	inf	0	0	0	0	0
Russia II	inf	1	0	0	0	0
Rwanda	inf	1	0	1	1	1
Serbia	inf	1	0	0	1	0
Sudan Ia	inf	1	1	1	1	0
Sudan Ib	CFSP	1	1	1	1	0
Togo I	Inf	1	1	1	1	1
Togo II	96	1	0	1	1	1
Turkey	inf	1	0	0	1	1
Uzbekistan Ia	CFSP	0	0	1	0	1
Uzbekistan Ib	CFSP	0	0	1	0	1
Zimbabwe Ia	96	1	1	1	0	0
Zimbabwe Ib	CFSP	0	1	1	0	0
Zimbabwe Ic	CFSP	1	1	1	0	0

Notes:

[a] Sanctions imposed against Guinea in 2009 are excluded from the dataset.

[1] For the purposes of the QCA analysis, the episodes Togo II and Togo III are considered a single episode.

Annex II

Truth table

Assumptions	*Raw coverage*	*Unique coverage*	*Consistency*
support*~grip*~eco	0.074074	0.037037	1.000000
respon*~grip*~eco	0.185185	0.148148	1.000000
support*respon*~grip	0.185185	0.148148	0.833333

solution coverage: 0.370370
solution consistency: 0.909091

Notes

1 Sanctions and their efficacy

1 For the sake of simplicity, the acronym EU will be used throughout this investigation to refer to both the European Community (EC) and the European Union (EU).
2 UN Charter, § 39 and § 41.
3 The function of control variables is to reduce the risk of attributing explanatory power to independent variables that are not in fact responsible for the occurrence of variation in the dependent variable. See Frankfort-Nachmias and Nachmias (1992:56)

2 EU sanctions

1 § 301 EC requires that any restrictive measure imposed by the Community should always be based on a CFSP decision (Wessel 1999).
2 In neither of these instances was the participation of all member states achieved without difficulties. Greece was exempted from implementing sanctions against the USSR, and Denmark ceased to apply the measures without being formally exempted. In the case of the Falklands crisis, Ireland and Italy originally agreed to the sanctions, but terminated them when the UK employed force.
3 In practice, this basic division is more complicated, especially as arms embargoes are not restricted to armaments, but encompass bans on assistance, advice and training related to military material. Such measures fall under the competency of the Community, and their implementation therefore requires an EC Regulation. See, for example, Council Regulation (EC) No 1727/2003 of 29 September 2003 concerning measures against the Democratic Republic of Congo.
4 See art.103 UN Charter.
5 Article number as in the original Maastricht Treaty. The exceptional clause § 297 EC allows member states to take measures that deviate from Community regulations 'in order to carry out obligations … accepted for the purpose of maintaining peace and international security'.
6 However, these documents are not official EU statements.
7 The reaction to the Indian/Pakistani nuclear tests in 1998, which prompted the temporary freezing of Community development aid and cooperation programmes, is the only exception. See Chapter 6 of this book.

3 What determines the efficacy of EU sanctions?

1 See e.g. Gauttier 2004
2 Refer to Annex II for truth table.

4 The efficacy of sanctions imposed under the Common Foreign and Security Policy

1 The first examples of CFSP Common Positions followed this model (see Common Position on Nigeria, 95/515/CFSP).

2 In 1991 the EC had suspended its bilateral trade and cooperation agreements with Yugoslavia, interrupting aid programmes and trade preferences, and introducing quotas on textile imports. The following year, positive trade measures in the form of benefits were offered only to Slovenia, Croatia, Macedonia, Bosnia-Herzegovina and Montenegro to encourage each republic to work towards a settlement by confronting them with a choice between benefits or sanctions (Wilde d'Estmael 2004). The fact that only Slovenia and Croatia had been recognised by all member states at the time shows how considerations of state sovereignty were overridden by the objective of encouraging progress on an agreement.

3 The UK eventually rallied to the majority position that the ban did not necessitate a termination of bilateral agreements, as it was warranted as a countermeasure against the breaches by the FRY of *erga omnes* obligations (Blockmans 2007:161).

7 Withdrawal of Trade Privileges under the Generalizaed System of Preferences

1 The number of countries suspended can only be small given that the EU can only withdraw GSP preferences from third states with which no contractual agreement - such as a bilateral free trade agreement - is in place. Although the present investigation does not contemplate cases where GSP plus preferences were downgraded to regular GSP, it is worth mentioning that the EU has withdrawn GSP-plus incentives from of Venezuela because of non-ratification of the Convention against Corruption.

8 Sanctions theory and the efficacy of EU sanctions

1 See relevant chapters of this book for full quotations and references.

Bibliography

ACP-EU Council of Ministers (2001) Press release 146b056E, Brussels, 5 February 2001.

Ahora (2007) 'The EU Lacks Moral Authority to Judge Cuba', 22 June 2007.

Anthony, I. (2002) 'Sanctions Applied by the European Union and the United Nations', in *SIPRI Yearbook 2002*, Stockholm: SIPRI.

Arikan, H. (2003) *Turkey and the EU. An Awkward Candidate for EU Membership?*, Aldershot: Ashgate.

Arts, K. (2005) 'Political Dialogue in a New Framework', in O. Babarinde and G. Faber (eds) *The European Union and the Developing Countries: The Cotonou Agreement*, Leiden: M. Nijhoff.

AsiaNews (2007) 'Myanmar Playing "Tricks" with the International Community', 22 November 2007.

Austin, G. (2005) *The 1989 China Arms Ban: Putting Europe's Position to Congress*, London: The Foreign Policy Centre.

Babarinde, O. and Faber, G. (2004) 'From Lomé to Cotonou: Business As Usual?', *European Foreign Affairs Review* 9: 27–47.

Baldwin, D.A. (1999) 'The Sanctions Debate and the Logic of Choice', *International Security* 24(4): 80–107.

Baldwin, D.A. and Pape, R.A. (1998) 'Evaluating Economic Sanctions', *International Security* 23(2): 189–98.

Bapat, N. and Morgan, C. (2009) 'Multilateral versus Unilateral Sanctions Reconsidered: A Test Using New Data', *International Studies Quarterly* 53: 1075–94.

Barber, J. (1979) 'Economic Sanctions as a Policy Instrument', *International Affairs* 55 (July 1979): 367–84.

Bartels, L. (2005) *Human Rights Conditionality in the EU's International Agreements*, Oxford: Oxford University Press.

Beichelt, T. (2007) 'Externe Demokratisierungsstrategien der Europäischen Union: Die Fälle Belarus und Moldawien', in M. Knodt und A. Jünemann (eds) *Die Externe Demokratieförderung der Europäischen Union*, Baden Baden: Nomos.

Biersteker, T. (2001) *Targeted Financial Sanctions: A Manual for the Design and Implementation. Contribution from the Interlaken Process*, Providence: International Institute of International Studies.

Bilandzic, B. (2007) 'Serbia Could Resume EU Talks "Very Soon"', *Reuters*, 17 May 2007.

Blagov, S. (2005) 'Uzbekistan and Russia Sign Mutual Defence Pact', *Eurasia Insight*, 15 November 2005.

Blanchard, J.F. and Ripsman, N.M. (2002) 'Asking the Right Question: When Do Economic Sanctions Work Best?', *Security Studies* 9, Autumn 1999/ Winter 2000: 219–53.

Blockmans, S. (2007) *Tough Love. The European Union's Relations with the Western Balkans*, The Hague: Cambridge University Press.

Boadle, A. (2008) 'EU Commissioner Wants Cuba Sanctions Abolished', Reuters, 9 March 2008.

Bohr, S. (1993) 'Sanctions by the United Nations Security Council and the European Community', *European Journal of International Law* 4(2): 256–68.

Bonetti, S. (1991) 'Sanctions and Statistics: Reconsidering "Economic Sanctions Reconsidered"', *University of St. Andrews Discussion Papers* 9103.

Bosse, G. and Korosteleva-Polglase, E. (2009) 'Changing Belarus?: The Limits of EU Governance in Eastern Europe and the Promise of Partnership', *Cooperation and Conflict* 44: 143–65.

Bourque, A. and Sampson, P. (2001) 'The European Union's Political and Development Response to the Democratic Republic of Congo', *European Centre for Development Policy Management (ECDPM): Discussion Paper No. 28*, Maastricht: ECDPM.

Bradley, A. (2005) 'An ACP Perspective and Overview of Article 96 Cases', *European Centre for Development Policy Management (ECDPM): Discussion Paper No. 64D*, Maastricht: ECDPM.

Brandtner, B. and Rosas, A. (1998) 'Human Rights and the External Relations of the European Community: An Analysis of the Doctrine and Practice', *European Journal of International Law* 9(3): 468–90.

Bridges, B. (1999) *Europe and the Challenge of the Asia Pacific*, Northhampton, MA: Edward Elgar.

Brummer, K. (2009) 'Imposing Sanctions: The not so "Normative Power Europe"', *European Foreign Affairs Review* 14: 191–207.

Brzoska, M. (2001) *Design and Implementation of Arms Embargoes and Travel and Aviation related Sanctions: Results of the Bonn–Berlin process.* Bonn: Bonn International Centre for Conversion.

——(2003) 'From Dumb to Smart? Recent reforms of UN Sanctions', *Global Governance* 9(4): 519–35.

——(2005) 'Gezielte Sanktionen als Mittel der Konflikteinhegung in Afrika – Erfahrungen und Aussichten', *Sicherheit und Frieden* 4/2005: 157–63.

Buchet de Neuilly, Y. (2003) 'European Union's External Relations Fields: The Multipillar Issue of Economic Sanctions against Serbia', in M. Knodt and S. Princen (eds) *Understanding the European Union's external relations*, London: Routledge.

Casarini, N. (2006) 'The Evolution of the EU–China Relationship: From Constructive Engagement to Strategic Partnership', *Occasional Paper 64*, Paris: ISS-EU, October 2006.

Castle, S. (2007) 'Zimbabwe and Trade Dominate Tense Europe-Africa Summit', New York Times, 8 December 2007.

Chand, S. (2006) 'Preference Erosion: The Case of Fiji Sugar', in S. Chand (ed.) *Pacific Islands Regional Integration and Governance*, Canberra: Asia Pacific Press.

Charnovitz, S. (2005) 'The World Trade Organisation: Sanctions for Non-compliance', in P. Wallensteen and C. Staibano (eds) *International Sanctions: Between Words and Wars in the Global System*, London: Frank Cass.

Chesterman, S. and Pouligny, B. (2003) 'Are Sanctions Meant to Work? The Politics of Creating and Implementing Sanctions through the United Nations', *Global Governance* 9(4): 503–18.

Combacau, C. (1992) 'Sanctions', in R. Bernhardt (ed.) *Encyclopedia of Public International Law*, Amsterdam: North-Holland.

Commission of the European Communities (1992) Commission Communication on the implementation in 1993 of the resolution of the council and of the member states meeting in the council on human rights, democracy and development, adopted on 28 November 1991, COM (94) 42 final, 23/02/92.

——(1995) Report on the Operation of the Treaty on European Union, Brussels, 10. May 1995.

——(1999) Commission Communication to the Council and the European Parliament on the co-operation with ACP Countries involved in Armed Conflicts, Brussels, COM (99) 240 final, 19. March 1999.

——(2000) Commission Communication on conflict prevention, Brussels, COM (2001) 211 final, 11 April 2000.

——(2003) 'Conflict Prevention and Crisis Management Unit: Civilian Instruments for EU Crisis Management', April 2003.

——(2005) 'Launching of EUBAM', Press release, Brussels, 29 November 2005.

——(2006a) 'What the European Union Could Bring to Belarus', non-paper, Meeting Doc. 265/06 rev 5, 21 November 2001.

——(2006b) Proposal for a Council regulation temporarily withdrawing access to the generalised tariff preferences to the Republic of Belarus, Brussels, COM(2006) 764 final, 2006/0255 (ACC), 30 November 2006.

——(2007a) 'European Union and its Main Trading Partners: Economic and Trade Indicators', Available HTTP: http://ec.europa.eu/trade/issues/bilateral/data.htm.

——(2007b) Commission Communication on the opening of consultations with Fiji under Article 96 of the Cotonou Agreement, COM (2007) 14 final, Brussels, 17 January 2007.

——(2007c) 'The EC–Burma/Myanmar Strategy Paper (2007–2013)', Brussels, 11 June 2007.

Cooper Drury, A. (1998) 'Revisiting "Economic Sanctions Reconsidered"', *Journal of Peace Research* 35(4), 99: 497–509.

Cortright, D. and Lopez, G.A. (1996) 'Smart Sanctions on Nigeria', *Occasional Paper Series*, 10:OP:1, Notre Dame: Kroc Institute for International Peace Studies.

——(2000) *The Sanctions Decade. Assessing UN Strategies in the 1990s*, Boulder: Lynne Rienner.

——(2002) (eds) *Smart Sanctions: Targeting Economic Statecraft*, Lanham: Rowman & Littlefield.

Cosgrove, E. (2002) 'The Efficacy of Sanctions', *International Security Policy Paper* No. 82, London: International Security Information Service.

——(2005) 'Examining Targeted Sanctions: Are Travel Bans Effective?', in P. Wallensteen and C. Staibano (eds) (2005) *International Sanctions: Between Words and Wars in the Global System*, London: Frank Cass.

Council of the European Communities (1982a) Council Regulation 596/82, 15 March 1982.

——(1982b) Council Regulation 877/82, 16 April 1982.

——(1991) Resolution of the Council and of the Member States meeting in the Council on Human Rights, *Democracy and Development*, EC Bulletin no. 11, 1991.

——(2006) Council Common Position (2006/267/CFSP) of 10 April 2006 concerning Restrictive Measures Against Certain Officials of Belarus, OJ L 101/5, 11 April 2006.

Council of the European Union (1989) Statement on China, Doc Nr 89/180, 27 June 1989.

——(1991) Statement by the Presidency concerning Burma/Myanmar, Press 91/238, 29 July 1991.

——(1994a) Council Decision (94/165/CFSP) of 17 March 1994 concerning the imposition of an embargo on arms, munitions and military equipment on Sudan, OJ L 075.

——(1994b) Council Decision (94/697/CFSP) of 24 October 1994 concerning the Common Position adopted by the Council on the Basis of Art. J.2 of the Treaty on European Union on the objectives and priorities of the European Union vis-à-vis Rwanda.

——(1995) Council Common Position (95/515/CFSP) of 20 November 1995 defined by the Council on the basis of Article J.2 of the Treaty on European Union on Nigeria, OJ L 298, 11 December 1995.

——(1996a) Council EC Regulation 1256/96 of 20 June 1996 applying multiannual schemes of generalized tariff preferences from 1 July 1996 to 30 June 1999 in respect of certain agricultural products originating in developing countries.

——(1996b) Council EC Regulation Nr. 1279/96 of 4 July 1996 concerning the provision of assistance to economic reform and recovery in the New Independent States and Mongolia, OJ L 165/1.

——(1996c) Council Common Position (96/635/CFSP) on Burma/Myanmar, 28 October 1996.

——(1996d) Council Common Position (96/697/CFSP) of 2 December 1996 defined by the Council on the basis of Article J.2 of the Treaty on European Union, on Cuba, OJ L 322, 12/12/1996.

——(1997) Council EC Regulation 556/97.

——(1998a) Council Common Position (98/374/CFSP) concerning the prohibition of new investment in Serbia, 8 June 1998.

——(1998b) Council Common Position (98/448/CFSP) of 24 September 2004 concerning restrictive measures against certain officials of Belarus, OJ L 301/67, 28 September 2004.

——(1998c) Joint Action (98/735/CFSP) of 22 December 1998 adopted by the Council on the basis of Article J.3 of the Treaty on European Union in support of the democratic process in Nigeria, OJ L 354, 30 December 1998, pp. 1–2.

——(1998d) Council Common Position (98/606/CFSP) of 26 October 1998.

——(1999a) Council Common Position (99/156/CFSP) of 22 February 1999 concerning restrictive measures against certain officials of Belarus, OJ L 52/1, 27 February 1999.

——(1999b) Council Common Position (1999/624/CFSP) concerning restrictive measures against the Republic of Indonesia, 16 September 1999.

——(1999c) Non-military Instruments of Crisis Management, 3. December 1999.

——(1999d) Presidency Conclusions of the Helsinki European Council, 10 and 11 December 1999, Annex II.

——(2000a) Conclusions of the General Affairs Council, 2000 document SN 0003/00, 24 January 2000.

——(2000b) Council Common Position (2000/345/CFSP) on Burma/Myanmar, 26 April 2000.

——(2000c) Conclusions of the General Affairs Council, 10 July 2000.

——(2000d) Council Common Position (2004/848/CFSP) of 13 December 2004 amending Common Position (2004/61/CFSP) concerning restrictive measures against certain officials of Belarus, OJ L 367/35, 14 December 2004.

——(2001a) Concluding consultations with Côte d'Ivoire under Art. 96 of the ACP-EU Partnership Agreement (2001/510/EC), 25 June 2001.

——(2001b) Council Common Position (2001/757/CFSP) on Burma/Myanmar, 29 October 2001.

——(2001c) Rapport de Mission à Lima (Pérou) du 26 novembre au 5 décembre 2001, Commission Européenne, Direction Générale Relations Extérieures, Direction Amérique Latine, Bruxelles, Décembre 2001.
——(2002a) Council Common Position (2002/831/CFSP) on Burma/Myanmar, 21 October 2002.
——(2002b) Council Common Position (2002/147/CFSP).
——(2003a) Council Common Position (2003/139/CFSP) concerning restrictive measures against the leadership of the Transnistrian region of the Moldovan Republic, 27 February 2003.
——(2003b) Council Common Position (2003/297/CFSP) on Burma/Myanmar, 28 April 2003.
——(2003c) Council Common Position (2003/345/CFSP) on Burma/Myanmar, 20 June 2003.
——(2003d) Concluding the consultation procedure opened with the Central African Republic and adopting appropriate measures under Art. 96 of the ACP-EU Partnership Agreement (2003/837/EC), 24 November 2003.
——(2003e) Guidelines on the Implementation and Evaluation of Restrictive Measures (Sanctions) in the framework of the EU Common Foreign and Security Policy, Council Doc. 15579/03, Brussels, 3 December 2003.
——(2003f) European Security Strategy: A Secure Europe in a Better World, Brussels, 12 December 2003.
——(2003g) EU Strategy against the Proliferation of WMD, Brussels, 12 December 2003.
——(2004a) Council Common Position (2004/31/CFSP) of 9 January 2004 concerning the imposition of an embargo on arms, munitions and military equipment on Sudan.
——(2004b) Council Common Position (2004/423/CFSP) on Burma/Myanmar, 26 April 2004.
——(2004c) Basic Principles on the Use of Restrictive Measures (Sanctions), Council Doc. 10198/1/04 REV 1, Brussels, 7 June 2004.
——(2004d) Council Common Position (2004/510/CFSP) of 10 June 2004 amending Common Position (2004/31/CFSP) concerning the imposition of an embargo on arms, munitions and military equipment on Sudan.
——(2004e) Council Common Position (2004/661/CFSP) of 24 September 2004 concerning restrictive measures against certain officials of Belarus, OJ L 301/67, 28 September 2004.
——(2004f) Conclusions of the General Affairs Council, October 2006.
——(2004g) Council Common Position (2004/694/CFSP) on further measures in support of the effective implementation of the mandate of the International Criminal Tribunal for the former Yugoslavia (ICTY), 11 October 2004.
——(2004h) Council Decision of 4 November 2004 concluding the consultation procedure with the Togolese Republic under Article 96 of the Cotonou Agreement.
——(2005a) 2636th Council Meeting (Minutes) General Affairs and External Relations Council, 31 January 2005.
——(2005b) Council Common Position (2005/792/CFSP) of 14 November 2005 concerning restrictive measures against Uzbekistan.
——(2005c) Conclusions of the General Affairs Council, June 2005.
——(2005d) EU Annual Report on Human Rights adopted by the Council on October 2005, Luxembourg: Office for Official Publications of the European Community.
——(2006a) Council Common Position (2006/276/CFSP) of 10 April 2006 concerning restrictive measures against certain officials of Belarus and repealing Common Position (2004/661/CFSP).

——(2006b) Council Common Position (2006/318/CFSP) concerning renewing restrictive measures against Burma/Myanmar, 27 April 2006.

——(2006c) Council Decision amending decision (2004/793/EC) of 6 October 2006 concluding the consultation procedure with the Togolese Republic under Art. 96 of the Cotonou Agreement, COM (2006) 577 final, Brussels.

——(2006d) EU-Uzbekistan Cooperation Council, Seventh meeting, Brussels, EU Press Release, 14947 (Press 308), 8 November 2006.

——(2006e) Council EC Regulation 1933/2006 of 21 December 2006 temporarily withdrawing access to generalised tariff preferences from the Republic of Belarus, OJ L 405, 30 December 2006.

——(2007a) Council Common Position (2007/734/CFSP) of 13 November 2007 concerning restrictive measures against Uzbekistan.

——(2007b) Council Common Position (2007/750/CFSP) on Burma/Myanmar, 19 November 2007.

——(2008a) Council Common Position (2008/160/CFSP) concerning restrictive measures against the leadership of the Transnistrian region of the Moldovan Republic, 26 February 2008.

——(2008b) Conclusions of 2865th External Relations Council meeting, Luxemburg, 29 April 2008.

——(2008c) Conclusions of 2897th External Relations Council meeting, Luxemburg, 13 October 2008.

——(2009a) Conclusions of 2933rd External Relations Council meeting, Brussels, 16 March 2009.

——(2009b) Council Common Position (2009/788/CFSP) concerning restrictive measures against the Republic of Guinea, 27 October 2009.

——(2009c) Conclusions of the 2971st External Relations Council Meeting, Luxembourg, 27 March 2009.

Crawford, G. (1997) 'Promoting Political Reform through Aid Sanctions: Instrumental and Normative Issues', *Working Papers on Democratisation*, Centre for Democratisation Studies, Leeds: University of Leeds.

Cuba News (2004) 'Cuba News Talks to Top Alarcón Adviser Miguel Álvarez', 12(1) January 2004.

Daoudi, M. and Dajani, M. (1983) *Economic Sanctions: Ideas and Experience*. London: Routledge.

de Jonge Oudraat, Ch. (2000) 'Making Economic Sanctions Work', *Survival* 42(3): 105–28: 1–21.

——(2001) 'UN Sanction Regimes and Violent Conflict', in C.A. Crocker, F.O. Hampson and P. Aall (eds) *Turbulent Peace. The Challenges of Managing International Conflict*, Washington, DC: United States Institute of Peace Press.

de Vries, A.W. (2002) 'European Union Sanctions against the Federal Republic of Yugoslavia (1998–2000): A Special Exercise in Targeting', in D. Cortright and G.A. Lopez (eds) *Smart Sanctions: Targeting Economic Statecraft*, Lanham: Rowman & Littlefield.

de Waal, A. (2008) 'Dilemmas of Multiple Priorities and Multiple Instruments: The Darfur crisis', in A. Griffiths and C. Barnes (eds) *Powers of Persuasion: Incentives, Sanctions and Conditionality in Peacemaking*, London: Conciliation Resources, Accord issue 19.

de Wilde d'Estmael, T. (1998) *La Dimension Politique des Relations Economiques Extérieures de la Communauté Européenne*, Bruxelles: Bruylant.

——(2000a) 'L'efficacité politique de la coercition économique exercée par l'Union européenne dans les relations internationales', *Annuaire Français de Relations internationales* (1) 2000: 502–21.
——(2000b) 'Les mesures coercitives de l'UE à l'égard de l'URSS et de la Russie', in T. de Wilde et L. Spetschinsky (eds) *Les Relations entre l'Union Européenne et la Fédération de Russie*, Louvain-la-Neuve: Institut d'Études Européennes.
——(2004) 'La Communauté Européenne face a l'implosion yougoslave: aléas d'une gestion de crise par la coercition économique', *Revue d'Histoire de l'Intégration Européenne* 19, 10(1).
Doxey, M.P. (1972) 'International Sanctions: A Framework for Analysis with Special Reference to the UN and Southern Africa', *International Organisation* 26: 527–50.
Dragovic-Soso, J. (2003) 'The Effect of International Intervention on Domestic Policy Outcomes. Western Coercive Policies and the Milosevic regime', in P. Siani-Davies (ed.) *International Intervention in the Balkans since 1995*, London: Routledge.
Drezner, D.W. (1999) *The Sanctions Paradox. Economic Statecraft and International Relations*, New York: Cambridge University Press.
Elliot, K.A. (1995) 'Factors Affecting the Success of Sanctions', in D. Cortright and G.A. Lopez (eds) *Economic Sanctions. Panacea or Peacebuilding in a Post-Cold War World?*, Boulder: Westview Press.
——(1998) 'The Sanctions Glass: Half Full or Completely Empty?', *International Security* 23(1), Summer 1998: 50–65.
Eriksson, M. (2005) 'EU sanctions: Three Cases of Targeted Sanctions', in P. Wallensteen and C. Staibano (eds) *International Sanctions: Between Words and Wars in the Global System*, London: Frank Cass.
——(2007) 'Targeting Zimbabwe's Leadership', Uppsala: Department of Conflict and Peace Research, Uppsala University.
EU Business (2007) 'Austria Opposes French Proposals for EU Sanctions Against Iran', 1 February 2007.
EU Observer (2008a) 'Bosnia Angered by Signing of EU–Serbia Seal', 30 April 2008.
—— (2008b) 'UN Prosecutor Wants More Progress from Serbia', 17 April 2008.
Eurasia Insight (2006) 'Uzbekistan Surprised by EU Move to Extend Sanctions', 14 November 2006.
European Council (1989) European Council Conclusions, Madrid, 27 June 1989.
European Parliament (2006) Note d'Information sur la situation politique et économique du Pérou et sur ses relations avec l'Union Européenne, Direction Générale pour les politiques externes de l'Union, Direction B, Département Thématique, PE 381.009, 18 Octobre 2006.
Ferrero-Waldner, B. (2006a) 'European Strategies for Promoting Democracy in Post-communist Countries', International Conference, Institute for Human Sciences, Vienna 20 January 2006.
——(2006b) 'Statement on Belarus' European Parliament plenary session discussion on Belarus elections, European Parliament, Strassbourg, 5 April 2006.
——(2006c) 'Suspension of Aid to the Palestinian Authority Government', SPEECH/06/260, Brussels, 26/04/2006.
——(2007) 'Statement to the Plenary', European Parliament Plenary Session, Brussels, 6 June 2007.
——(2009) 'The European Union and Belarus: Moving Closer Together?', Europa Hotel, Minsk, 22 June 2009.

Fierro, E. (2003) *The EU's Approach to Human Rights Conditionality in Practice*, The Hague: M. Nijhoff.

Foran, V. and Spector, L. (1997) 'The Application of Incentives to Nuclear Proliferation', in D. Cortright (ed.) *The Price of Peace. Incentives and International Conflict Prevention*, Lanham: Rowman & Littlefield.

Frankfort-Nachmias, Ch. and Nachmias, D. (1992) *Research Methods in the Social Sciences*, 4th edn, New York: St. Martin's Press.

Frankfurter Allgemeine Zeitung (2008) 'EU stimmt Abkommen mit Serbien zu', 29 April 2008.

Galtung, J. (1967) 'On the Effects of International Economic Sanctions, with Examples from the Case of Rhodesia', *World Politics* 19: 378–416.

García-Pérez, M. (2007) 'How to Deal with Human Rights among Partners: Consultations under the Cotonou Agreement', in M. Salomon, W. Vandenhole and A. Tostensen (eds) *Casting the Net Wider: Human Rights, Development and New Duty-Bearers*, Antwerpen: Intersentia.

Gauttier, P. (2004) 'Horizontal Coherence and the External Competencies of the European Union', *European Law Journal* 10(1): 23–41.

George, A. (1991) *Forceful Persuasion. Coercive Diplomacy as an Alternative to War*, Washington DC: United States Institute of Peace Press.

Gibert, M. (2006) 'The European Union in the IGAD-Subregion: Insights from Sudan and Somalia', *Review of African Political Economy Nr. 107*: 142–50.

Goldirova, R. (2007) 'EU Relaxes Palestine Aid Embargo', *EU Observer*, 12 June 2007.

Grant, C. and Leonard, M. (2006) 'The EU's Awkward Neighbour: Time for a New Policy on Belarus', *CER Policy Brief*, April 2006.

Grünfeld, F. (1999) 'The Effectiveness of United Nations Economic Sanctions', in W.J.M. van Genugten and G.A. de Groot (eds) *United Nations Sanctions. Effectiveness and Effects, Especially in the Field of Human Rights*, Antwerpen: Intersentia.

Haass, N. and O'Sullivan, M.L. (eds) (2000) *Honey and Vinegar: Incentives, Sanctions, and Foreign Policy*, Washington, DC: Brookings.

Hafner-Burton, E.M. (2005) 'Trading Human Rights: How Preferential Trade Agreements Influence Government Repression', *International Organization* 59, Summer 2005: 593–629.

Hamilton, D.S. (2008) 'The United States: A Normative Power?', *CEPS Working Document* Nr. 291, May 2008, Brussels.

Harris, P.B. (1968) 'Rhodesia: Sanctions and Politics', *Rhodesian Journal of Economics* (2): 5–20.

Hazelzet, H. (2001) 'Carrots or Sticks? EU and US Reactions to Human Rights Violations (1989–2000)', unpublished thesis, European University Institute.

——(2005) *Suspension of Development Cooperation: An Instrument to Promote Human Rights and Democracy?* European Centre for Development Policy Management (ECDPM): Discussion Paper No. 64B, Maastricht: ECDPM.

Heller, R. (2008) *Normensozialisation in Russland*, Wiesbaden: Verlag für Sozialwissenschaften.

Holland, M. (2004) 'When is Foreign Policy not Foreign Policy? Cotonou, CFSP and External Relations with the Developing World', in M. Holland (ed.) *The Common Foreign and Security Policy: The First Ten Years*, 2nd edn, London: Continuum.

House of Lords (2007) *The Impact of Economic Sanctions*, Second Report of Session 2006–7, Select Committee on Economic Affairs, Volume I: Report, 9 May 2007, London: The Stationery Office.

——(2008) *The Treaty of Lisbon: An Impact Assessment*, 10th Report on Session 2007–8, European Union Committee, Volume I: Report, 13 March 2008, London: The Stationery Office.

Hovi, J., Huseby, R. and Sprinz, D. (2005) 'When do (Imposed) Economic Sanctions Work?', *World Politics* 57 (July 2005): 479–99.

Hufbauer, G.C. and Oegg, B. (2000) 'Targeted Sanctions: A Policy Alternative?', paper submitted to the symposium 'Sanctions Reform? Evaluating the Economic Weapon in Asia and the World', 23 February 2000, Washington DC: Institute for International Economics, pp. 11–21.

——(2003) 'The European Union as an Emerging Sender of Economic Sanctions', *Aussenwirtschaft* 4: 1–20.

Hufbauer, G.C., Schott J.J. and Elliot, K.A. (1985 and 1990) (1st, 2nd edn) *Economic Sanctions Reconsidered. History and Current Policy*, Washington, DC: Institute for International Economics.

Hufbauer, G.C., Schott J.J. and Oegg, B. (2001) 'Using Sanctions to Fight Terrorism', *Policy Brief 01–11*, Washington D.C.: Institute for International Economics.

Hufbauer, G.C., Schott J.J., Elliot, K.A. and Oegg, B. (2007) (3rd edn) *Economic Sanctions Reconsidered. History and Current Policy*, Washington, DC: Institute for International Economics.

Hughes, C.R. (2007) 'New Security Dynamics in the Asia Pacific: Extending Regionalism from Southeast to Northeast Asia', *The International Spectator* 42(3): 319–36.

International Crisis Group (2006) 'Moldova's Uncertain Future', *Europe Report* 175, August 2006.

——(2007) 'Zimbabwe: An End to the Stalemate?', *Africa Report* 122, March 2007.

——(2009) 'Zimbabwe: Engaging the Inclusive Government', *Africa Briefing* 59, April 2009.

Jarabik, B. and Silitski, V. (2008) 'Belarus', in R. Youngs (ed.) *Is the European Union promoting democracy in its neighbourhood?*, Madrid: Fride.

Jentleson, B.W. (2000) 'Economic Sanctions and Post-Cold War Conflicts: Challenges for Theory and Policy', in P.C. Stern and D. Druckman (eds) *International Conflict Resolution after the Cold War*, Washington, DC: National Academy Press.

Jentleson, B.W. and Whytock, C.A. (2005) 'Who "Won" Libya? The Force-Diplomacy Debate and its Implications for Theory and Practice', *International Security* 30(3): 47–86.

Jones, S.G. (2007) *The Rise of European Security Co-operation*, Cambridge: Cambridge University Press.

Kaempfer, W. and Lowenberg, A. (1999) 'Unilateral versus Multilateral International Sanctions: A Public Choice Perspective', *International Studies Quarterly* 43(1) March 1999: 37–58.

Kirshner, J. (1997) 'The Microfoundations of Economic Sanctions', *Security Studies* 6 (3): 32–64.

——(2002) 'Economic Sanctions: the State of the Art', *Security Studies* 11(4): 160–79.

Klenner, W. (2005) 'Economic Relations between the EU and China: Evolution of an Exclusive Partnership?', *China: An International Journal* 3(2), 331–46.

Kononenko, V. (2006) 'EUBAM Moldova after One Year: Assessing the EU's Security Promotion at the Separatist Border', *CFSP Forum* 4(5), 1–4.

Koutrakos, P. (2001) *Trade, Foreign Policy and Defence in EU Constitutional Law*, Oxford: Hart.

Kreikemeyer, A. and Zellner, W. (eds) (2007) 'The Quandaries of Promoting Democracy in Central Asia: Experiences and Perspectives from Europe and the USA', Report of a Transatlantic Workshop at the Centre for OSCE Research in Hamburg, *CORE Working Paper*, February 2007, Hamburg: Zentrum für OSCE Forschung.

Kreutz, J. (2004) 'Reviewing the EU Arms Embargo on China: The Clash between Value and Rationale in the European Security Strategy', *Perspectives* 22/2004, Summer 2004.

——(2006) *Hard Measures by a Soft Power? Sanctions Policy of the European Union*, BICC Paper 45, Bonn: Bonn International Centre for Conversion.

Kryvoi, Y. (2007) 'Why European Union Trade Sanctions Do Not Work', *Harvard European Law Working Paper* no. 4/2007: 119–37.

Laakso, L., Kivimäki, T. and Seppänen, M. (2006) *Evaluation of the Consultation Processes under Article 96 in the Cotonou Partnership Agreement – Comparative Overview*, Albertslund: Conflict Transformation Service.

——(2007) *Evaluation of Coordination and Coherence in the Application of Article 96 of the Cotonou Partnership Agreement*, Amsterdam: Aksant Academic Publishers.

Lehtinen, T. (2001) *The European Union's Political and Development Response to Sudan*, European Centre for Development Policy Management (ECDPM): Discussion Paper No. 26, Maastricht: ECDPM.

Lektzian, D. (2003) *Making Sanctions Smarter. Are Humanitarian Costs an Essential Element in the Success of Sanctions?*, Oslo: International Peace Research Institute.

Lerch, M. (2004) *Menschenrechte und europäische Außenpolitik*, Wiesbaden: Verlag für Sozialwissenschaften.

Lindner, R. (2008) 'Belarus gerät in Bewegung', *SWP Aktuell 73*, Berlin: Stiftung Wissenschaft und Politik: 55–73.

Lindsay, J.M. (1986) 'Trade Sanctions as Policy Instruments: A Re-examination', *International Studies Quarterly* 30: 153–73.

Lukaschek, A. and Weidel, B. (2002) 'Economic Sanctions and the European Union Legal Framework', in S. Grille and B. Weidel (eds) *External Economic Relations and Foreign Policy in the European Union*, Vienna: Springer.

McGowan, P.J. (2003) 'African Military Coups d'état, 1956–2001: Frequency, Trends and Distribution', *Journal of Model African Studies* 41(3): 339–69.

Mack, A. and Khan, A. (2000) 'The Efficacy of UN Sanctions', *Security Dialogue* 31(3): 279–92.

Mair, S. (2008) 'Simbabwe zwischen den Wahlen', *SWP Aktuell* 39, Berlin: Stiftung Wissenschaft und Politik.

Mandelson, P. (2006) 'Trade Policy and Decent Work Intervention', EU Decent Work Conference, Brussels, 5 December 2006.

Mbangu, L. (2005) *Recent Cases of Article 96 Consultations*, European Centre for Development Policy Management (ECDPM) Discussion Paper No. 64C, Maastricht: ECDPM.

Meier, O. (1999) *Involving India and Pakistan*, BITS Research Report 99.2, Berlin: BITS.

Mitchell, R. (1997) 'International Control of Nuclear Proliferation: Beyond Carrots and Sticks', *The Non-Proliferation Review*, 5(1): 40–52.

Morgan, T.C. and Schwebach, V.L. (1997) 'Fools Suffer Gladly: The Use of Economic Sanctions in International Crises', *International Studies Quarterly* 41(1): 27–50.

National Centre of Legal information of the Republic of Belarus (2009) 'Belarus attracted by free trade with EU', 27 August 2009.

Niño-Perez, J. (2005) 'EU Instruments for Conflict Prevention', in V. Kronenberger and J. Wouters (eds) *The European Union and Conflict Prevention. Policy and Legal Aspects*, The Hague: Asser Press.

Noutcheva, G. (2007) 'Fake, Partial and Imposed Compliance: The Limits of the EU's Normative Power in the Western Balkans', *CEPS Working Paper* nr. 274, Brussels: Centre for European Policy Studies.

Olcott, M.B. (2007) 'Democracy Promotion in Central Asia: From High Expectations to Disillusionment', in A. Kreikemeyer and W. Zellner (eds) *The Quandaries of Promoting Democracy in Central Asia: Experiences and Perspectives from Europe and the USA*, *CORE Working Paper*, Zentrum für OSCE Forschung: Hamburg.

Olson, R.S. (1979) 'Economic Coercion in World Politics, with a Focus on North–South Relationships', *World Politics* 31(4): 471–94.

Orbie, J. (2010) 'Promoting labour standards through trade: Normative power or regulatory state Europe?' in R. Whitman(ed) *Normative Power Europe: Empirical and Theoretical Perspectives*, Houndsmills: Palgrave

Orbie, J. and Tortell, L. (2009) 'The New GSP + Beneficiaries: Ticking the Box or really Consistent with ILO Findings?', *European Foreign Affairs Review* 14, 663–81.

Orbie, J., Vos, H. and Taverniers, L. (2005) 'EU Trade Policy and Social Clause: A Question of Competences?', *Politique Européenne* no. 17, automne 2005: 159–87.

Osteneck, K. (2004) 'Die Umsetzung von UN-Wirtschaftssanktionen durch die Europäische Gemeinschaft', *Beiträge zum ausländischen öffentlichen Recht und Völkerrecht* 168(1).

Paasivirta, E. and Rosas, A. (2002) 'Sanctions, Countermeasures and Related Actions in the External Relations of the European Union: A Search for Legal Frameworks', in E. Cannizzaro (ed.) *The European Union as an Actor in International Relations*, The Hague: Kluwer.

Pabst, R. and Klein, M. (2006) 'Information Note on the Political and Economic Situation of Nigeria and EU–Nigeria Relations', Directorate-General for External policies of the Union, Directorate B, Policy Department.

Paes, W.C. (2009) 'The Challenge of Measuring Success: Yugoslavia Sanctions Decade (1991–2001)', in M. Brzoska and G. Lopez (eds) *Putting Teeth in the Tiger: Improving the Effectiveness of Arms Embargoes,* Boulder: Lynne Rienner.

Pape, R.A. (1997) 'Why Economic Sanctions Do Not Work', *International Security* 22 (2): 90–136.

——(1998) 'Why Economic Sanctions *Still* Do Not Work', *International Security* 23 (1): 66–77.

Parry, R.L. (2000) 'Indonesian Army Will Use EU arms in Creeping Coup', *The Independent*, 18 January 2000.

Partsch, K.J. (1994) 'Reprisals', in R. Bernhardt (ed.) *Encyclopaedia of Public International Law*, Amsterdam: North-Holland.

Patten, C. (1999a) 'Declaration on Chechnya', SPEECH/99/166, European Parliament, Strassbourg, 17 November 1999.

——(1999b) 'The Future of the European Security and Defence Policy (ESDP) and the Role of the European Commission', speech at the Conference on the Development of a Common European Security and Defence Policy, Berlin, 16 December 1999.

——(2005) *Not Quite the Diplomat*, London: Penguin.

Pelczynska-Nalecz, K., Strachota, K. and Falkowski, M. (2008) 'Para-states in the Post-Soviet Area from 1991 to 2007', *International Studies Review* 10, 366–96.

Petiteville, F. (2003) 'Exporting "Values"? EU External Co-operation as a "Soft Diplomacy"', in M. Knodt and S. Princen (eds) *Understanding the European Union's External Relations*, London: Routledge.

Poeschke, O. (2008) 'Maastrichts langer Schatten', *Hamburg Review of Social Sciences*, Spring 2008, 37–69.

Popescu, N. (2005) 'The EU and Moldova: Settling Conflicts in the Neighbourhood', *Occasional Paper 60*, Paris: ISS-EU.

Portela, C. (2003) 'The EU's Role in the Non-Proliferation of Weapons of Mass Destruction: The Way to Thessaloniki and Beyond', *PRIF Report 65*, Frankfurt/M.: Hessische Stiftung für Friedens-und Konfliktforschung.

——(2005) 'Where and Why does the European Union Impose Sanctions?', *Politique Européenne* nr 17, autumne/hiver 2005, 83–111.

——(2007a) 'Sanktionen der EU: Wirksamkeit durch Stigmatisierung?', *SWP Aktuell 63*, Berlin: Stiftung Wissenschaft und Politik.

——(2007b) 'Aid Suspensions as Coercive Tools?', *Review of European and Russian Affairs*, 3(2), 38{-53}.

Ragin, C.C. (2000) *Fuzzy-set Social Science*, Chicago/London: University of Chicago Press.

Rajkovic, N.M. (2007) 'The Limits of Consequentialism: ICTY Conditionality and (Non)Compliance in Post-Milosevic Serbia', paper presented at 6th Pan-European International Relations Conference, Turin, September 2007.

Rehn, O. (2007) 'Serbia's European Road', European Parliament Plenary Session, Strassbourg, 24 October 2007.

Reuters (2007a) 'Cuba Says No Talks with EU until Sanctions Dropped', 22 June 2007.

—— (2007b) 'Zimbabwe should be at EU–Africa Summit', 4 September 2007.

Rogers, E. (1996) 'Economic Sanctions and Internal Conflict', in M. Brown (ed.) *The International Dimensions of Internal Conflict*, Cambridge, MA: MIT Press.

Rosas, M.C. (2003) *Sanciones, Zanahorias y Garrotes*, México D.F.: Universidad Nacional Autónoma.

Rotschild, D. (1997) *Managing Ethnic Conflict in Africa. Pressures and Incentives for Co-operation*, Washington, DC: Brookings Institution Press.

Santiso, C. (2003) 'Responding to Democratic Decay and Crises of Governance: The European Union and the Convention of Cotonou', *Democratization 10–3*, Frank Cass: London.

Schelling, T. (1966) *Arms and Influence*, New Haven: Yale University Press.

Schimmelfennig, F. and Sedelmeier, U. (eds) (2005) *The Europeanization of Central and Eastern Europe*, Ithaca, NY: Cornell University Press.

Schmalz, U. (1997) Kohärenz der EU-Aussenbeziehungen? Der Dualismus von Gemeinschaft und gemeinsamer Aussen-und Sicherheitspolitik in der Praxis, *Arbeitspapier*, Sankt Augustin: Konrad Adenauer Stiftung.

Smith, K.E. (1997) 'The Use of Political Conditionality in the EU's Relations with Third Countries: How Effective?', *SPS Working Paper 1997/7*, San Domenico di Fiesole: EUI: 1–37.

——(2000) 'The End of Civilian Power Europe: A Welcome Demise or Cause for Concern?', *The International Spectator* 23 (2): 11–38.

——(2003) *European Union Foreign Policy in a Changing World*, Cambridge: Polity Press.

——(2005) 'Beyond the Civilian Power debate', *Politique Européenne* 17: 63–82.

——(2006) 'The Limits of Proactive Cosmopolitanism: The EU and Burma/Myanmar, Cuba and Zimbabwe', in O. Elgstöm and M. Smith (eds) *The European Union's Roles in International Politics. Concepts and Analysis*, London: Routledge.

Soler, E. (2005) 'Debating Turkey's Accession: National and Ideological Cleavages in the European Parliament', in E. Barbe and A. Herranz (eds) *The Role of Parliaments in European Foreign Policy. Debating on Accountability and Legitimacy*, Barcelona: Office of the European Parliament.

Stangos, P.N. (2000) 'La conditionnalité politique, en termes de protection des droits de l'homme, de démocratie et d'état de droit, des relations économiques extérieures de la Communauté de l'Union Européennes', in H. Ruiz-Fabri, L.A. Sicilianos and J.M. Sorel (eds) *L'Effectivité des Organisations Internationales: Mécanismes de Suivi et de Contrôle*, Paris: Pedone.

Steinberg, D.I. (2003) 'Burma/Myanmar: The Triumph of the Hard-Liners', *South China Morning Post*, 15 August 2003.

Stephanides, J. (2002) 'Foreword', in D. Cortright and Lopez (eds) *Smart Sanctions: Targeting Economic Statecraft*, New York: Rowman and Littlefield.

Stokke, O. (1995) (ed.) *Aid and Political Conditionality: Core Issues and State of the Art*, London: Frank Cass.

Taylor, B. (2009) *American Sanctions in the Asia-Pacific*, London: Routledge.

Tocci, N. (2007a) 'What Went Wrong? The Impact of Western Policies towards Hamas and Hizbollah', *CEPS Policy Brief*, Nr. 135, July 2007.

Toledano, E. (2001) 'Les relations entre l'Union Européenne et la Biélorussie entre 1991 et 2001', *Transitions* XLII(1).

Tonkin, D. (2006) 'Burma (Myanmar): A Case Study', evidence submitted to the House of Lords, Select Committee on Economic Affairs, SC/05–06/EA285.

Tostensen, A. and Bull, B. (2002) 'Are Smart Sanctions Feasible?', *World Politics* 54 (3): 373–403.

Tsebelis, G. (1990) 'Are Sanctions Effective? A Game Theoretical Analysis', *Journal of Conflict Resolution* 34(1): 3–28.

Tull, D. (2005) 'Der Sudan nach dem Naivasha Friedensvertrag: Noch kein Anlass zur Euphorie', *SWP Aktuell 2005/ A01*, Berlin: Stiftung Wissenschaft und Politik.

United Nations Security Council (2003) Resolution 1493 adopted by the Security Council at its 4797th meeting, on 28 July 2003 concerning sanctions against the democratic republic of Congo.

——(2004) Resolution 1554 (2004) adopted by the Security Council at its 5013th meeting, on 29 July 2004.

——(2005) Resolution 1591 (2005) established by the Security Council on 29 July 2004 concerning Sudan.

Usborne, D. (2007) 'Cuba Frees Political Prisoners Ahead of Talks on EU Sanctions', *Belfast Telegraph*, 26 April 2007.

van Bergeijk, P.A. (1994) *Economic Diplomacy, Trade and Commercial Policy. Positive and Negative Sanctions in a New World Order*, Aldershot: Edward Elgar.

——(1999) 'Economic Sanctions: Why Do They Succeed; Why Do They Fail?', in W.J.M. van Genugten and G.A. de Groot (eds) *United Nations Sanctions. Effectiveness and Effects, Especially in the Field of Human Rights*, Antwerpen: Intersentia.

von Bömcken, M. (2009) 'UN Arms Embargoes in the Great Lakes (1994–2004)', in M. Brzoska and G. Lopez (eds) *Putting Teeth in the Tiger: Improving the Effectiveness of Arms Embargoes*, Boulder: Lynne Rienner.

Vysotskaya, A. (2008) 'Opening of the European Commission Delegation in Minsk: Do EU–Belarus relations need a rethink?', Briefing Paper 18, Finnish Institute for International Affairs: Helsinki.

Wacker, G. (2004) 'Ende des EU-Waffenembargos gegen China?', *SWP Aktuell 13*, Berlin: Stiftung Wissenschaft und Politik: 1–8.

Wagemann, C. and Schneider, C.Q. (2007) *Qualitative Comparative Analysis and Fuzzy Sets: Ein Lehrbuch für Anwender und jene, die es werden wollen*, Leverkusen: Barbara Budrich.

Wallensteen, P. (1968) 'Characteristics of Economic Sanctions', *Journal of Peace Research* 3: 248–67.
Wallensteen, P., Staibano, C. and Erikson, M. (eds) (2003) *Making Targeted Sanctions Effective. Guidelines for the implementation of UN policy options. Final report of the Stockholm process on the implementation of targeted sanctions*, Uppsala 2003.
Ward, C. (2005) 'The Counter-terrorism Committee: Its Relevance for Implementing Targeted Sanctions', in P. Wallensteen and C. Staibano (eds) *International Sanctions: Between Words and Wars in the Global System*, London: Frank Cass.
Watson Institute (2007) 'EU Bureaucracy Stalls Action on Sanctions', 15 February 2007.
Weiland, H. (2004) 'EU sanctions against Zimbabwe: A Predictable Own Goal?', in M. Holland (ed.) *The Common Foreign and Security Policy: The First Ten Years*, 2nd edition, London: Continuum.
Weintraub, S. (1982) *Economic Coercion and US Foreign Policy: Implications of Case Studies from the Johnson Administration*, Boulder: Westview Press.
Wessel, R.A. (1999) *The European Union's Foreign and Security Policy. A Legal Institutional Perspective*, The Hague: Kluwer.
White, H. (2008) 'The Road to INTERFET', *Security Challenges* 4(1): 69–87.
Will, G. (2003) 'Wege aus der Isolation. Birmas nationaler und internationaler Aussöhnungsprozess', *SWP Studie* 36, Berlin: Stiftung Wissenschaft und Politik.
Wohlgemuth, L. (2005) 'African Sanctions: The Case of Burundi', in P. Wallensteen and C. Staibano (eds) *International Sanctions: Between Words and Wars in the Global System*, London: Frank Cass.
Wulteputte, V. (2004) 'The EU Embargo on Trade in Arms to China', in M. Dumoulin and G. Duchenne (eds) *L'Europe et l'Asie*, Bruxelles: Peter Lang.
Zanon, F. (2005) 'The European Parliament: An Autonomous Foreign Policy Identity?', in E. Barbe and A. Herranz (eds) *The Role of Parliaments in European Foreign Policy. Debating on Accountability and Legitimacy*, Barcelona: Office of the European Parliament.
Zurawski, P. (2005) 'Belarus: The Unrecognised Challenge', in D. Lynch (ed.) *Changing Belarus, Chaillot Paper 85*, Paris: ISS-EU: 103–19.

Index

For Product Safety Concerns and Information please contact our EU representative GPSR@taylorandfrancis.com
Taylor & Francis Verlag GmbH, Kaufingerstraße 24, 80331 München, Germany

www.ingramcontent.com/pod-product-compliance
Ingram Content Group UK Ltd.
Pitfield, Milton Keynes, MK11 3LW, UK
UKHW021720240926
475702UK00029BA/1721
9780415502740